THE MARXISM OF MARX

By the same author

THE OLD TESTAMENT IN THE 20TH CENTURY
A FAITH TO LIVE BY
CHRISTIANITY AND THE SOCIAL REVOLUTION *(Ed.)*
TEXTBOOK OF MARXIST PHILOSOPHY *(Ed.)*
DOUGLAS FALLACIES
THE PHILOSOPHY OF THE SOVIET STATE
THE CASE AGAINST FASCISM
MARXISM AND MODERN IDEALISM
AN INTRODUCTION TO PHILOSOPHY
MARXISM AND THE IRRATIONALISTS
MARXISM AND THE OPEN MIND
RELIGIONS OF THE WORLD
SCIENCE, FAITH AND SCEPTICISM
ANTHROPOLOGY
SOCIALISM AND THE INDIVIDUAL
A HISTORY OF PHILOSOPHY
MAN AND EVOLUTION
THE LIFE AND TEACHING OF KARL MARX
BERTRAND RUSSELL
NAKED APE AND HOMO SAPIENS
THE LEFT BOOK CLUB

THE MARXISM OF MARX

by
JOHN LEWIS

1972
LAWRENCE & WISHART
LONDON

PRINTED BY Unwin Brothers Limited

THE GRESHAM PRESS, OLD WOKING, SURREY, ENGLAND

A MEMBER OF THE STAPLES PRINTING GROUP

Produced by Letterpress

CONTENTS

PREFACE

It is one of the ironies of history that a thinker of the importance of Karl Marx can be held by one philosopher of repute to "exercise a stronger influence upon the present age than the theories of any of our contemporaries",[1] while another, equally distinguished, can declare that "Marxism is the illegitimate and rebellious offspring of nineteenth century Liberalism".[2] Or again, that Marx's theories can be rejected out of hand by Professor Karl Popper as sheer "historicism", while the Oxford political philosopher, John Plamenatz, declares that "Marxism still remains the most important of all systematic political theories".[3] More volumes of weighty scholarship have been published on Marx over the past ten years than on any other political theorist, but in literary circles and in the pages of the serious weeklies Marxism is regarded with little more than contempt as a social philosophy. How are we to account for this strange gap between the criticism of Marxism as effete, and the increasing recognition of the extent and importance of Marx's theories?

One reason is undoubtedly a surprisingly careless or superficial reading of Marx's own works by writers with a considerable reputation in their own sphere. Both Sir Karl Popper and Professor A. J. Ayer find fault with Marx for his metaphysical theory of history which as they see it reveals history as moving irresistibly to its foreordained end, every event part of the necessary unfolding of the Absolute. Ayer never condescends to quote a single sentence from Marx in support of this view. E. H. Carr, in reply to both of them, has only to point out that there is not the slightest evidence in anything that Marx wrote to support such a theory. On the contrary Marx explicitly rejected any view of his work which saw it in "a general historico-philosophical theory", and pointed out that *Capital* was no more than "an historical sketch for the origin of capitalism in Western Europe".[4]

[1] Professor Sidney Hook, *Marx and the Marxists*.
[2] Carew Hunt, *Theory and Practice of Communism*.
[3] John Plamenatz, *German Marxism and Russian Communism*.
[4] Letter to editor of *Notes on the Fatherland* (end of 1877).

Have the critics been neglecting their homework? It would seem so when Popper frankly admits that his refutation of Marx's historicism is not based on anything that Marx ever said:

> "I have not hesitated to construct arguments for its support which have never, to my knowledge, been brought forward by historicists themselves. I hope that, in this way, I have succeeded in building up a position really worth attacking."[1]

If not "really worth attacking," it is certainly the way to construct a case that can very effectively be demolished. Is not this a perfect example of a procedure too common in controversy: namely, representation of the position of an opponent in the terms it would have *if* the critics held it; that is, not in its own terms, but after translation into the terms of another, indeed an opposite theory, that lends itself perfectly to devastating criticism?

Dr. George Steiner is also prepared to make sweeping generalisations about Marx on the slenderest evidence. In his recent *Eliot Memorial Lecture* he says "Marx seems to paraphrase the vision of Isaiah and of primitive Christianity . . . his 1844 manuscripts are steeped in the tradition of messianic promise". So Marx is to be explained as a combination of Jewish Messianism and Christian utopianism. Unfortunately for Dr. Steiner Marx had no Jewish upbringing. His father was a Voltairian sceptic; he was baptised into the Christian Church with the other children as a formality, educated in a Jesuit school, and never betrayed the slightest interest in Biblical or religious matters either Jewish or Christian. His later philosophical account of religion has nothing to do with pietism.

Marx's attitude to messianic utopianism is also perfectly clear—it had value for earlier periods when social conditions were undeveloped and man could do no more than hope for a better future, but in his own time, since conditions had revealed the ripened potentialities of advancing capitalism, utopianism had become wholly reactionary, and moral exhortations as the way to better things "so much worthless earnestness". So much for primitive Christianity. Surely all this would be perfectly obvious to anyone who had read the *Economic and Philosophical Manuscripts* of 1844 or *The Holy Family*?

Perhaps the most widespread idea of Marxism is that it represents a doctrine of economic determinism. Once again there is not the

[1] Karl Popper, *The Poverty of Historicism*, p. 3.

slightest ground for this view in Marx himself. The text most often quoted about the laws of *capitalist* production "which work out with an iron necessity towards an inevitable goal", refers, as Marx says, to the economic laws of capitalist economists, then, and now, the results of which are catastrophic. Marx points out that they are not, however, laws of nature, but historically conditioned, and to be replaced by an economic system controlled by the rational organisation and disposition of resources. Economic determinism belongs essentially to capitalism, not to socialism. It was in reply to some of his determinist disciples that Marx cried in anger, "Then all I know is that I am not a Marxist!"

It has been widely accepted that Marxism stands for a philosophy of existence concerned with the ultimate substance of the world, which is matter, and certain immanent laws of progress driving it irresistibly forward—such as the law of contradiction, and the law of transformation of quantity into quality. If we turn to Marx's own works, however, we do not find any of these doctrines; on the contrary his own views are strictly empirical and naturalistic, and his approach anthropological and not in the least metaphysical. We must no longer assume that every doctrine subsequently taught by Marx's followers is identical with the teachings of Marx himself. Engels never suggests that the views on controversial issues which he expressed in *Anti-Dühring* in their entirety agreed with Marx. He merely observed many years later that he had read the manuscript to Marx, but he says nothing about Marx's approval. At the time, as we know, Marx was old and ill, and exercising his remaining powers on the uncompleted volumes of *Capital*.

Another, and perhaps one of the most significant reasons to account for the gap between the Marx of popular understanding and the Marx of history, is the attempt by some students of Marxism, among whom one might mention Professor Acton, to create a synthesis of Marx and his later exponents, who were in fact not following Marx at all. The resulting confusion could well explain John Plamenatz's remark that "there has never been any such thing as a coherent Marxist doctrine that a man could hold consistently".[1]

Recently it has become much plainer to what degree Marx developed an approach of his own which cannot be presented in the form of any system of philosophy. The publication of a whole series of Marx's hitherto unpublished works, extending from his essays of 1842 to the

[1] John Plamenatz, *German Marxism and Russian Bolshevism.*

full length *Outlines* (*Grundrisse*) of his theories in 1858, provide very important material which has now to be taken into account in any exposition of Marxism, and naturally therefore in any critical examination of Marx's thought. What emerges from these writings is not, however, a collection of additional philosophical statements to be built into our already formulated conception of Marxism, but the fuller exposition of the real Marx *implicit* in all his later works, but only here stated in precise terms. This is the point of view which marks a fundamental departure from systematic philosophies of every kind. It is what Marx himself called the "actualisation" of what philosophers had been straining towards through all the centuries of thought, and expressing in their speculations and "explanations". It is Marx's attempt to understand through involvement in the movement of events, which he called "praxis". That is the theme of the whole body of Marx's writings which now becomes the source of our understanding of the mind behind *Capital* and all his later works.

From this point of view much of the current theoretical criticism of Marx becomes irrelevant, but on the other hand we begin to see more clearly the source of the prevailing power of the Marxist method and the force behind the world-wide movement which the *Times Literary Supplement*[1] on the hundred and fiftieth anniversary of Marx's birth in 1968 recognised as the expression of his faith.

"More than any other great figure of the past, Marx has succeeded to an unusual degree in breaking through the geographical, cultural, professional and even ideological barriers which normally confine human reputations . . . He forms part of the living universe both of intellectuals and, through the medium of the movement inspired by his ideas, of vast sections of the world's population. His reputation is genuinely global."

To understand a new point of view is much more difficult than to venture on the elaboration of an accepted one, however difficult. To press on into the deeper obscurities of an already obscure system of thought, or to wrestle with a radical criticism still expressed in its own terms and within the same universe of discourse, is not so difficult as the fundamental revolution of the mind demanded by a Copernican change in the whole pattern of thinking. When Marx announced that "Philosophers have only interpreted the world differently; the point

[1] *Times Literary Supplement*, May 9, 1968.

is, to *change* it", what he meant was that by understanding the way changes operate, and participating in the intelligent interplay of events, man gradually brings about the rational ordering of the world and discovers, progressively, how best to fulfil his needs.

In taking this position Marx anticipates, on the negative side of the question, the anti-metaphysical position of contemporary philosophy, which has been telling us for many years that "metaphysics is out".[1] But whereas these philosophers do not get any farther than a return to the world as it is, the reality comprehended by "ordinary language", Marx, while entirely empirical and naturalistic in his approach, sees reality in process of change, not change just happening, but brought about by human intelligence and action—change not only *within* the system of things now familiar to us, but change *of* that system into another.

It is important to see what Marx means by abandoning all philosophical *explanations*. He means by these, as metaphysics always means, theories attempting to deal with the universe as a whole, the ultimate reality behind the confusing, apparently meaningless world of everyday, of appearances. This is the traditional approach which gives us, as it were, the world in two editions—an eternal edition, complete from the start, a pre-existent perfection, in which there neither is nor can be growth or change or novelty; and an inferior world, a sort of side-show, the temporal edition, in which things seem to be moving towards that perfection which already abides in the Whole, in the eternal, in the ultimate.

This is what Whitehead called "the bifurcation of nature", which expresses itself in all sorts of philosophies and all sorts of ways: for instance as reality in itself rational, but which does not appear as such, but underlies and seeks to control the outer, phenomenal world of imperfection and disorder—which is therefore less than real. For Marx and all empirical thinkers there is only one world, this one. It is imperfect; it has no predetermined goal. Man himself takes the responsibility of improving it, of giving it whatever purpose it comes to have, and to that end creates it anew in his civilisation, remaking it either well or ill, or both at once. It can be none other than *his* values and *his* aims which he seeks to realise, and to seek for some transcendental origin or guarantee for these is useless.

If this is so, the ideas with which one works must take their origin

[1] *The Nature of Metaphysics*, Essays by Quinton, Hampshire, Ryle, Warnock, Williams and Strawson.

from the world and its happenings, and from the complex structures of society, and from the arts and sciences which man himself has built. No ideas descend from the heavens from a world of pre-existent truth. Man is himself a part of nature and in constant interaction with it. His knowledge is for action, and is tested and corrected in action. It has been forged in action to enable men to deal effectively with the problems of the natural, social and economic environment, in all its multifarious aspects. Human knowledge is derived from experience by patient and sustained activity which is itself inseparable from knowing, but this immediacy shifts continually from past origins to future consequences, since action is directed towards the future.

This activist involvement, interpenetrated by thought or it cannot be at all, and working all the time to change and improve, to extend and perfect control, discards entirely all intention of formulating any complete, sociological, economic or political theory—a Marxist *system*. The importance of the new material, of Marx's philosophical and political studies, and of his anthropological and economic essays, is neither that they provide ideas to be incorporated in any such Marxist *system*, nor that they will help us to frame a new one. They will show us, if we take the trouble to understand them, how to take an entirely different course. And if we have been foolish enough to misunderstand what Marx was up to, and have made for ourselves one of those explanatory systems which he wanted to leave behind, they will show us that we must get rid of it, and come back to his more pragmatic approach. The more we study this newly published work, and also the older *German Ideology* to which too little attention has been directed, the more we see that Marx had finished altogether with any systematisation of his theory, and intended to do the rest of his thinking in the contemporary situation.

There is therefore no Marxist task of careful exegisis of the sacred texts, no endless discussion as to how the final truths are to be applied in practice. All this implies a Marxist theory over and against the facts, a system of abstractions (as all generalised propositions must be) which itself remains unchanged, but is applied to the changing world. This is exactly what Marx has finished with. He works instead with the concept of *praxis*, which means the intimate and inseparable connection of understanding and action which we find on every side of effective human activity, in medicine, in engineering, in scientific experimental work, and in such sports as sailing and climbing. The competent physician learns from the reaction of his patient to his treatment as well as from his medical textbook. There is a science, but it is constantly being tested and modified in use, often in fact radically revised. There is a science of sailing, and of climbing, and neither are unimportant, but in the last resort it is judgement as to wind and tide, as to foothold and approaching storm, that tests the judgement. Marx's Marxism exists not in the book, but *in media res*, in the understanding applied to the complexity and novelty of the actual situation, and being tested in the event, leading to a new understanding for the future.

The rejection of *system* by no means implies that Marx has no methodology, and no empirically obtained principles of social development and history; but these will be found to be more in the nature of working hypotheses than philosophical theories. Moreover their constant application necessarily leads to their frequent revision and extension, as is the case with all scientific theories—but not with metaphysical ones. The indestructible quality of Marxism is based on the fact that it transfers its theories from the study to the world, and keeps them there.

If this is so then the Marxist himself must not stand above the battlefield arguing about his orthodoxy and its opposing heresies. He will not be speaking about "Marxism" at all, he will be immersed in affairs, using all his judgement and sense not only to convince himself as to the next most practicable step, but to convince others too. What insight he obtains from his Marxism will be tested not by arguments as to how consistent his views are with those of the author of *Capital*, but by the results of his actions and of those who act with him. The proof of the pudding will be in the eating.

This might be called the *new* Marxism, but better, Marx's Marxism. It makes no claim to be an all-embracing philosophy, or to do the work of the professional metaphysician or logician. It is not a total theory of history, or a system of economics or economic sociology. It is a highly practical and contemporary policy about *modernisation*. Originally it was about the modernisation involved in the transition from pre-industrial society to capitalism; but Marx saw also the beginning of the modernisation demanded by the muddle and confusion of a capitalism itself in difficulties, of the transition from the age of anxiety to the rational disposal of the immense potentialities available, in order to grapple with the still menacing problems of poverty and economic insecurity.

But Marxism today is not an hypothesis confronting the dubious future. It is already in process of experimental testing on the plane of history. Far from being advanced as an "explanation" consistent with whatever might result, it can now be refuted by the results of its working—refuted, or of course, verified. Unlikely indeed that even the most hopeful consequences would prove every experimental venture as successful as optimism would expect. But, as in all scientific progress, right enough to warrant further advance with a modified and enlarged hypothesis, and not wrong enough to warrant abandonment of the whole concept.

Its most effective exponents in our time have been concerned with the direction of affairs rather than with the exposition and defence of Marxist theories. Their theorising has been linked with and emerges from their day to day struggles. This was especially so with Lenin. This is Marxism, growing and changing, being tested and modified on the field of experimental action—a process still in active progress. This is the kind of Marxism that is not concerned with doctrinal orthodoxy, but demands constant criticism and revision of one's working hypotheses. And as Lenin firmly said;

"We do not want anything to be accepted with the eyes shut, to be an article of faith. Everyone should keep his head tight on his own shoulders, and think out and verify everything for himself."

WHAT IS MARXISM?

It is the fate of genius after it has surprised and uplifted the world to find its message dealt with very strangely even by the most devoted of disciples. They wish to propagate and explain, to apply to life and history on the widest scale, but the result is too often an unwitting distortion, vulgarisation, even perversion of the original insight.

What appears as a new understanding of reality, a new approach to experience, is converted into an orthodoxy. The followers of the prophet find it impossible to resist the impulse to construct a system and an organisation out of a vision whose supreme intention was to transcend everything of that nature.

Distortion also enters in another way. On the plane of history it is impossible for principles not to suffer distortion when they are used to set in motion millions of people, and become the ideology of political movements. Hegel called this "the cunning of reason".[1] History lets men's passionate convictions do their own work, though in doing so what is translated into action and achieved may be very different from, and quite other than, the original intention. When the ideas of a great thinker are put to work in the real world, operated by men who are themselves the product of the tangled history of their times, it is not surprising that the path they take is never one of simple fidelity to the ideals and principles of the founders of their faith. How is it possible that there could have been a great movement which kept its principles unsullied and its practice consistent? "The web of history is not woven with innocent hands." This is not cynicism, for in its own way and at a stumbling pace history advances. Russell Lowell makes his Yankee poet regretfully admit that

"Civylyzation *doos* git forrid
Sometimes upon a powder-cart."

This does not mean that it is useless to look for fundamental principles or that the search for rational theories should be abandoned. They play

---

[1] *Die List der Vernuft*: *Encylopedia* (1817, §158), also in his introductory lectures on the philosophy of history.

their essential role. They *do* work, but not as it was hoped they would, not as completely or as rapidly as enthusiasm would wish.

Among the influential figures whose work has been carried forward historically in a way never anticipated, we must surely include Marx. The days are past when his ideas could be dismissed. The historian acknowledges that he has contributed more to historical scholarship than most critics like to confess.[1] The social philosopher who finds Marx's doctrines questionable nevertheless concludes that "Marxism is, in its own right, and apart from having inspired great political movements, a social theory of the utmost importance",[2] while a leading social philosopher, who is very far from being a Marxist, admits that the teachings of Marx "have proved more successful than any other set of doctrines which the West has brought forth, swifter, more final in its conquest of the world than ever Christianity was."[3]

The Times declared, when discussing the centenary of the publication of *Capital*,

"there is no country in which at this moment someone is not discussing Marx's ideas. His intellectual stature is recognised, with enthusiasm or reluctance—rarely with indifference—wherever there are people capable of reading books. He is one of the rare nineteenth century thinkers who are part of our present and not part of our history."

It is no longer a touchstone of political wisdom or of intellectual integrity to refute "Marxism" or to exorcise the Red Menace; nor is it an expression of genuinely critical thought when it is felt to be invidious to express any opinion which might be thought Marxist, or to advocate any reform which could be regarded by political opponents as possibly to have been thought desirable by disciples of Marx. The whole question of Marxism has to be lifted from this phase of controversy and, like other profound social changes and religious and intellectual upheavals, considered historically.

When we do so we may well discover that the doctrines that have proved least acceptable are precisely those arising from the kind of distortion that has been the fate of every other important prophet and

[1] Butterfield, *Christianity and History*.
[2] Plamenatz, *German Marxism and Russian Communism*, p. 309.
[3] Peter Laslett, reviewing Robert Tucker's *The Marxian Revolutionary Idea* in *The Guardian*.

thinker in the course of history. They frequently depend on imperfect acquaintance with Marx's own works, or the selection of certain striking phrases, casual propositions, or metaphorical remarks as comprising the essence of his teaching. Nor have the critics always been able to distinguish the original doctrines from inevitable distortions arising from the work of Marx's successors in systematising and explaining them, and, even more so, in applying them. Practical men who use the ideas of genius instrumentally also vulgarise them. Then, again, perhaps the most serious kind of misunderstanding arises from assuming that the most influential of the immediate followers of a great thinker truly represent faithfully and develop the ideas of the master. Were the Platonists the real followers of Plato? How close is the theology of St. Paul to the Sermon on the Mount? Able thinker and loyal collaborator though he was, is everything that Engels writes just what Marx really taught?

A great deal depends upon what texts are considered to represent the real Marx, *and what portions of those texts*. *Capital*, long regarded as essential, was never intended to be the final and complete exposition of Marxism. The first of four huge volumes on the development of capitalism, and nothing more even in its entirety[1] (and Marx himself only finished Volume I), was only the first on a series of treatises on Law, History, Government, Ethics and so forth. It is a difficult book and does not lend itself to brief quotations. In consequence the understanding of Marx often seems to be derived from striking phrases from the Prefaces and a few well-known passages from other works, which lend colour to the current interpretation, while the main trend of the work is hardly grasped. The teaching of Marx must be viewed as a whole. The separate themes are intimately related and cannot be assessed in isolation. We do not arrive at the truth of his theory as a whole by considering only the striking phrases and isolated paragraphs. On the contrary it is only the understanding of the whole that will enable us to see what these brief sentences really mean. Still more essential is it to grasp the exposition of Marx's basic theories before turning to *Capital*, where we find their application in a single (unfinished) study in economic history. But this is seldom even attempted, partly because the texts are only available in libraries and in some cases have only recently been published, partly because their importance has been overlooked.

[1] "My historical sketch of the genesis of capitalism in Europe", *Correspondence*, February 11, 1878.

Excursus on the lesser known writings of Marx

It is seldom realised how little Marx's actual work played any part in the early development of the political movement that went by his name. *Capital* was not translated into English until 1887, and then had a very limited circulation. It is by no means a popular exposition of Marxism, or a polemical tract like the *Manifesto* on an extended scale. What really came to represent Marx's views and to play by far the most important part in their popularisation was Engel's *Socialism, Utopian and Scientific* (1892)[1], a brilliant exposition which was translated into many languages and had an enormous circulation. *Anti-Dühring* was by no means so influential; and Engels refused to have it translated into English on the grounds that "the English-speaking public would not swallow that controversy", and that the Hegelian philosophising was incomprehensible and out of date.[2] It did not appear in English until 1934.

The breadth of Engels' interest, the range of his knowledge and his loyalty to Marx are unquestionable. But he had no training as a philosopher and his occupation was that of a highly successful Manchester business man. He was a fine expositor of many of Marx's views, but he made no pretentions to being an original thinker and always deferred to Marx on questions of fundamental theory. His digressions into metaphysics, while interesting, cannot have the same authority as the views of Marx himself, or be regarded as identical in meaning with them; yet for half a century or more they were far more accessible, brilliantly stated, and widely disseminated.

Lenin attempted no systematic re-statement of basic Marxist theory, but saw the necessity of a party to act as the vanguard of the working class, to work for its enlightenment and to give political leadership. He contributed to Marxist theory an exposition of economic imperialism, and also a refutation of Mach's phenomenalism many years before the academic philosophers had dealt with it. His talent lay in the application of Marxism to the concrete situation—which was exactly how Marx wanted his theories to be dealt with.[3]

---

[1] This consisted of the essential chapters from *Anti-Dühring* omitting not only the philosophical controversy with Dühring, but also the extremely interesting sections on ethics, freedom, and other important questions.

[2] Letter to Florence Kelly, February 25, 1886.

[3] Lenin's philosophical notebooks are of absorbing interest. Coming *after* he had read a good deal of philosophy, they differ considerably from some of his earlier views on philosophical subjects. They were of course only jottings accompanying his reading and he never contemplated publication, nor would he have wished them to be taken as authoritative.

From 1938 to 1956 the theoretical views of Stalin as set out in his *Dialectical and Historical Materialism* were held to be the real substance of Marxism. After 1956 this pamphlet was discredited. Although treated as a basic text for twenty years it departs radically from the approach of both Engels and Lenin. It ignores "the negation of the negation" altogether, and is the least Hegelian of all the versions of Marxism. Yet in one important particular it returned to Marx's own insistence on the importance of human understanding, on men "becoming philosophical", by stressing the essential importance of ideas as a liberating and organising force on the one hand, and as obstructive forces on the other. Stalin was far from supporting any theory which saw the process of history as an irresistible tide sweeping mankind forward to a pre-determined goal.

This episode itself might suggest that the fact that popular formulations are accepted and become current even over a considerable period of years is not a sufficient reason for them to be regarded as authoritative statements of Marx's own views, and that popular versions of Marxism may fall short of Marx's own thought. That this is indeed the case has been brought home by the publication in recent years of a considerable volume of Marx's own writings hitherto unknown or largely inaccessible.

The rediscovery of Marx is an interesting story. The *Economic and Philosophic Manuscripts of 1844*, probably the most talked about philosophical work of the century, appeared in an incomplete edition in Russia in 1927. The first German edition was by Landshut and Mayer, Leipzig 1932. An English translation appeared in 1959, though it was being studied in England in a seminar under the direction of Professor John MacMurray in 1938. Marx's *Critique of Hegel's Philosophy of Right* was not published until 1927; and the essays contributed to the *Deutsch-Französische Jahrbücher* were only to be found in Mehring's *Nachlass* (1902) until they were made available in the Collected Works *Marx-Engels Gesamtausgabe* (1931 and after). They appeared in English in Bottomore's *Karl Marx, Early Writings* in 1963.[1] This included the important *Introduction to the Critique of Hegel's Philosophy of Right*, which contains the well-known phrase used by Marx in his discussion of religion—"the opium of the people"; much quoted, never in context, and invariably misconstrued. *The Holy Family*, written jointly with Engels, was published in Frankfurt in 1845. Marx had

[1] Some *Selected Essays* (H. J. Stenning) appeared in 1926, poorly translated. The volume has long been out of print.

no copy and was surprised when a friend presented him with one. The first English translation appeared in 1956. A fascimile of the original was published in Leipzig in 1953.

The German Ideology, also written jointly with Engels, was the first and only book in which Marx set forth his economic theory of history. It was never printed in Marx's lifetime, the prospective publisher taking fright on account of Marx's part in the German revolution of 1848. Thereafter, as Engels says, "it was consigned to the growing criticism of the mice" (some of the pages are entirely lost). It appeared in Professor Pascal's edition here in 1938, but this covered only Parts I and III. The first complete English edition was published in 1964.

Finally there appeared in 1939, for the first time in Moscow, the 1000 page draft on which Marx based his Capital, the Grundrisse der Kritik der Politschen Ökonomie (1857). There is an English translation of the part of it known as Pre-capitalist Economic Formations (1964), and valuable extracts edited by D. McLellan in 1971. The Grundrisse is really the centre-piece of Marx's work, but it was not until 1953 that there was an accessible edition. As Marx himself said, it was, "the result of fifteen years research, that is to say, the best years of my life". What is particularly interesting is the fact that far from indicating a sharp break with the early Marx and his theory of alienation, it is manifestly a continuation and development, as was The German Ideology. Instead of "alienation" having disappeared from his thought, "it maintains," as Meszaros[1] says, "its massive presence throughout the whole manuscript and appears in some 300 contexts".

It is interesting that when Marx raised the question of the relation of his later work to the philosophy of Hegel in the Preface to the Second Edition of Capital he referred back for a full statement of his views to the essay entitled Critique of the Hegelian Dialectic in the Manuscripts of 1844; and yet this is one of the least read of Marx's works.

It is a mistake to call these Marx's "early writings". The Economic and Philosophic Manuscripts were written when he was 26 and the last of these unpublished works, the Grundrisse, in 1857 when he was 40. Moreover in 1872, in the Preface to the Second Edition of Capital, he still refers to his treatment of Hegel in the Manuscripts of 1844 as representing his present views.

In these writings, and especially in The German Ideology and The Grundrisse, Marx works out in considerable detail his fundamental theoretical position and his method of applying it. Thereafter he does

[1] Istvan Meszaros, Marx's Theory of Alienation.

apply it, notably in *Capital*, which he intended to be the first of a series of treatises covering every aspect of social and political theory. So far from *Capital* making a break with the exposition in the earlier works we find here its development and application; above all the development of his conception of alienation through economic exploitation; the theory of man making his own history and at the same time making himself; and the attainment of a classless society in which man can fully develop his own personality. All these views are consistently and progressively developed from their beginnings in 1844 to the last volumes that came from his pen. The early writings in fact contain all the subsequent themes of Marx's thought and show them in the making. Their discovery has shifted the emphasis of Marxist studies from the conflicting theories of rival Marxist parties, and the debate between Marxist and non-Marxist, to the richness of Marx's fundamental philosophical thinking.

What then is the Marxism that emerges from the entire body of Marx's philosophical and sociological writings? Marx's whole approach was a welding of understanding and actual practice into something more like a working hypothesis than a theory standing over against the reality it purports to explain. Marx emphatically rejected the kind of theory which, to use his own words, "resides outside the world", and is then applied. For him theory belonged inseparably to action; it was "society becoming conscious of itself", of its situation, its perils and its opportunities. If, then, Marxism in the course of history developed into a system, this was to depart a long way from what Marx himself wanted. He never believed that it was possible to create a conceptual system applicable at all times, in all situations, "a key to open all locks", as he phrased it. Knowledge for Marx was the process of going to meet reality, getting to grips with it, and verifying one's understanding in practice, and then modifying it in the light of that experience; and trying again. Marx's Marxism was never a pre-critical, dogmatic philosophy, never suggested that the meaning of life and history was laid down once and for all, independently of our understanding and will in a process which unfolds in accordance with irresistible laws. The meaning of history, for Marx, is man's work—men learning to master their world and control their destiny.

The basic doctrines which emerge are three: the nature of man and his alienation; the making of history and at the same time of man himself; the conscious participation of man in the transformation of society.

First we have Marx's understanding of the *nature of man*. This has nothing to do with some abstract conception of the Platonic "principle" of Man. It is social and anthropological. Man is inherently a maker—*homo faber;* and he makes in co-operation with his fellows and fulfills himself in such labour and by his mastery of the external world. In our time, since he created for himself the capitalist system, he is enmeshed in a mechanical system in which he is merely an instrument, and whose economic laws are increasingly hostile to his interests and personality. This is what Marx means by alienation. In such circumstances the aim is to establish the conditions, not to be found under capitalism, in which man at last can be fully human.

Secondly, we come to the *making of history*. We have already seen that man himself creates the social structure which then shapes him; and then continuously reshapes it to improve its efficiency and secure the satisfaction of his ever-growing needs, thus remaking himself at every advance. In our time capitalism by its own development creates the conditions for its supersession and for overcoming the alienation involved in its economic system. That is to say it creates the conditions for fulfilling all needs, the potentiality of plenty in place of the obligations of scarcity, and the only way out from the insuperable and increasing difficulties which capitalism itself creates. This situation is the one in which, to use Lenin's words, "socialism looks out at us through all the windows of capitalism".

The third principle of Marx's Marxism is the *consciousness* in men of the possibilities and demands of the situation. The task of Marxism thus becomes that of bringing the world to understanding of itself, that is to say of the possibilities and necessities of a highly developed capitalism. Such an understanding is primarily a revolution of the mind, a change of focus, a new conceptual pattern without which no political and social change is possible.

Thus Marx sees the development of society as dependent upon the discovery that all formulations of the present state of the world, and especially its economic laws, are inadequate—as inadequate as the Ptolemaic conception of a fixed earth before Copernicus, or as the pre-Darwinian view of the nature and origin of species. The possibilities of human life are not limited by the economic laws of capitalism, or by the philosophy and ethics of competitive individualism. But the transition to socialism requires the enlightenment and willed participation not of a minority but of the overwhelming majority. Whatever the role of leading groups, nothing is possible without that. Nor can it be attained without struggle, since, as in every social advance, the interests of the majority must take precedence over the interests of the privileged, who are disposed to resist radical social change. Marx saw no inevitable victory in such a struggle, which must end, he said, "either in the total transformation of a society or in the common ruin of the contending classes".[1]

It follows that Marx does not present us with a philosophy of history, which, as Professor Popper supposes, serves no other purpose than to prophesy the coming of the millenium which is "predicted with the certainty of an eclipse".

Popper exemplifies the result of deriving one's understanding of Marxism from an insufficient familiarity with the text. In the whole of his *Poverty of Historicism* Marx is actually only quoted three times. One of these references is to the Preface to *Capital*, and a second to Marx's declaration that "philosophers have only interpreted the world differently; the point is, to change it". Popper purports to be in conflict with the view of Marxism he is expounding, and refuting—"the communist belief in an inexorable law of historical destiny"; but since he is reduced to but one brief quotation and that not even running to a complete sentence ("to lay bare the economic law of motion of human society"), he is under the necessity of constructing his own theory of Marxism before knocking it down; and naturally what he constructs in order to be demolished is very well done for that purpose. But surely in philosophical controversy it should be the rule to deal with the actual position of one's opponent, not one that misrepresents him.

Another common misunderstanding is that Marxism preaches a utopian alternative to the "capitalist system", the demand to make all things new, to reject the past history having no lesson for us. And yet no-one more contemptuously rejected the widely prevalent utopian socialism of his time than Marx, though he paid a generous tribute to the idealism of the utopians St. Simon, Owen and the rest. The most popular presentation of Marxist doctrine in its early days was Engel's *Socialism: Utopian and Scientific* which was written to show the inadequacy of millenial hopes and the importance of a critical, realistic form of socialism. And far from rejecting the past, Marxism has consistently explained the historical sequence of social orders as preparing the way for those changes which are now on the agenda,

---

[1] *Communist Manifesto.*

and asserted that past achievements are not negated but "taken up" (*aufheben*) into the new order where they play their part as a permanent and essential constituent of civilisation.

Marxism is also frequently said to demand the overthrow of a system which is seen as a malevolent conspiracy to defraud the people of their birthright. No doubt propagandists of all shades of socialism have frequently talked of capitalism in this way—but not Marx. It was his anarchist opponents whom he spent his life combating, from Proudhon to Bakunin, who made that kind of statement. Marx saw that the immense achievement of the "system" had to be preserved and developed by radical social reconstruction. Particularly in Volume III of *Capital* he shows how within modern capitalism the outlines of socialism are already appearing, and that the changes taking place in the last phase of capitalism already point the way to socialism. Nor did Marx ever attack "capitalists" as malevolent, or conspirators. On the contrary his view was that however well-intentioned and praiseworthy their character and motives, the economic laws within which they worked, and which they regarded as absolute, would not permit them to do any better.

One last illusion is worth mentioning—the idea that Marx believed in the "perfectibility of man". Marx had no belief at all in any permanent condition of "human nature". On the contrary his most fundamental teaching was that it is entirely malleable and constantly changing. Man is a social being, and the form of society he constructs, appropriate to his economic methods at any time, moulds the type of man that comes into being. If man decides to institute a co-operative type of society as necessary, as required by the economy, man will adapt himself to this pattern of social life, as he has frequently adapted himself to other patterns in the past. What he has so often done before, he can surely do again. This implies no suggestion of perfection. The idea is wholly foreign to Marx for whose thinking the nature and potentialities of man are always presented as relative to changing circumstances and conditions.

Thus Marxism appears not as a vast scheme, a total explanation to be imposed on society, but as the indication of how to *grapple with the concrete situation;* a methodology involving a close welding of understanding and action. The Marxism of Marx is a critical and non-dogmatic philosophy which makes *practice* the source and criterion of every truth. It is a *philosophy of act*, that is, one which makes a true reading of consciousness and the human practice which engenders it, and constantly enriches it, constantly going beyond and continually adding to reality by a creative act.

Marxism is in this sense pragmatic. It knows in order to act, and by action enlarges and corrects the understanding on the basis of which it acts, and then advances again.

We cannot turn to the Marxist texts for the guaranteed formulae of sound action. Does that sound disappointing? It should not be, for that is a treatment of Marx's works that renders them useless, that embroils "Marxists" in furious arguments as to what interpetations are "correct", what policies are sanctioned by the infallible word, and who are the heretics. The more Marx is treated as the source of final truth, or as providing a system of dependable political principles and precepts, the farther do we get from the real Marx.

Marxism is not the kind of philosophy that looks at the world from outside and tries to understand it, to interpret it. It is not, therefore, an explanation of existence. It does not conceive the world as in its essential nature just what it is now, and therefore to be explained, justified, shown to be rational or purposive. It is man who gives the world its purpose, who makes it more rational or less irrational, who makes life worth-while, or turns it into a tragedy. Our task is not to show how rational and meaningful the world is, as we have made it so far, but to make it as rational and meaningful as we can in the future.

Nor, on the other hand, are we discovering an irresistible movement of history, or creating a system to explain the sequence of historical changes in world history. For Marx, what is going to happen is not decided by natural laws pursuing their irresistible course independent of man; but on the contrary, the future of society will depend wholly on our comprehension of the situation and what we do about it.

This means much more than finding a theory which may then be applied in practice. Marx was not concerned with "theory" over against "practice" but with a more intimate and indissoluble connection of thinking and acting. Instead of philosophical understanding being embodied in a systematic theory or explanation of existence, Marx seeks an understanding of the actual situation in which men find themselves. Nor is this the work of the theoretician. It is the dawning of the historical self-consciousness of man. As such it is always and necessarily expressed both in thought and action—the action required by the understanding. Thought is conceived in the sense of knowledge, rational insight into the actual as relative to actual need, even to the *urgent* demands of a threatening situation, and therefore involving *doing* what must be done now, comparable to awareness that the train is just going and that you must jump in; that the house is on fire and you must get out; that here is water at last and you can quench your thirst.

When Marx examines the historico-economic situation in Europe, and especially in England in the eighteen-sixties, he sees history coming to a consciousness of itself, of its problem, of its contradictions, of its possibilities. And since it seemed to him that the working class was in a position to see most clearly the next step in social change, he speaks of this as "the working class becoming philosophical", and of "philosophy actualising itself". As *understanding* takes hold of *people*, philosophy as an attempt to explain the world as it is and is likely to remain, disappears. There is for Marx, then, no longer a philosophical theory in the head of philosophers, or in his own, but only the awareness in men of their present condition and their dawning future.

Marxism, therefore, as we understand it today propounds no orthodoxy at all. It does not close discussion; it begins it.

2

THE CHANGING FACE OF MARXISM

Karl Marx is perhaps the most difficult of the considerable thinkers of the 19th century to come to terms with, firstly because the most widely disseminated formulation of his ideas has come to be treated as an accepted doctrine rather than a philosophy open to discussion and modification, an attitude to his theories that there is no reason to believe Marx himself would have approved; and secondly because, like the teaching of other leaders of human thought, "Marxism" has become so completely involved in certain historical developments that it is as difficult to distinguish what Marx actually taught from the pragmatic politics of his followers, as it is to separate the teaching of Christ from the policies and institutions of the historical Church.

The difficulty is increased by the fact that it was of the essence of Marx's own teaching that it deliberately turned away from system-isation, and indeed from any attempt to create some comprehensive philosophical system comprising the principles of explanation that underlie all things without exception, "the first *whence* and the last *whether* of the whole cosmic procession".[1]

Yet several forms of Marxism have moved in the direction of creating from the writings of Marx, Engels, Lenin and their followers a unitary doctrine embodying and synthesising all their interpretations of Marxism. The best known and most authoritative represents the Marxism of the socialist countries of Eastern Europe. Mao Tse-tung has drawn up his own version, which owes a good deal to Chinese philosophy and is highly critical of all Western varieties of Marxism. In Yugoslavia there is a good deal of new thinking both concerning Marxist philosophy and worker's control in industry. Italian, French and British Marxists are not tied to any established orthodoxy, and are working out for themselves, separately, developments both in con-stitutional methods for entering upon the democratic road to socialism, and in Marxist theory.

On the extreme left are many splinter groups, mostly varieties of

---

[1] William James, *Selected Papers on Philosophy*.

Trotskyism, which also has parties of its own in India, Ceylon and elsewhere.

Often calling themselves Marxist are some anarchist groups aiming at the total overthrow of "the system", a catastrophe to end our corrupt world, which, after its destruction, will be built again, though how and on what lines no one knows. Anarchist doctrines were well known to Marx. Advocated by Bakunin, they were vigorously attacked by him and eventually he demanded Bakunin's expulsion from the International.

Of greater interest than the vagaries of the ultra-left are the theories of the French Marxist Althusser, who has been alarmed by the growing influence of the recently published writings of the Young Marx. These he regards as Hegelian, utopian, humanist and of a moralising nature. He is attempting to restate what he calls a "scientific" form of Marxism to counter these heretical tendencies.

It is hardly surprising that the recovery of these writings has caused some alarm in certain quarters. In the thirties, before alienation was seen in the light of Marx's philosophy of history and its economic basis developed in *Capital*, it seemed to suggest an "early Marx" who was simply concerned with any condition adverse to human freedom. This simple humanism could then be seen as more idealistic and ethical than Marx's later concern with economics and politics. It is only the more careful study of the whole concept, and particularly its relation to "the fetishism of commodities", labour as a commodity, and the process whereby the anti-human forces of the market both develop and are to be overcome in historical development, that transcends this simplistic version of the "Young Marx" and shows the mistake of imagining a break with his developed thought.

A more fundamental objection to Marx's humanism is connected with what Althusser describes as "the aberrant and 'criminal' forms Marxism took during the period of the cult of personality" and with "the historical reality of the supersession of the dictatorship of the proletariat and of the 'abusive' forms it took"[1] in Eastern Europe. It is in these terms that Althusser discusses the real significance of the opposition which has appeared in some quarters to *alienation* and *humanism*.

This has led to a rejection not only of Marx's writings prior to 1845 (condemned as idealist), but of all passages in his later works in which these concepts of alienation and humanism appear and also

[1] Althusser, *For Marx*, Part Seven: Marxist Humanism, p. 237.

of such notions as "the negation of the negation", transcendence, supersession, "going beyond" existing forms, and the idea of man "making his own history".[1]

What reveals this view to be a complete misunderstanding of Marx is the fact that the *Grundrisse*, which is as late as 1858, is entirely concerned with these issues, and we have Marx's own words for seeing it as the matrix of the final form which his developed theories were to take in *Capital* and the whole series of his future works.

The question of Marxism however goes beyond the texts and the conclusions of scholars on Marx's theories. It is a contemporary and historical problem on the plane of reality and not alone a question of theory. Whatever may be said of its expositors and their interpretation, Marxism has appeared upon the stage of history and has indisputably played its part in the history of the past fifty years. Our understanding of it is inseparable from the part it has actually played in Eastern Europe, China and other parts of the world, and the new forms of political and economic life which have appeared there. Clearly the way in which Marxism developed was by no means determined solely by the ideas of Marx. The circumstances giving rise to the struggle for "revolution in one country" not anticipated by Marx, the consequent intervention, boycott, isolation, and war, sometimes cold and sometimes hot, could not but profoundly modify the political forms of Marxism as it developed, and must have determined which elements in the writings of Marx could provide help and guidance under various circumstances.

This is the way history happens. Whether we consider the influence of Plato or John Locke, Buddha, Christ, or Thomas Jefferson, the ideals and theories of the founders do their work in the matrix of reality. History cannot be expected to conform to pure theory, and that is why Marx never produced a system of philosophy, or a utopian dream, or a strategic plan. What happened to Europe in the Middle Ages had much to do with the permeation of society by the historical forms of Christianity. There is no pure Christianity, and yet no Europe is imaginable without the interwoven ideology and institutions of the Church. It is thus that we have to see Marxism. Looking at the socialist fifth of the earth, we realise what history has done with Marxism and what Marxism has done with history; and we are not called upon either to wring our hands over it or idealise it. It is folly not to recognise progress because it is marred and imperfect. This

[1] Althusser, *For Marx*, pp. 197, 227.

is so whatever social and political developments we are considering, whether it be those of constitutional democracy, the principles of the American and French Revolutions, the ideals of the Renaissance, or Socialism in the 20th century.

The plain fact is that Marxism has changed the world. Speaking of Lenin, John Plamenatz says:[1] "No man ever changed the world more and more quickly than he did".

And as another critic of Marxism observed after casting grave doubts on the validity of Marx' teaching:[2] "Nevertheless, if a name had to be found for the age in which we live, we might safely call it the Marxian era."

The great variety of forms taken by these political upheavals and revolutions have given the term "Marxism" to widely different policies, theories and forms of socialist organisation. The difference of theory as well as of policy must be stressed. Mao's Marxism is not Stalin's, or Tito's, or that accepted by Western Communist parties. Castro has little to do with any of these versions of Marxism. Different from all of these are the theories and policies of communists in established democracies like Italy, France and Great Britain.

Beyond the more important and highly organised Marxist groups, parties, and political powers, are the innumerable Marxist trends and minor associations, from the Naxalites in India, to groups here at home engaged in constant propaganda, like the tiny Socialist Party of Great Britain and the numerous sects of the Ultra Left. Many of these have come to mean by "Marxism" no more than the rejection of all forms of capitalist and authoritarian government and a revolutionary romanticism which appeals to those who are disillusioned with society. They are all driven by much the same motives: experience of social injustice or degradation; a sense of insecurity bred by war, slumps and social crises; and the craving for a great ideal or purpose, or for a reliable intellectual guide through the bewildering labyrinth of modern society.

Yet this Marxism often has little real knowledge and understanding either of the man or his teaching. In some cases the name "Marx" is hardly more than a symbol of revolution; in others we find much quoting of Marx and pre-occupation with verbal exegesis and text-slinging, in the spirit of religious sects quarelling about the Second Coming, or the rival systems of Pauline and Petrine theology. A

[1] Plamenatz, German Marxism and Russian Communism.
[2] Leopold Schwarzschild, The Red Prussian.

passionate affirmation of Marxist orthodoxy would not be daunted
by being shown that Marx provided no real support for its theories
when understood in the light of his whole theory. To go back to Marx
may even be denounced as "dogmatism"; while to hold any other
version of Marxism than theirs is "revisionism". On this basis you are
bound to have a dozen rival Marxisms, all of them quite immune to
reasoned and critical study of Marx himself.

What has caught the imagination of this varied assembly of rebels
and reformers is the traditional picture of the great revolutionary,
the image of a bearded figure of power and overwhelming authority,
the illumination of some vivid phrase or epigram attributed to him
—"you have nothing to lose but your chains, and a world to win"
—and then the sense of belonging somehow to a great movement,
with a great promise, and of having done with the inhumanity and the
sordid money values and the heartless philistinism of a corrupt society.

There is a semantic question here. The word "Marxism" is supposed
to stand for *one* thing, if a conceptual thing, or an historico-social
reality. Some terms do have a referent of this kind, as in science,
or geography, or when referring to events in history. But have vague
emotive concepts like "freedom", "democracy", "peace", recognisable
referents? Can we say "freedom" is a good thing, in all circumstances
for all purposes and for all kinds of people? Can we say *"this* is democracy?" *"this* is Marxism?" Have they one *real* meaning? Are they
definable as *words* which just have a single meaning in ordinary usage?
This is not so. All these terms, including "Marxism" and many others,
are *concepts* that mean many different things.

Therefore when someone says: "I am a Marxist", we do not know
what he means. If it is said of some writer, or thinker, or politician,
or man in the street: "he is a Marxist", this is not a simple designation
as would be the case if it were said of someone—"he is Japanese",
or "he has red hair", or "he is lame in his right leg". In consequence we
may describe some theory by the term "Marxist" and do no more
than convey a pejorative implication (or the reverse) and in doing so
attribute to it whatever vague ideas, or indeed definite ideas, we ourselves may have on the subject. But there is no objective referent which
really characterises or designates the theory or person we call "Marxist". The term is vacuous and usually more emotive than informative.

Marxism has thus been many things historically, and its various forms
have taken their origin only in part from Marx himself. From all
these forms there is much to learn, but in the special circumstances

of Western Europe in our time, perhaps most from the rediscovery of Marx himself. What new facets of his teaching are going to contribute to the problems of out time has yet to be seen. Of one thing we may be quite certain—illumination does not lie in any Marxist system waiting for authority to state it and apply it.

Marxism as Marx held it is the discovery of the self-criticism which is in society itself, and reaches the level of consciousness in man.

"Communism is not a state of affairs to be established, an *ideal* to which reality will have to adjust itself. We call communism the *real* movement which abolishes the present state of things."[1]

It depends wholly on men themselves realising how the contradictions of society can be overcome, and taking the necessary steps to utilise the maturing forces at their disposal and realise the new possibilities of a ripening situation.

The clear consciousness of what is necessary, the assumption of responsibility, the convictions of the intellect, and the decisions of the will, are the *sine qua non* of social progress.

So far from Marxism being a new system, a theory, a set of ideas, men

"need no longer seek this science in their minds, they have only to take note of what is happening before their eyes, and to become its mouthpiece",[2]

and the intelligent instruments of their own understanding.

[1] Marx and Engels, *The German Ideology*, Part I.
[2] Marx, *The Poverty of Philosophy* (translation by Quelch. Kerr edition). The last phrase re-translated from "to make of that their medium", p. 136.

3

THE MAN NOBODY KNOWS

It is one of the paradoxes of Marxism that the severest critics of Karl Marx can yet pay the highest tributes to his intellectual strength and pervading influence in our time. John Bowle, for instance, is compelled to admit that Marx has "created a social philosophy of massive range and insight which radically altered and even enriched economic and political thought".[1] Every part of his teaching has been attacked, but still it has to be confessed even by his critics that the history of social thought in the last hundred years cannot be understood without taking into account Marx's contribution to the classical tradition in sociological thinking.

He is indeed representative of the whole European tradition, and his thought has a vitality which in its growth was able to absorb a variety of elements—the philosophies of three countries, the experience of Western culture, the history of the working class, and the fruits of many other departments of human thought. He summed up, in fact, an immense accumulation of knowledge in the course of his life. His range of reading and study was limitless.

Marx was never satisfied with the scope of his studies for the work in hand. Engels, impatient to see the first volume of *Capital* finished, writes to him: "As long as you still have a book unread that you think important, you will not get down to writing." Marx wanted to get everything right and he was never satisfied. "It is self-evident", he wrote in 1846, "that an author, if he pursues his research, cannot *literally* publish what he has written six months previously". When young Kautsky asked Marx whether the time had not come to publish his complete works, Marx's reply was, "They would first have to be completed".

We have a vivid picture of Marx as he was seen in Brussels in 1846 by Pavel Vasilyevich Annenkov, a young Russian intellectual who had a letter of introduction to him. Marx presented, he says,

"A type of man all compact of energy, force of character and unshakeable conviction—a type who was highly remarkable too for

[1] John Bowle, *Politics and Opinion in the 19th Century.*

B

his outward appearance. With the thick black mane of hair, and his coat buttoned up askew, he gave one the impression of a man who had the right and the power to command respect, even though his aspect and his behaviour might seem to be rather odd. His movements were awkward, but bold and self-assured; his manners violated all the social conventions. But they were proud and slightly contemptuous, and the metallic timbre of his voice was remarkably well adapted to the radical verdicts which he delivered on men and things. He never spoke at all except in judgments that brooked no denial and that were rendered even sharper by the harsh tone of everything he said."[1]

His voice is still heard, and it is still critical and discordant. His ideas at once haunt and attract the non-Marxist world. Perhaps this should persuade us to put aside for the moment what has been written about him, and go back to the laughing young philosopher of the Doctors' Club in the University of Berlin, high spirited, vivacious, charming, but even then devastating in argument, and with a trenchant wit; to the brilliant editor of the Liberal journal *Rheinische Zeitung* in Cologne; to the newly-married philosopher in Paris in 1844; to the exiled socialist and his young family living in utter poverty in the slums of Soho after the collapse of the Liberal revolution in Germany in 1848, in which he had played a not undistinguished part; to the heavily bearded scholar spending his days in the British Museum and his nights sustained by endless cups of coffee, in tireless writing amidst the smoke of cigars.

It is astonishing how little has been written about Marx's life, either here or even in socialist countries; and still more astonishing what little interest there is in the man and his works rather than in what are supposed (too often mistakenly) to be his ideas. If that seems too extreme a statement, one must protest that while Marx is mainly known by his mighty *Capital*, which everybody talks about and few read, and by the brilliant pamphlet of his youth *The Communist Manifesto*, the actual substance of his available and quoted writing often consists of no more than extracts from the *Selected Works*,[2] none of which contain anything he wrote before 1859 except a short pamphlet on economics and the *Manifesto*. A good deal of attention and controversy centres round extracts not from the works themselves but from

[1] *Reminiscences of Marx and Engels*, p. 270.
[2] Karl Mark, *Selected Works*, 1935; also *The Handbook of Marxism*, ed. Emile Burns.

the Prefaces, of which two pages from the Preface to the *Critique of Political Economy* are often for many people the beginning and the end of any acquaintance with Marx's theoretical position. Single sentences taken out of context, casual asides, half-humorous illustrations, deliberate exaggerations not intended to be taken seriously, are used to reveal the alpha and omega of the life work of a genius. Yet the reverse ought to be the method of understanding him. One cannot take the detached remark as in itself containing the essence of a man's philosophy, making it superfluous to read any further: on the contrary, it is only the *whole*, and the understanding of the whole, that enables one to grasp the meaning of the fragment.

But Marx is also one of those men whose writings alone are not enough to fathom his thoughts, if only because he was from the first very much a man of action, and involved in many practical responsibilities; and also because he was a man of immense erudition and wide culture. His culture was not something for his hours of leisure, but first and last an integral part of his philosophy of life. He ends his *Introduction to a Critique of Political Economy* with a fascinating discussion on classical Greek tragedy. Even in his old age he still read Aeschylus in the original for recreation, and teased his academic friends by discussing the more difficult passages. The Marx of *Capital* and the *Manifesto* was never just the revolutionary pamphleteer, or utopian doctrinaire, which he is to so many who have never read him. He was a child of the philosophical Enlightenment and of German Romanticism, steeped in the culture of his day, in French and German literature, Dante, Cervantes, Heine, and above all Shakespeare.

Marx and the Enlightenment

The rationalism of the Enlightenment had inspired three revolutions —those of England, America and France. The aim of this philosophy had been to submit all ideas and institutions to rational criticism, sweeping away a vast mass of superstition and out-of-date forms of social and political life. Its main effort, as the name Enlightenment suggests, was the freeing of the mind from superstition, dogmatism, authority; thus freeing man's spiritual and moral activity by its development and progress from medieval and authoritarian tutelage to adult responsibility. As far as society was concerned it rejected the notion of an eternal and immutable pre-established order; it criticised the existing state of things as irrational, and declared the necessity of changing the world in order to give it a content and a character in keeping with reason. Yet even so liberating a philosophy had its narrow limits, chiefly in thinking of reason only in terms of mathmatical knowledge, and of nature as a mechanism—a dead thing, incapable of change and growth.

Very closely linked with this idea was faith in man's increasing mastery over nature, and in so far as these new conceptions accompanied and fostered the development of science and industry, this integration of man and his world became a concrete reality in the new world of capitalism.

From this spirit came the French Revolution, which was universally welcomed by those who professed the liberating ideas of Voltaire, Helvetius and Rousseau, among whom were Marx's father and a close friend of the family, Marx's future father-in-law Baron von Westphalen.

Marx's father Heinrich Marx, a lawyer, was a man of wide culture, a real disciple of the Enlightenment, who knew Voltaire and Rousseau by heart, according to Marx's daughter Eleanor. His neighbour Baron von Westphalen was also a product of 18th-century culture, whose father had been secretary to the liberal Duke of Brunswick, the friend of Voltaire and Winckelmann. Westphalen loved Shakespeare and knew Homer by heart. He used to take Karl Marx, when a boy, for walks among the vine-covered hills of the Moselle. It was through him that Marx first learned about the great socialist St. Simon.

Marx's father had abandoned the Jewish faith, and Karl as a small boy, was baptised into the Christian Church in 1824 and was educated in the Jesuit School at Trier. His home influence was entirely rationalist, and his schoolmaster was a disciple of Kant.

Marx went first to the University of Bonn to study law, and from there went on to Berlin. In an interesting letter to his father about his studies and his future hopes the young undergraduate raised a significant philosophical problem. Criticising the legal studies he was engaged in he says: "Here the same opposition of 'is' and 'ought' which is the hallmark of idealism was the dominating and very destructive feature, and engendered a hopelessly mistaken division of the subject matter."[1] It was Hegel who in his union of subject and object, of the rational and the real, overcame this dualism in his own philosophy. Marx abandoned law and became a devoted disciple of Hegel. He was quickly recognised as a talented scholar and joined the famous Doctor's Club

[1] Marx, Letter to his father, November 10, 1837.

of graduate philosophers. Here he met all the brilliant Young Hegelians of the University who were engaged in controversy about the next phase in the Hegelian philosophy. Was it to be the acceptance of the static system in which philosophy could only explain events after they had happened; or was the emphasis to be on the other aspect of Hegel, the dialectic of change? Hegel had declared that the rational was the real. Then if the world were not rational, neither was it yet real. In that case had it not to be made real, to be altered? But how?

It was now that Marx came under the influence of Feuerbach, who persuaded him and the little group who parted company with the Bauers—the "Holy Family" with whom Marx was soon to enter into violent controversy—that man and history were not the manifestation of the Idea. Ideas arise in the course of our material life. Of these, religious ideas are especially important because they are the projection of man's real nature: God represents all that man on earth lacks and is deprived of. Feuerbach went on to show that metaphysics is only a further form of abstraction, deriving from the fantasies of religion. Feuerbach made a great impression on Marx, and this marked his conversion to materialism—but it was materialism with a difference.

After Marx had taken his degree at Jena he went to Cologne to edit a new liberal journal, the *Rheinische Zeitung*, the organ of the rising German bourgeoisie and their opposition to the Catholic Church and the Prussian monarchy. Within a year the censors closed it down. Marx, glad to get his freedom, married Jenny von Westphalen and went to Paris.

Marx and the Utopian Socialists

On arriving in Paris Marx commenced a serious study of socialism which he knew nothing about at that time. Paris was the very centre of socialist theory and utopian hopes for a new and better world. The leaders of socialist thought were men of great ability and warm humanity, who had come to understand that the French Revolution, with its watchwords Liberty, Equality and Fraternity, had emancipated the bourgeoisie but reduced the workers to greater misery than they had experienced under the Bourbons. St. Simon, Fourier and Baboeuf saw the whole problem in socialist terms. They denounced all who lived without working as "parasites on the community" and declared that "all men ought to work". They looked with horror and indignation at the wholesale destruction of the life and liberty of the individual by the monstrous regime of financiers, industrialists, judges, soldiers and administrators. The new economic freedom had only enslaved men.

St. Simon saw a new ruling class arising of scientists, technicians and administrators to replace King and Church. This meant a new stage in historical development, the creation of new institutions to fit the present age. All the socialists proposed various plans for model social systems, but the basic idea was that the clever and the good would take charge and build a better world for the grateful poor. It was to such benefactors that the poor should look for help.

Marx and his friend Engels had a great admiration for these men.

"We delighted in the stupendously grand thoughts and genius of thought that everywhere breaks out through their fantastic covering and to which philistines are blind."[1]

But they believed that their utopianism, like religious dreams and like the speculations of German philosophers, belonged to the age of impotence, to the period of historical and economic backwardness which could only solve its problems *in the mind*, in the realm of ideas; Marx believed that this was because social development in Germany had not yet made their concrete solution practicable. But that very possibility was now, at last, because of the development of capitalism, becoming a real possibility.

In his study of the utopian socialists Marx was greatly influenced by the ideas of St. Simon, who died in 1825. St. Simon belonged to a younger branch of an aristocratic French family, and even his socialism was élitist. He believed in a social hierarchy in which each man would be placed according to his capacity and government would be in the hands of a ruling group of scientists and cultural leaders. He saw it as something like a church of a new kind representing science and industry, and clearly as a kind of technocracy.

St. Simon demanded that all should work, but his workers were going to include the manufacturers and bankers. What is important about his utopia is that economics entirely absorbs politics—the administration of things replaces political rule over men.

He had an evolutionary theory of social development based on technological advance. In each age man's needs are met and institutions are created to suit that stage of progress. Hitherto the law of humanity had been the exploitation of man by man on three successive levels—

[1] Engels, *Anti-Dühring*, Part III, chapter 1.

slavery, serfdom and the proletariat; but in the future the principle would be "the exploitation of the globe by man associated with man". It is clear how much of Marx's thought is derived from this man.

From Fourier Marx enthusiastically accepted his rejection of "the frenzy of speculation, the spirit of devouring commercialism" Fourier saw the workers as "the suffering class" and the upper classes as their enlightened benefactors. For the last ten years of his life he waited in his apartments at noon every day for the wealthy capitalist who would supply the means for the realisation of his schemes!

Unlike St. Simon's socialism which was based on authority, that of Fourier made every possible provision for local and individual freedom. He envisaged his socialism with an organised group called a phalange as the basic unit, each to consist of four hundred families. These would freely organise themselves into wider combinations.

Marx recognised both the virtues and the mistakes of such utopian forms of socialism. What he particularly objected to was the notion that socialism was to be bestowed from above by disinterested members of the ruling class. Marx believed that the emancipation of the working class must be the task of the working class itself:

"We must not say to the world, listen to us, for we possess the real truth. Instead we must show the world why it struggles. As history develops and with it the struggle of the proletariat, this consciousness is a thing it must acquire whether it likes it or not." [1]

When Engels made the acquaintance of Marx in Paris in August 1844, he was able to tell him of the powerful Chartist Movement in England, of the British trade unions, of the strong feeling of class solidarity and the militancy of the organised workers. They both realised that the utopian socialists had entirely failed to understand the role of the workers themselves in effecting the transition to socialism. Marx now complemented his belief that only common ownership would overcome alienation with the further conviction that this was not something the wise and good would do *for* the poor, but something the workers would have to do for themselves.

The Utopians had not been able to conceive of the workers acting as an independent social force. They looked upon the proletariat as a sore and nothing else, and watched with horror the spread of this sore with the growth of industry. Marx based his hopes upon the growth

[1] Marx quoted by Mehring in his *Karl Marx*, p. 61 (letter dated September 1843).

of the proletariat, *and their enlightenment:* "the lightning of thought" must penetrate them, and "then they would become men".

The Gospel of Mammonism

One of the most influential literary figures of the 19th century in England was Thomas Carlyle. With the style of a Hebrew prophet, a vigorous intellect and great courage, Carlyle attacked the mean scepticism of his day, the languishing debilitated negativism and flimsy superficialities of Victorianism. In the face of its doubt and hesitancy he affirmed "the Everlasting Yea". One trumpet blast from the prophet was heard from as far away as Paris.

Carlyle was a great hater. Most of the things he hated deserved his indignation, and the one that awakened most of all his wrath was the sordid commercialism of that nation of shopkeepers, the English. Occupying all minds at that time was the new political economy, the inspiration and guiding light of the business world, based on the theory of "the economic man" who, the Benthamite philosophers said, rightly and necessarily followed his own interests, leaving it to the "unseen hand" of Adam Smith, by the subtle alchemy of the utilitarian philosophy, somehow to bring golden results for all mankind from the leaden instincts of a competitive economy.

There were spirits which revolted from the whole thing—Charles Kingsley, Frederick Denison Maurice, William Morris, and in the forties and fifties, Thomas Carlyle and John Ruskin. In 1843 Carlyle published his *Past and Present*.[1] Engels was immensely impressed and wrote a full length review article for the first Marxist publication, the *Deutsch-Französische Jahrbücher* of 1843. It was an attack on the impersonal, mechanical relations between men in a capitalist economy— the dehumanising "cash-nexus". This became the theme of Marx's *Economic and Philosophic Manuscripts of 1844.* Here the expression "cash-nexus" appears in his writings for the first time, taken directly from Thomas Carlyle.

The relevant chapter is called *The Gospel of Mammonism.* It is a critique of the new economics, widely read and discussed, and generally accepted as the philosophy of the rising capitalist economy. Carlyle repudiated this philosophy:

"Supply and demand is not the Law of Nature: Cash payment is not the sole nexus of man with man—how far from it. We for the

[1] The actual volume may be seen in the Marx Museum, Moscow.

present, with our Mammon Gospel, have come to strange conclusions. We call it a society; and go about professing openly the mutual helpfulness but rather, cloaked under due laws-of-war, named 'fair competition' and so forth, it is a mutual hostility."[1]

And what must follow is not the automatic working of natural laws to secure the harmony and happiness of man; quite otherwise:

"perpetual mutiny, contention, hatred, isolation, execration shall wait upon his footsteps, till all men discern that the thing which he attains, however golden it look or be, is not success, but the want of success."

It may surprise those who think of Marxism as no more than the hard-headed and hard-hearted struggle of the "have-nots" to improve their economic position, to find Marx in the company of Thomas Carlyle. In fact the recent discovery of the thinking involved in these basic principles and Marx's clear recognition of human values, has caused resentment amongst some Marxists. It runs counter to the operation of the programmes, and the propaganda supporting them, which some socialist political parties believe to be Marxist. Hence the tendency to write off the *Manuscripts* of 1844, as a relic of "idealism", and "immature"; and hence, therefore, the total neglect of these basic theoretical writings of Marx and the attempt to blot out every trace in Marx's writing which showed the influence and importance of the Western philosophical tradition. This is strange when we recall Engels' assertion that he and Marx had always recognised that "the German working-class movement is the inheritor of classical German philosophy".[2] Lenin himself, far from discounting the Hegelian basis of Marxism, insisted on its importance and declared that its neglect was responsible for the fact that "none of the Marxists of the past half-century has understood Marx".[3]

Marx and the Philosophers

Chief among those who influenced Marx were the German philosophers who in the 19th century were the leading thinkers of Europe; Kant, Fichte, and Hegel. Heine had said that these men

[1] Thomas Carlyle, *Past and Present* (Routledge edition, 1888), pp. 114 and 141.
[2] Engels, *Feuerbach* (ed. Dutt, 1935), p. 70.
[3] Lenin, *Philosophical Notebooks*, Collected Works, Vol. 38 (section on Hegel).

had accomplished on the intellectual plane a revolution comparable to that of Danton and Robespierre on the political plane—a revolution still to be realised beyond the intellectual world—one that would radically transform society both in its economics, its political structure, its culture and its religion.

Marx was not an isolated thinker who appeared on this planet fully armed with a complete philosophy of man and history. On the contrary he owed much to his predecessors, to the great European tradition of philosophy, itself the product of two thousand years of philosophical thinking. Nor did he sweep away the whole of classical philosophy as tendentious bourgeois ideology.

Marx had learnt from Hegel not to fight against the systems of the philosophers of the past, but to consider them as different stages in the development of thought corresponding to successive phases of civilisation. Every particular philosophy is the daughter of its own time.

"The latest birth of time is the result of all the systems which have preceded it and must include their principles, and so, if it deserves the title of philosophy will be the fullest, most comprehensive, and most adequate system of all."[1]

Marx was to develop this idea in a new and unexpected direction. No-one more completely than he was the inheritor of the whole philosophical development which he was to transform. But believing as he did that the work of philosophy was finished, that it had played its essential role in history, he was concerned with "making the world philosophical" rather than creating metaphysical fantasies of a rational world. In consequence he spent the years 1843 to 1846 in settling accounts with his erstwhile philosophical friends, the Young Hegelians—and also it must be noted with "all hitherto existing materialism including that of Feuerbach". This task accomplished, he never mentions them again; he turns to the world of economics, of politics, of imminent social change, and for the rest of his life he philosophises in concrete terms. Now all systems are finished—nor is he going to create a Marxist system. The very idea he regards as preposterous: "one will never arrive there by the universal passport of a general historico-philosophical theory, the supreme virtue of which consists in being super-historical!"[2]

---

[1] Plekhanov, Essays in the History of Materialism, p. 180.
[2] Marx-Engels Correspondence. Letter to Editor of "Notes on the Fatherland" (end of 1877).

His last vigorous and vehement engagement with his philosophical opponents will be found in *The Holy Family* (the brothers Bauer) and *The German Ideology*. There follows a rather over-emphatic criticism of Proudhon's *Philosophy of Poverty*. Proudhon, a hard-working socialist who had been a printer and was entirely self-educated, was congratulating himself on having written a Hegelian defence of socialism based on the famous triad—*thesis, antithesis, synthesis*. Marx tore his arguments to pieces in a caustic reply which he entitled *The Poverty of Philosophy*.

In all this critical work, which occupied him for several years, we recognise the characteristic method of Marx. His own opinions, says Edmund Wilson,

"seem always to have been arrived at through a close criticism of the opinions of others, as if the sharpness and force of his mind could only really exert themselves in attacks of the minds of others, as if he could only find out what he thought by making distinctions that excluded the wrong opinions of others."[1]

Marx and Engels are certainly exhilarating and often very funny when they are knocking philosophers' heads together, though Marx could waste an unconscionable amount of time and energy demolishing paper tigers like Herr Vogt. But his polemical style was often put to better use. No one ever had so deadly a sense of the infinite capacity of human nature for remaining oblivious or indifferent to the pain we inflict on others when we have the chance to get something out of them for ourselves. And Marx can show himself a master of satire in the manner almost of a Swift. This is true of much of the first volume of *Capital*, once we have got through the difficulties of the opening chapters. The horrors of the industrial revolution depicted there are not only the result of the operation on humanity of a remorseless non-human force. There is also a human principle at work—"those passions which are", says Marx, "at once the most violent, the basest, and the most abominable of which the human beast is capable—the furies of self-interest." Here is a vision that appals us and yet fascinates, the evolution of mechanical production and the magnetic accumulation of capital, rising out of the feudal world, wrecking it and over-spreading it; accelerating, reorganising, reassembling, in ever more ingenious complexity, sending its commerce across the oceans and the continents as it lays hold on the destinies of the nations of the world,

[1] Edmund Wilson, *To the Finland Station*.

reducing men to productive units, overriding their personalities and aspirations, without their really grasping what has happened to them.

Hegel had called this the unconscious action and reaction of industrial and spiritual forces which so strangely brings about the unintended, "the cunning of reason". Marx, unlike Hegel, believed that what had been an unconscious process in the past must now become the conscious and intelligent work of men; but he continues to affirm to the end his immense indebtedness to Hegel. Marx will be totally misunderstood unless we put him back into the great philosophical tradition of Western Europe rather than detach him wholly from it and link him. with the empiricism and rationalism of the positivists.

Nobody knows Marx who has not recognised the basic principles which Marx derived from Hegel and then translated into material terms, thus revealing them as operating in the real world and not in the world of pure thought: they are the self-creation of man through labour—alienation and its overcoming—and transcendence, "going beyond" present categories, legal principles and all existing political and economic systems.

It was his task now to find his theory in practice, and make his practice the realisation of his theory. This does not mean *applying* his theory *to* the facts, but understanding the ever changing situation in order to control and change it, a proceeding which will itself modify the theory and correct it. From now on Marx teaches by participation in events as well as by unveiling their meaning in his critical writings. What is happening before his eyes is history moving towards the transcendence of a great social and political system, still sure of itself but with its dissolution already implicit. His part is to secure the understanding and involvement of the people in this change, as the necessary condition of society becoming at last, as Hegel anticipated, rational.

"The realisation of reason implies the overcoming of this alienation, the establishment of a condition in which the subject knows and possesses itself in all its objects."[1]

This is how the Hegelian sees it. For Marx it is the transcendence of the class system and of the alienation it inevitably brings with it; the healing of the breach between the subject, man, and his work; the arrangement of the empirical world "so that in it man experiences and

[1] Marcuse, *Reason and Revolution.*

becomes accustomed to what is really human and becomes aware of himself as man".[1]

Let us consider *Capital* from this point of view. Does it show the working out of Marx's already finished theory? Where is there such a theory? The creation of any such thing is far from Marx's intentions. Or is the theory gradually coming to light in *Capital*, so that we can extract it, and build it into a complete system from which all the facts and laws of capitalism and socialism can be deduced from now to eternity? This is to go back to Hegel's Absolute Idea of which all history is the explication. Surely Marx expects us to have finished altogether with "the labyrinth of systems"—*all* systems past and present, and we shall go wrong if we look for one. What we have to do is to confront the actual situation with the basic principles of Marxism to help us. But even such principles will mean nothing, except in so far as they are seen to be at work in the actual situation. By themselves, principles are vacuous. They are nothing apart from our firm grip on the facts. From now on we do not philosophise or systematise any more. "We make the fossilised conditions dance to their own tune."

The intention of Marx was to develop this understanding over the whole field of economics, law, sociology, history and culture. He never got farther than his "historical sketch of the genesis of capitalism in Western Europe", an unfinished fragment even of that.[2]

What, then, is *Capital?* It is not the quintessence of Marxism. It is not "The Revolutionists Handbook". Still less is it a text-book of Marxist economics. Marx was anxious to get it over and done with (indispensable preliminary though it was), so that he could get on to something more interesting.[3]

He set his hand to other tasks under the compulsion of the events and political problems of the times. Some of the most illuminating expositions of Marxism resulted. Events in France gave rise to *The Eighteenth Brumaire of Louis Bonaparte, Class Struggles in France,* and *The Civil War in France* which dealt with the Paris Commune. Marx provides a chart of the currents running below the surface of French politics during the turbulent years between 1830 and 1871, during

---

[1] Marx and Engels, *The Holy Family.*
[2] The rest of the material which Marx had accumulated was subsequently put together by Engels in the Second and Third Volumes of *Capital.* The Fourth is Kautsky's arrangement known as *Theories of Surplus Value,* subsequently re-arranged and re-edited at the Institute of Marxism–Leninism, Moscow.
[3] "I am beginning to be tired of it" (Marx, Engels *Werke,* Vol. xxvii, p. 228).

which there were three revolutionary upheavals. In these studies he discovers the influence of class interests operating beneath the surface phenomena of party slogans and abstract concepts. Never relinquishing the economic thread, he is able to penetrate all the pageantry of Legitimists and Orleanists, Bonapartists, Republicans and The Party of Order, and to show what had really happened in France after the abdication of Louis-Philippe. The great industrialists, the big landlords and the financiers, had combined against the small bourgeoisie and the workers. Never after we have read *The Eighteenth Brumaire* can the language, the conventions, the combinations, the pretensions, of parliamentary bodies seem the same to us. They lose their consistency— evaporate before our eyes. Now for the first time we can see through the shadow play to the conflicts of interests which, partly unknown to the parties themselves, are the driving force beneath the surface.

There is the real stuff of Marxism, too, in the letters. Almost a treatise in itself is the long letter to the German Social Democratic leaders about their provisional political formulation known as *The Gotha Programme*. His enormous correspondence with people in every land reminds one of the letters of Voltaire and the Encyclopedists in the 18th century, as both apply their new methods to current events, and to the historical questions that came their way. There was, too, the remarkable range of personalities who found their way to London to see Marx and afterwards started and continued a correspondence with him, or were sometimes waspishly discussed in Marx's letters to Engels. Among them were Russian, French and Italian exiles, Germans later to become the revisionist leaders of the German Social Democrats like Bernstein and Bebel, or men of the left like Kautsky and Mehring. We hear about Bakunin and the anarchists, about the romantic and baffling figure of Lassalle, of the early trade union leaders in Britain, Applegarth, Burt and John Burns. In these letters, and in all his occasional writing dealing with affairs of the day all the world over, in articles and pamphlets on Palmerston, on the American Civil War, on revolution in Spain, on India, we are constantly made to feel the excitement of a new intellectual insight into the march of history. Marx's writing is vigorous and vivid, with the energy that both comprehends and expresses with wit and sometimes tragic invective the illusions and manoeuvres that characterised European politics in his day.

It was with considerable surprise that in the autumn of 1868 Marx learned that a Russian translation of *Capital* was in hand and would shortly be submitted for publication in St. Petersberg. The Tsarist censorship gave permission with the following interesting justification:

"Although in his convictions the author is undoubtedly a socialist and the whole book reveals a definitely socialist character, yet, noting that its treatment cannot be called accessible to everyone and that, on the other hand, its form is that of a scientific-mathematical argumentation, the committee recognises that for this book prosecution in the Courts is impossible."[1]

The original edition of *Capital* had been in German and had been published in 1867. The first English translation did not appear until 1887, four years after Marx's death. Marx had begun to show an interest in Russian affairs some years before in connection with the Third Volume of *Capital* (much of which was actually written before Volume One). He learnt Russian, read widely in the Russian classics, and made exhaustive studies in Russian agriculture, the development of capitalism, and the prospects of revolution. He believed that the village communes might develop in a revolutionary direction and that Russia "had the finest chance ever offered to escape the fatal vicissitudes of capitalist development."[2] The Russian Marxist, Vera Zasulich, discussed this possibility with him again in 1881. Riazanov[3] discovered among Marx's papers several drafts of a reply, among them the suggestion that "the physical configuration of the Russian land invited mechanical farming organised on a vast scale and cooperatively run".[4]

This was one of the last of Marx's unfinished writings. He was now old and very ill, almost unable to work. Much earlier he had suggested that the contradictions of capitalism might come to a head not in the industrially advanced countries, but when similar contradictions arose in a country with a backward industry, but coming within the orbit of Western capitalism.[5] These were exactly the conditions that were found in Russia in 1917.

Marx died on March 14, 1883, after suffering the two heavy blows of the death of his wife and his eldest daughter. The ferocious Marx was a devoted family man. On reading the letters he wrote, in failing health,

[1] Quoted in Leontiev's *Marx's Capital*, p. 120.
[2] Marx to the Editor of *Notes on the Fatherland* (end of 1877).
[3] Founder and Director of the Marx-Engels Institute, Moscow.
[4] Marx-Engels Archives, Vol. I, pp. 318-43.
[5] Marx and Engels, *The German Ideology*.

to his daughter Eleanor, we find in this stern man a spring of tenderness. He never posed either as saint or hero. When, as is sometimes the case, he is represented in such terms, we might remember that he himself in answer to the question as to what was his favourite motto, replied, "I am a man, and nothing human is alien to me."[1]

[1] From a manuscript by Marx's daughter Laura, in *Reminiscences of Marx and Engels* (Moscow).

4

MARX AND PHILOSOPHY

"Every genuine philosophy is the spiritual quintessence of its time," said Marx. It is more than a system examining the world from without, it is within its world as well as above it, it informs and controls the thinking, feeling and activities of its age. The philosophy of the second half of the 19th century was that of Hegel, and no one understood him better than Marx. But Hegel himself felt that philosophy had come to a new phase in the development of human thought and in the process of history; like the present world, philosophy itself was becoming worldly, and the world at the same time was becoming philosophical. It was the living soul of a contemporary culture. "It is something not difficult", Hegel said, "to see that our time is a time of birth and transition to a new period."

But Hegel and Marx drew dramatically opposite conclusions from this. Hegel believed that all his concepts terminated in the existing social and political system in Germany. Marx, on the contrary, saw the philosophy of the age turning against the existing social order, because the latter was supremely un-philosophical, not rational, not a unity but divided. Thus the closer philosophy draws to the world the more it creates a condition of violent tension.

Indeed, Hegel himself spoke of transition as though conscious of a truth beyond his own acceptance of the *status quo* as already the embodiment of reason. For Marx, thought entering into the world was not merely at work giving itself a new form, it was becoming the very consciousness of change, all its categories not conforming to the world but criticising it, an indictment not a justification, breaking with all traditional formulations and trends.

The philosophy that is the quintessence of *this* world is the consciousness of its forthcoming and immanent social transformation moving under the law of its own development to the moment of revolutionary change.

Whitehead says that as long as things drift along in the old way men take things as they come, with a good deal of grumbling. "But when for human experience quick change arrives human nature passes into hysteria. While for some, heaven dawns, for others hell yawns open." The essence of life is to be found in the frustration of established order and in the sheer confusion of an old system unable to unify and rationalise the facts of economic and political life. It is the realisation that this heralds a new pattern of human life that elicits the excitement of life in our time. "One must not let oneself be alarmed by the storm that accompanies a new world philosophy."

Of course some hasten to assure us that all is well, and attempt to repair the damage; it is the historic role of others to take in hand the business of changing the world, of beginning to make it rational. The categories of Hegel's philosophy are reflected in existing institutions; the categories of Marx's philosophy do not conform to the world but criticise it and contradict it. They are an indictment, not a justification, of the existing order, breaking with traditional formulations and values.

Thus the transition to a new age begins with a conflict of ideas, the war of the philosophies. Marx applied this conception in a totally unexpected way. Who were the enlightened? Who were to make society rational? Was it the intellectual élite? Was it an enlightened ruling class? No, it would be the people themselves, the chief sufferers of the alienation which capitalism had imposed upon mankind. A class will arise, said Marx, which has suffered the loss of its humanity, and which can only redeem itself by a total redemption of humanity.

The attack on existing society and its justifying ideology is more than an intellectual assault, though it is that. It is the coming to political consciousness of the working class. "Theory becomes a material force as soon as it lays hold of the masses."

This is both a critical and a political movement.

Marx argues that the criticism of philosophy does not remain on the level of theoretical discussion but "leads to tasks which can only be solved by means of practical activity". If this is effective in making the social order more genuinely rational, thus achieving what Hegelian philosophers mistakenly imagined to be already the case, the setting free of people to realise their potentialities, then philosophy as a theory is in process of entering the world, of reaching the position of its actualisation—Hegel's own belief and hope—and therefore of its abolition as a philosophy. "You cannot, however, abolish philosophy without realising it."[1]

The rationalists who think that metaphysics can simply be thrown

[1] Marx, *Critique of Hegel's Philosophy of Right* (Bottomore's translation), p. 50.

overboard are wrong. "Philosophy can only be realised by the abolition of the proletariat, and the proletariat can only be abolished by the *actualisation* of philosophy",[1] of the rational order it has imagined and dreamed about.

This movement of philosophy in the direction of a critique of both the ideology and the reality of bourgeois society owed a great deal to a Polish philosopher von Cieszkowski who in 1838 was arguing that with Hegel philosophy had reached its culmination, and had achieved everything of which pure philosophy was capable. But its highest achievement in this form could only look back on history to explain it. Hegel himself had said, "The owl of Minerva only takes its flight when the evening shadows fall." That is to say, philosophy can only explain history after it has happened. It cannot anticipate the future.

But why cannot philosophy look to the future? Hegel had not been able, as we might have expected, to proclaim the unfolding of the Idea whose future development could be foreseen. Cieszkowski on the other hand saw philosophy as embracing the field of action and acceptance of responsibility for the future. This called for a synthesis of thought and action which he called *praxis*. Philosophy was "to become a practical philosophy or rather a philosophy of practical activity, of 'praxis', exercising a direct influence on social life and developing the future in the realm of concrete activity".[2]

It is here that we find the powerful intellectual influence that turned the thought of Marx to the realisation of philosophy by making *the world* really philosophical, and by transcending, "going beyond", the existing order and structure of society altogether. But this cannot happen until people understand the limitations of the present order which is holding them back, see the reality and possibility of their situation, and are ready to act. This enlightenment of the people Marx saw as the people "becoming philosophical", in order to actualise the dream of rationality and of a society which fulfils the lives of its members, and by doing this going beyond philosophy as an intellectual system, as a theory standing over against the world, to the realisation of its dream.

Marx never sees this process otherwise than as human fulfilment. What he had learned from Feuerbach was that man must pass beyond his present state of compensating for his frustrations by inventing religions and philosophies, in which all he sought to be was achieved

[1] Marx, *Critique of Hegel's Philosophy of Right* (Bottomore's translation), p. 59.
[2] Cieskowski, *Prolegomena*.

—in fantasy. Man must come to recognise that he dreams and philosophises and creates the image of the divine just because he is deprived. But he must actualise *himself*, and become what he really can be instead of losing himself in the illusion of a pre-existent perfection, either philosophical or theological.

Marx does far more than see this as a rationalist argument against religious illusion. He relates it immediately to the point in history at which we are. The state of alienation, of de-humanisation, a falling short, will cancel itself when it sees its own plight for what it is. This cannot take place merely by argument and education. It demands a stage in social development in which the conditions are prepared both for understanding and for action. Marx sees the history of the world as a process by which man gradually makes himself fully man. This, at the period of history we are entering, said Marx, presents us with urgent tasks to perform, rather than more and more philosophical attempts to explain why things are and have to be as contradictory, as irrational and as frustrating to human hopes as they are.

The philosophies of his day, as of ours, set themselves the task of revealing the ultimate meaning of our perplexing life; of finding an answer to the problem of evil. But Marx rejects all theories which seek merely to offer us a solution to the mystery of human life as it is. There is no "problem of evil", but only problems not beyond solution and evils not past the possibility of alleviating.

Man, who lives in a world of hazards, is bound to seek for security; and there are two ways in which he can obtain it. He may propitiate the powers which stand above the chances and changes of this mortal life, and place his trust in another world. By such means he can adjust himself to his environment by modifying his own attitude to his sufferings. The other way is to change the world through action, as the first is the method of changing the self in emotion and idea.

Marx chose the way of making clear to man the immediate perils it was in his power to escape, and the immediate possibilities it was within his scope to realise—this being the recognition of a developing historical situation which had enlarged the possibilities while at the same time it intensified the peril.

Marx saw the explanatory philosophies of the past as proclaiming a higher realm of reality of which alone true knowledge is possible, in opposition to the imperfect world of changing things with which practical matters are concerned. They glorified the invariant at the expense of change and held before man the vision of the *antecedently real*, rather than, as is the case in practical affairs, the necessity of gaining the understanding which is necessary to deal with the problems immediately confronting us. Marx's new approach might well be described as loosening philosophy from the theoretical tyranny of a transcendental perfection, from mistaking such conceptual systems for reality and as having the authority of reality.

This attitude involves a new conception of knowledge itself. Mind is no longer a spectator beholding the world as it is and seeking to explain it in terms of a transcendental reality. Mind is within the world as a part of the world's own process of development. It is marked off by the fact that wherever it is found, change takes place in a *directed* way, from confusion to clarity, from obstruction to overcoming. This means, in philosophy, a shift from knowing which simply makes a difference to the knower but none to the world, to knowing which is a directed change within the world.

When we compare Marx's attitude to that of the great explanatory and reconciling philosophies, with their answers to every problem, we find a philosophy that breathes a strikingly different spirit. Practice becomes the life of theory; theory the guide to practice. *The subject-matter of philosophy is not "the whole universe indivisible" but the specific problems of man, history and culture.* An answer to those problems may be recognised as genuine only in so far as it gives us a leverage to deal with the concrete difficulties out of which those problems have arisen.

For the philosophers the irrationalities of existence were to be overcome by further reflection, by pure logical analysis, for there was nothing intelligible outside of the system. For Marx activity was an essential, and the making and remaking of society was the process of achieving rationality.

We must choose between actualising the possibility of a more rational state of affairs or accepting the actuality at hand, between speculating about possibilities without enquiring whether they can be converted into existence or grappling with the necessities and possibilities of radical change.

To theorise about the nature of the good state without trying to make the existing state good is in effect to accept the existing state. In this way, a theory proud of its impracticality is in reality viciously practical. Pretending to be indifferent to the effects of thought, it has very definite effects of its own. Contemplative philosophies are not so far removed from life as they are taken to be. They represent a way of life, and as such must be judged by their consequences. In his analysis of social and philosophical theories, Marx shows himself to be intensely alive to the social practices with which, no matter how reconditely, those theories are involved. The purpose of his own social theories was to provide that knowledge of social tendencies which would most effectively liberate *action*. *Philosophy is not speculative insight* into the nature of existence to assure us that in spite of appearances it is really good and rational. That is to look back to the past, to the ultimate origin. *Its function is prospective anticipation of the future, to explain why the present is what it is in order to make it different.* So often an expression of social quietism, or a means of individual escape, philosophy in the future must function as an instrument of social liberation. The world is not inherently reasonable, as Hegel claimed. It must be made reasonable.

It was Feuerbach who showed Marx that speculative philosophy and religion were trying to derive the world of man from their own abstractions. It is not the Idea which manifests itself in history, or God that creates the world; it is men who objectify their fantasies, hopes and compensating illusions. All properties of the grand Idea, the subject whose objects are things and men, the creations which it contemplates, are nothing more than representations of powers of the human mind expressed in metaphors and abstractions. But here Feuerbach stopped, and it was Marx who then showed how man is not a mere object within nature acted upon by his material environment, as he was for Feuerbach's materialism; but is engaged in creating his world and himself, by his work, in society, and through his knowledge. Thus men, their urgent needs, their ever-growing and changing needs, and the means they discover to satisfy them, become the basis of all our thinking, and of the whole course of human development. Thus the movement of history is not imposed by Absolute Mind, nor is it the result of a dynamic urge within matter; it develops out of man's changing and improving methods of satisfying his needs.

Feuerbach, and after him Marx, thus came to lay the whole stress of his thinking upon man, man not as a unit, but as essentially social, knowing himself and his world only in cooperatively mastering and developing the material environment. Philosophy, therefore, begins and ends, in Marx's words with "real active men, and on the basis of their real life processes".[1]

Aristotle described man as a *zoon politikon*, a political animal. He did not mean, of course, a man who is interested in politics, but a man who lives and moves and has his being in a civil society. Marx

[1] Marx and Engels, *The German Ideology*.

makes this the basis of his understanding of human nature. When he speaks of "essential man", or "species man", he emphatically disclaims meaning man as an abstract entity, he means that man is everywhere involved in social relations and is constituted by them.

"Man is in the most literal sense of the word a political animal: not only a social animal, but an animal which can develop into an individual only in society. Production by isolated individuals outside society is as great an absurdity as the idea of the development of language without individuals living together and talking to one another".[1]

Although Marx now passes beyond the phase of philosophical speculation, he declares his permanent indebtedness to the whole tradition of German philosophy from Kant and Fichte to Hegel, which Engels described as "the glory of Germany in the days of its deepest political humiliation".[2] Those who merely abandoned philosophy, said Engels, were no more than philistines. "If German philosophy, particularly that of Hegel, had not previously existed, scientific socialism would never have existed".

Marx and Engels regarded Hegel's philosophy as the last and greatest of the philosophies, bequeathing to his successors the conception of the world as a changing and developing organism, transforming itself endlessly in a constant process of "becoming" and passing beyond its present condition to the embodiment of reason in society. It thus extended to the entire world the notion of development and progress which the rationalist had limited to mental development and emancipation. The German philosophers thought of mind not as observing the world from outside, but penetrating what it worked on, and controlling its historical evolution. This lifted the rationalist understanding of man's control of nature on to a new and vitally important level.

Kant's great contribution to philosophical thought was his insight into the creative and constitutive activity of minds, which did not reflect, but created the world of knowledge—a view which did not of course, deny the existence of the material world. Kant had begun by showing that the mind selects and organises its data in the very

---

[1] Marx, *Grundrisse, General Introduction,* originally printed as the Appendix to the *Critique of Political Economy* to which it is not, of course, the Introduction.
[2] Engels, *Ludwig Feuerbach,* Ch. I.

act of knowing. Fichte showed that in our life in the world we make it over again, we modify it, we recreate it. Only thus does it come to be *our* world. Thus, has not man at the same time as he makes his world *made himself*? Can any ego, any self, come into existence except as man makes his world?

Fichte had a very great influence on Marx. From him came the notion that man creates himself as he creates his world, so that the external world is not the "given", but a creation, expression and instrument of the thinking, active subject. This dialectical development determines the radical transformation of reality, and at the same time the successive stages in the development of human personality. So much for Fichte. As Marx interpreted Fichte's idea, man manipulates the world, tills it, builds, organises transport, makes machines, and by so doing makes himself at the same time. Man *is* what he *does*. Both the world and human nature are not things which are *given*, but things which man makes. But Marx was always careful to add that "in all this, the priority of external nature remains unassailed."[1]

Marx saw these philosophers as engaged in a problem which the materialists had abandoned by separating sense knowledge from the material world and restricting knowledge to the sense impressions in their minds. The world itself lay outside and beyond their knowing. This the idealist philosophers, and Marx, regarded as quite unacceptable. The knower and the known had been separated. The idealist philosophers reunited them in their new theory of knowledge, which was also a new theory of science, a new theory of nature, and a new theory of man.

This philosophical development reached its climax in Hegel, whom Marx continued to the end of his life to regard as his teacher.

In addition to Hegel's theory of knowledge which united subject and object, as we have seen, Marx recognised three great truths which he interpreted in materialistic terms and embodied in his own philosophy.

1. That the material and spiritual powers of mankind had reached a degree of maturity which made it possible to reorganise social and political life in accordance with reason.
2. That philosophy is the age's consciousness of itself, and that idealism had revealed the world not as a dead mechanism but as a changing developing organism within which man plays a creative role as he makes and remakes his world.

[1] *The German Ideology*, Part I.

3. That in creating his world and at the same time himself, through labour, man finds that what he has made stands over against him as an oppressive and hostile force—man is alienated.

Where Marx departed from Hegel was in seeing the history and development of man wholly in terms of a natural process, whereas Hegel saw it as essentially the unfolding of the Absolute Idea so that the goal was already, in essence, achieved, and the course of history its inevitable actualisation. This theory was an attempt to explain the whole world and everything in it, and the whole course of events, in terms of an order of reality transcending experience.

Marx, on the other hand, was not seeking an explanation transcending experience in a metaphysical way, but looking at real men as gaining an increasing control over nature and thus the better able to improve their conditions of living. There is no mysterious necessity about this, nor any belief in a predetermined utopia. Nor is there any attempt to explain history as the outcome of either a deterministic process or an overriding destiny of some philosophical kind.

In the years following the death of Hegel there was a widespread feeling that philosophy had come to an end, and that there was now only one form in which the truth could be found and manifested, not in the realm of thought but in society, in man's actual existence. While some religious thinkers began to speak of the realisation of God through the deification of man, and Hegel declared that the embodiment of Reason in history reaches its completion in Germany (where mind and all that is rational is objectified in the institutions of society), Marx, relating the origin and development of the individual to co-operative labour, found in the extension of social ownership and co-operation the real basis for man's emancipation and the realisation of philosophy.

Marx came to Berlin to study philosophy just as the younger philosophers were packing up to come out into the world. In all the books published by these vigorous and earnest men, from Hess's *Philosophy of Action* in 1834, to Marx and Engels' *German Ideology* in 1846 the central theme was how to get a grip on political events, how to solve the problems of modern Europe, and especially Germany. "There are moments", said Marx, "when philosophy turns its eyes to the external world."

But the followers of Hegel soon became at variance. While all

of them wanted to come out into the world and face reality most of
the "Young Hegelians" saw the road to future rationality as the way
of intellectual criticism of dogma and illusion; but Marx took a
different line. The process of realising this ideal appeared to him to
depend upon the maturing of social and economic conditions, and
especially the full development of the machine age and the industrial
proletariat.

In the course of history, says Marx, progress takes place through
the appearance of contradictions between the developing forces of
production and the existing method of organising that production.
To *get beyond* these contradictions man must face the task of reorganising society, of changing the pattern of his economy.

This in briefest summary is the process of technological advance
and change of pattern that characterises the successive phases in social
development. However, for many thousands of years each socio-
economic system had been a form of class society involving exploitation, whether of slaves, or serfs, or wage earners. The next advance in
history, says Marx, will pass beyond this kind of class structure and
eliminate economic exploitation altogether. Man today is not simply
making a technological advance, as he might have done a thousand
years ago, and then bringing his social organisation into line with it;
he is facing the necessity of a major transformation of the whole of
society, ultimately involving not only its economy, but its class structure,
its institutions and its ideology.

This long process Hegel saw as giving rise to three great epochs of
history—the Graeco-Roman, the Medieval, the Germanic-Christian, as
we might briefly designate them. This process, always induced by the
maladjustment of form (organisation, economic and political) to
function (productive potentiality), Hegel calls "transcendence" or
"supersession"—the key to his dialectic. (In German the word is
Aufhebung, which means lifting up, cancelling, transcending, going
beyond.)

This is the essential meaning of dialectics—beginning in the reciprocal process of primitive man making his world and so making
himself, and then energetically developing his techniques under the
stimulus of the first forms of human organisation. The very success
of this development soon demands fresh organisational changes,
institutions, and economic categories—the next *Aufhebung* or "going
beyond". These once established, we have a new pattern of society,
and a new man. Under the encouragement of this improved economic

organisation, the forces of production again move forward. Thus the reciprocity of changing social forms, changing methods of production, and changes in the habits and character of man proceed *dialectically*; ever transcending one form by another.

Marx sees the overcoming of alienation, of the contradictions of capitalism, as heralded by the disintegration of its ideological forms, its ethics, its philosophy, as demanding "going beyond" its categories, its economic laws, its political institutions, and its class basis.

Such social change depends on men thoroughly understanding the nature of the contradictions and obstacles which confront them, bringing all the resources of intelligence to devise a way out that will overcome the difficulties, set men's energies free, and create new patterns of economic and social life.

This process, constantly repeated, is the dialectic of history, the driving force of which is insight into the objective situation which allows man to release the forces making for fulness of life, liberty and rationality. This alone puts an end to external determination and sets men free. Freedom is not stepping outside the realms of law on the one hand, or acquiescing in the inevitable on the other, but *understanding* the situation and doing what without invention and intelligence would never happen at all.

In this way Marx interprets Hegel not in Hegel's own terms of the logical unfolding of the Idea in history, which would appear as some immanent principle of historical development—and would be precisely that objectionable type of speculative metaphysics which he rejected, but translating Hegel's position into wholly realistic terms, accepting no premises but man at work in the material world.

So long as the conditions were not ripe, capitalism itself not sufficiently advanced, and the productive forces themselves not sufficiently developed, philosophies, religions and utopias would necessarily continue. For instance, an unjust society, says Marx, inevitably produces religion, which is the "inverted consciousness" of an "inverted world". It is the imaginary realisation of the true human being, and at the same time the expression of and protest against real suffering. It is through religions and philosophies that we seek to overcome our unhappy lot and seek for some alleviation. Therefore religion cannot be attacked by itself. The criticism of religion must become the criticism of society. We must turn theological questions into social and political questions.

Marx placed together philosophies of this kind, religion, and utopian socialism, as ideological expressions of man's imperfect condition, but also as the promise of a future transformation of society to overcome that condition. All of them, he argued, point to their supersession, to the necessity of "going beyond" the conditions which make them man's protest and answer to the evils of human life. Their "truth", like that of capitalism, lies in what the present is developing into, what is concealed in the present irrational and depressing forms. For within the present is the potentiality and promise of the future. It is in this sense that Marx speaks of the "realisation of philosophy", and also the realisation of the dreams of utopian socialism, and the ideal of the State. Marx and Engels paid a warm tribute to the utopian socialists whose theories, crude as they were, corresponded to the crude conditions of economic development at that time. The real solution "as yet lay hidden in the undeveloped economic conditions", so that the utopian could only create ideal solutions out of their brains.

These ideologies, before the time of radical transformation has arrived, conceal the germ of that time within themselves, but when the development of events and of the resources of production create the necessary conditions for practical measures, they must be opposed as offering only illusory hopes at the very time when men should be turning to the task of changing society.

Marx thus explains and justifies both religion and philosophy as they arise in earlier times, but considers them now in a different light. But, as he goes on to say, neither the evil conditions, nor these ideologies which have arisen from them, will pass away automatically. If philosophy is to disappear it will only be by the people themselves becoming philosophical, that is to say coming to the consciousness of their situation, of the actual causes of their plight, and of the potentialities now within their grasp. It is man himself who must now proceed to make his own history, deliberately and responsibly, for the first time. That, and only that, represents for Marx at once the negation of philosophy and its realisation.

5

THE DIALECTIC

"As a consequence of the neglect of Hegel, no one has understood Marx for the last fifty years." (Lenin)[1]

In 1872, in the Preface to the Second Edition of *Capital*, Marx proclaimed himself to be still "a disciple of that great thinker [Hegel] . . . who was the first to expound the general forms of the dialectical movement in a comprehensive and fully conscious way". Hegel and Feuerbach were the two most powerful influences on Marx's thought. Feuerbach's "positive humanist and naturalistic criticism", he says, "certain, profound and lasting in its influence, contains the real theoretical revolution of our age"; while Hegel's *Phenomenology*, "the true birthplace and secret of Hegel's philosophy", is the basis of Marx's dialectical theory of social development. In the Preface to *Capital* Marx looks back to the *Economic and Philosophic Manuscripts of 1844*, that time "nearly thirty years ago", when he attempted, as he says, to separate the *kernel* of Hegel's teaching, Hegel's unique theory of how man creates himself and society and develops them both in the course of history, which he accepts, from the *husk*: "the mystifying aspect" of this process, which he rejects. In that theory, he says, "all the elements of criticism are implied, already prepared and elaborated", waiting to be unfolded and developed in a realistic way.

But what was the Hegelian principle that Marx adopted and transformed from the unfolding of the Idea to the development of history? It is not the well-known triad *thesis–antithesis–synthesis* which is not an essential part even of Hegel's system and is entirely absent from his philosophy of history. The terms are indeed Fichte's, and more properly belong to Fichte's method of thinking. Marx never used them and ridiculed poor Proudhon's use of them unmercifully in his *Poverty of Philosophy*. There is therefore no foundation for the idea that Marx, too, attempted to deduce the movement of history from the sequence of the logical categories. The dialectical theory is meant to conform to the actual movement of reality, which, however,

[1] *Philosophical Notebooks*, Collected Works, Vol. 38, p. 180.

is not as it appears to observation, any more than is the movement of the sun.

Neither is the dialectic a general philosophical theory of history imposed upon the actual pattern of historical events. The Russian sociologist Michailovsky thought so, and was speedily disillusioned by Marx[1] who informed him that *Capital* was not intended to be anything more than an historical outline of the origins and development of capitalism in Western Europe. Lenin underlined Marx here: "No Marxist has ever regarded Marx's theory as a general and compulsory philosophical scheme of history, or as anything more than an explanation of a particular social and economic formation."[2]

Marx's theory of social development, as we find it in *Capital*, may be said to possess a general validity only in the sense that any searching, empirical analysis of a given social structure has a relevance transcending its own particular subject matter.

Lenin also rejected "the stereotyped charge of Hegelian dialectics", quoting Engels to the effect that "Marx never even thought of 'proving' anything by means of Hegelian triads".[3]

Nor is Marxism an attempt to force all experience into the design of a monistic construction of the universe in order to build a unified system of knowledge—a science of the sciences. Marxism while accepting the material world as the origin of man and history is not concerned with cosmology or geology, or even with biology, it is

"primarily interested only in the phenomena of interrelations of historical and social life . . . only in what occurs within a short period of time and into whose development it can enter as a practical, influential force".[4]

Neither have Marxists any right to claim the undeniable superiority of Marxism in the field of sociology as grounds for creating a Marxist theory of the natural sciences. This can only result in the contempt bestowed upon such efforts even by those by no means unfriendly to socialism. This is now recognised by Soviet scientists like Kapitsa and Asmus. Asmus declared emphatically that "the socio-historical

---

[1] Letter to editor of *Notes on the Fatherland*, 1877.
[2] Lenin, *What the "Friends of the People" Are*.   [3] Lenin, *loc. cit.*
[4] Korsch, "Why I am a Marxist", American *Modern Quarterly*, Vol. IX, No. 2.

sciences do not allow in principle the identification of their problems and methods with those of the natural sciences."[1]

The physicist Kapitsa said in 1960

"Had our scientists back in the year 1954 paid attention to the philosophers, who applying the principles of dialectics were proving the unsoundness of relativity, we may safely say that our conquest of space could never have been made a reality."[2]

These attempts to extend dialectics to physics, quantum mechanics and biology have now ceased. Science has, so to speak, been "declassified"; and dialectics is now, at any rate in Russia, regarded as concerned with the social and not the physical sciences. Marxism is neither a positive materialist philosophy nor a positivist theory of science. From beginning to end it is a theoretical as well as a practical *critique* of existing society. Thus Marxism returns to its real province.

What was the essential principle which Marx accepted and made the basis of his theoretical work? Although Hegel saw all history as the manifestation in the real world of the Absolute, Idea, Spirit, he saw this in completely realistic terms. It is the *actual* world, as we experience it and see it, that is the manifestation of Reason and Reality. It was this *realism* of Hegel's that impressed Marx.

The *Phenomenology*, which is the work that Marx discusses at length in the *Manuscripts* of 1844, is Hegel's exposition of his theory of man creating himself and his world in the course of history, and he sees this as taking place through *work*. "He grasps the nature of *work*", says Marx, "and comprehends objective man, authentic because *actual*, as the result of *work*." Hegel is also realistic enough to see the appearance, in this world which man builds, of a master–slave relationship, which in modern industry affects man's life so that he is "alienated" and unfulfilled.

This theory, and in particular Hegel's theory of man's creation of the object by his labour, Marx adopted as the clue to his own account of human history; but his basis, the source of the whole process, is not, as with Hegel, the unfolding of Idea, but the activity of man as a living thinking working organism. Marx is thus taking the Hegelian theory and *inverting it*. Finding it standing on its head, he turns it right way up,

[1] Professor V. Asmus, "Marxism and the Sciences" (*Voks*, 1933).
[2] Kapitsa, "Theory, Experimentation and Practice" (*Soviet Review*, June 1962).

revealing the whole process, explained by Hegel in metaphysical terms, as the material reality discovered by scientific investigation. Hegel considered beings and things in their ceaseless transformation arising from the oppositions and contradictions that are inherent in reality. Marx rejected the mystifying derivation of this but accepted the description as what indeed was happening in the world. Hegel saw the contradictory elements in reciprocal interaction and their transformation determining the evolution of the real. Marx explained this in terms of the economic and social development of society, and, in particular, gave the abstract theory the rich content of contemporary capitalism in the course of its transformation into socialism.

The "inversion" of Hegel means just that. It does not mean putting the metaphysical notion of a self-evolving principle into nature and history. This would be to perpetuate the metaphysical error of Hegel, making the history the manifestation of an abstract principle. Engels believed that he *could* discern such a principle in nature and life, the evidence for it provided by "contradictions" and by quantitative changes passing over into qualitative ones. But no such all-embracing metaphysic, covering the whole of inorganic and organic nature, and all the phenomena of history and man, could possibly be derived by logical inference from the evidence available. As Lenin said, you could not possibly demonstrate any theory of that sort from a handful of *examples* of contradiction and quantitative change.[1]

Such an all-embracing theory would provide an explanation covering all nature and history, "a law of motion both of the external world and of human thought", asserting itself unconsciously until man himself discovers it and finds his freedom in the acceptance of its necessity. But this was precisely what Marx emphatically rejected as what *he* was trying to do. He described it an an attempt to "metamorphose my historical sketch of the genesis of capitalism in Western Europe into an historico-philosophic theory of the general path imposed by fate upon every people."[2] But nowhere in Marx's writings is there, in fact, any attempt to frame such an explanatory philosophy, embracing the whole of reality.

Marx's conception of dialectics is concerned entirely with man and history, not with nature at all. It is the notion of man's self-creation, man's intelligent activity in handling the material world and organising society. Both Hegel and Marx interpreted man's intelligent mastery

---

[1] Lenin, *Philosophical Notebooks* (on the question of Dialectics), *Collected Works*, Vol. 38.
[2] *Marx-Engels Correspondence*, end of 1877.

of his environment as culminating in the realisation in history of the real nature and destiny of man, by his successful overcoming of the economic and social contradictions of society and the achievement of a rational social order.

Thus, throughout his work, from its first sketch in the *Economic and Philosophic Manuscripts of 1844* to the end of *Capital*, the dialectic is concerned with man and history, not with nature, except, as we shall see, that all our *knowledge* of nature, mediated as it is through human experience, human aims and values, and all the historical conditions of the movement, is essentially dialectical. We must not and cannot say that nature "in itself" is changing dialectically in accordance with certain laws of motion. There can be no question of a dialectic of external nature independently of man, because all the essential moments of a dialectic in that case would be absent. Material reality as we know it is always socially mediated. Its essence is in the coincidence of changing circumstances with human activity, with man's ability to rearrange the world of which he is a part, with the discovery by man that history is his own creative act. Dialectics, as far as Marx is concerned, is not a universal process at work in the stars, in outer space, in the geological origins of the earth, in chemistry, in biology. Nor is Marx ever concerned with contradiction in *nature*. And the only sort of contradiction he is concerned with is that between the forces of production and the economic system, with those "fetters" on the productive forces when "the material forces of production come into conflict with the existing relations of production",[1] from which comes the social revolution.

But the basic dialectical process involved here is closely related to the Hegelian and the Marxist theory of knowledge; and this itself is inseparable from the relationship of man, his world and society, in their endless interaction and creative activity. We come to know the world, says Marx, only as we make it, that is to say as we pursue our positive aims in handling, manipulating, using and controlling it.[2] We know what we *make*, what we *change*, what we *use;* and only in the process of handling the material world, guided by our needs and interests, does it become for us our objective world and do we ourselves come to be men. Marx at this point explains that he rejects the earlier materialist view which thought of man and nature as two separate things, man

[1] Marx, Preface to the *Critique of Political Economy*.
[2] Marx, *First Thesis on Feuerbach*.

C

knowing the external world through its impressions on his sense organs, as though the physical world around us were "given direct from all eternity, ever the same". But, says Marx, "it is not, it is the product of industry and the state of society. It is an historical product. the result of the activity of a whole succession of generations, developing its industry and its intercourse. . . . Even objects of the simplest sensuous certainty are only given to man through social development, industry and trading intercourse."[1] Man by this same process is creating himself. He *is* what his work, his conditions of life, *his social relations*, have made him "as a real, existing, active man".

But what did Marx mean when he said "It is not the consciousness of men that determines their existence, but on the contrary, their social existence determines their consciousness"?[2] It could mean that consciousness is a glow on the surface of matter, and itself only the self-consciousness of matter, wholly ineffectual except perhaps to acquiesce in the necessity it becomes conscious of. This is not what Marx believes. Or it could mean that consciousness is a reflection, a copy, of the external world and its laws, and can utilise them by conforming strictly to them. But this is not what Marx means either.

Marx's whole intellectual effort is directed *against* this dualistic approach of mental phenomena being regarded as copies of the material world. That is why he says that the physical world is not "given direct" "ever the same", but is *made* by us and *known as made*. As Vico[3] says, and Marx knew about that 18th century genius, we unite the *factum* with the *verum*, that which we *make* with that which we *know*.

The epistemology which sees man's mind only as being created and impressed by its environment, merely determined by what exists, by the institutions, the categories of the world as it is, can only have a mind that wholly accepts the *status quo*, and can never alter it. This is the ultimate consequence of the materialistic dualism of sensation and fact that Marx so severely criticised.

What Marx means he makes clear in everything he says about man creating his world, developing his technology, and organising the economy and social institutions in the way to secure the fullest

---

[1] *The German Ideology*. Adding, "Of course, in all this the priority of external nature remains unassailed".
[2] Marx, Preface to the *Critique of Political Economy*.
[3] Giovannis Battista Vico was the first philosopher who asked, "Why have we a science of nature, but no science of history?"

satisfaction of human needs. Marx is saying that economics, laws, morals, ideas of all kinds, don't descend from heaven, but arise as man's intelligent understanding of his actual problems in the world he is changing. Idealist philosophers thought of eternal principles of a legal, economic, political and ethical nature, which man derives from above and embodies in social life. Marx rejects this entirely.

Hegel's dialectic was aimed at maintaining the unity of material existence—it was a monism, overcoming the Cartesian dualism of matter and mind, as object and subject; and secondly it was an evolving material unity of intelligent beings and their world, proceeding to *realize* its potentialities. Hegel saw as mediating change what he called *objectification*, the projection of the object to stand over against the subject, and he saw that this took place through labour. All this Marx regarded as of supreme significance and going far beyond the materialism of his day, even that of Feuerbach. But in Hegel the whole process was represented as taking place *within consciousness*, even the overcoming of the alientaion involved in objectification. But Marx in giving the whole process a materialistic setting, finds in Hegel's idealism the paradigm of actual social and human development in the world. It has not to be rejected, but translated into materialistic or naturalistic terms.

The key to the translation lies in one word—*production*. It is real man, in his world, producing his means of subsistence, producing all that satisfies his growing and changing needs, who creates society, technology, civilisation, culture, and makes and remakes himself at the same time. It is a process that involves not an undifferentiated unity (as Althusser believes) but a duality within an undivided unity—the world that remains *one*. Within that world mind and matter, subject and object must never be separated. They are distinct but inseparable and inter-dependent. If they are separated as they were when Descartes split the universe into mind and matter, and when the materialists ("*all previous materialism*"), saw matter as known in its reflection, the sensations in the mind, then it is impossible to rebuild the integrated concept of the whole organic world of man by juxtaposing these two *abstractions*—for that is what they are.

So the key to Marx's dialectics is the overcoming of the dualism of Feuerbach and the other materialists. "The secret of Marx's success in radically transforming the limitations of dualistic, contemplative materialism is his unparalleled dialectical grasp of the category of mediation,"[1] that is to say of *productive activity* between subject and object, and creating both in *work*, in production. This gives us a valid differentiation between subject and object, not found in Hegel; and at the same time a valid unity of both in man's self-made world which is *one* world, in which he belongs.

Within this unity production is the source of development and change *continuously*. There can be no objective change that is not a subjective change, and a cultural organisational and social change, for man works not as a unit, but always in co-operation, in society.

Thus we have in the dialectic an approach to the understanding of history and society in that it

"includes in its comprehension and affirmative recognition of the existing state of things, at the same time also, the recognition of the negation of that state, of its inevitable breaking up; it regards every historically developed form as in fluid movement, and therefore takes into account its transient nature not less than its momentary existence; it lets nothing impose upon it, and is in its essence critical and revolutionary".[2]

This is not merely a philosophical and anthropological question. The psychologist concerned with the development of the child's personality sees him becoming a person as he handles material objects and has connection with other people. Consciousness is functionally related to activity, powers of the mind are simply differentiations of consciousness with reference to the needs of action. Self consciousness only comes into existence in relation to consciousness of other people in the earliest forms of social activity.

The literary critic, from quite another point of view, comes to see human personality in much the same way. Professor L. C. Knights in his Shakespearian studies says,

"What is coming into consciousness is nothing less than an awareness of how men make the world they inhabit, an understanding of the relation between what men are and the kind of perceptions they have about the nature of things. It is this growing awareness that explains our source of fundamental issues coming to expression."[3]

---

[1] Maszaros, *Marx's Theory of Alienation*.
[2] Marx, *Capital*, Afterword to the second German edition.
[3] L. C. Knights, *Some Shakespearean Themes*.

Thus, as consciousness progressively takes possession of concrete reality, as man increases his mastery over nature, he begins the development of his own personality. And always, insists Marx, it is a *social* personality involving social habits, attitudes and values, felt and accepted relationships with and obligations to others—for he cannot create his world alone. Man only becomes man by accepting social responsibilities, by co-operative activity.

The history of mankind is the history of technology and science, and of the organisational forms corresponding to these. The dialectics of man's increasing control of nature is seen in the development of new needs which form the motives for improvements, in technology and science, in the organisational forms, and in new ideological system, laws, institutions and morals. No one of these can be separated out as operating independently of the other.

This is the pattern of social development which Marx finds suggested and sketched in general terms in the philosophy of Hegel, which he takes over and develops in economic and historical terms in his major works.

Marx lays the greatest stress, in this whole process from the earliest beginnings of human existence, on man as a *social* being. Men must co-operate and unite to operate any system of organisation related to any technological level, whether it be the stone axe or the modern factory. And it is the pattern of co-operation, even if it be at the same time one of exploitation, that creates the web of thought and action, of values and duties, the moral codes and religion, the institutions, that make up man's ever changing civilisation.

The historical development which Marx thus describes is the culmination of the process that begins with the appearance of man: the mastery of the environment, *the humanisation and rationalisation of the external world*. It is at the same time the making of man, for he only makes himself in so far as he humanises his environment and his relations with other men.

What do we mean by *humanising the environment*? Man changes the external world: he cultivates it, builds on it, develops transport, roads, harbours. He breeds new varieties of cattle and plants. Everywhere he sees his own handiwork. But at the same time *the environment makes man*. Wherever he changes the world, whether by invention, discovery of new sources of power, or modernised industry, he must change his own habits and forms of organisation in order to use the new methods to best advantage. Thus he brings into being all the complex ways of living and thinking, ideas, laws and customs which prove necessary for this purpose. He has changed himself.

Hegel and the young Hegelians were not only concerned with social progress. They were keenly aware of a fundamental contradiction in the process of mastering the external world and developing the potentialities of mankind. Progress there certainly was, but along with it frustration, repression, exploitation and tragedy—the condition the Hegelians and Marx called "alienation". Just as much deep consideration was given to this negative element in the development of society as to the dialectic of enlargement and fulfilment. Hegel, as we have seen, saw the solution of the problem of alienation in the rise of consciousness to a higher level, in a deeper understanding, as the *transcendence* of irrationality and contradiction. Feuerbach saw the problem in religious terms. But Marx saw it as an economic question, originating as the inevitable result of the appearance of a class system and of capitalism, under which the worker becomes a propertyless purveyor of his labour power. If that is the case, alienation can only be transcended by going beyond such a class system. "Man recovers himself only in a higher form of human society in which the means of production are communally owned and not privately owned. Only in such a community will man find in his relations with others the realisation of his true self."[1]

The *Economic and Philosophic Manuscripts of 1844* are largely concerned with the alienation involved in wage labour and the inescapable contradictions of capitalism. *The German Ideology* and the *Grundrisse* carry this analysis even further and attempt to show that only the total economic reoganisation of society on socialist lines offers the possibility of going beyond, of transcending, alienation, and emancipating the working class from its inferior, humiliating status. This advance is not conceived as a utopian project, but as rendered necessary by the development of capitalism itself—the discovery that the economic structure of capitalism at this advanced stage of industrial development calls aloud for the reconstruction of the economy that will provide a system of organised production more appropriate than private enterprise to the immense possibilities of modern industrial production.

Contemporary economic theory and sociology are prone to see society, empirically, as simply what it is now, as it presents itself to their observation, as though the patterns they observe were of the eternal nature of things; they do not countenance or allow the possi-

[1] Marx, *Economic and Philosophic Manuscripts.*

bility of radical change of pattern. Dialectical thinking sees the situation as one to be altered and developed, as only a stage in the humanisation of the environment. Therefore, Marx and Hegel see the whole history as a "passing beyond", transcending stage after stage in economic and social and political development.

The word constantly used, as we have said before, for this aspect of dialectics is *aufheben*. It has a variety of meanings all of which indicate dialectical change. It means lifting up, cancelling, transforming, going beyond, supersession. Thus the historical process is essentially a "transcending" of the existing pattern of economic and political life with the contradictions inseparable from it. But this takes place not as Hegel himself imagined, and other theorists who conceive of the Immanent Reason as an irresistible process of social progress, but by man's discovery of how to find more rational methods of realising the possibilities of modern industrialism, and, indeed, of the potentialities which have matured in the present phase of society and prepared the conditions for a new step forward.

In *Capital* Marx develops this dialectic in entirely concrete and realistic terms to show how the necessity arises for transcending the existing capitalist order and passing from the competitive war of individuals to common ownership and the rational utilisation of economic resources for the use of mankind.

This aspect of dialectic is of importance not only for the larger changes we see in the development of society. We are constantly "going beyond" present ways of doing things, on the one hand, by means of inventions and improvements, but also, on the other hand, by the constant alterations of our habits, our methods, our ideas, and, of course, our institutions to correspond to these improvements. It is just common sense and part of man's way of life. There is no mysterious philosophical principle involved; we can't get on at all unless we think and act like this.

It is a *reciprocal* business, that is the point. Good social organisation and good ideas stimulate invention, scientific and technological progress. But then this very development carries us beyond the ways of thinking and organising that stimulated it. They themselves have to be brought in line with new developments. This applies to economic organisation, to our ideas, our habits, our attitudes, even our personalities. The modern soldier, for example, has to become far more of a technician, virtually a different type. It is the same in farming, in industry, in the scientific laboratory, in local government.

Consider for a moment the dilemma we get into if we miss this *reciprocal* process of change. We say "people are made by circumstances." They are conditioned by them. So how can they be expected to change those circumstances, or to change themselves? But then one reflects: Those very circumstances were not always as they are. They were created by social change, men made them, and then they conditioned people. It is clear that though conditions make men it is always men, in the last resort, who make conditions. They do so when the old ways, the old habits and ideas become inefficient, are not useful in working the new machines, techniques, improved methods they have developed.

We find ourselves faced with a lack of correspondence between our ideas and our practice, between possibilities and our economic organisation. Objective facts may contradict our ideologies, the economics we learn at the university, our current theories. A tension is generated which will ultimately bring about the appropriate modification of our theories, even of our habits and institutions. As these are gradually altered we ourselves are, of course, changing.

Marx applies this concept to the much more radical question of antagonisms which reflect the basic contradiction of society's economic production. The class structure of capitalism, for all its harshness, was once very appropriate and fostered production. But in its later stages obstruction and a slowing down of growth appears, and a growing clash of interests between business and wage demands. This critical situation compels new and critical thinking, because it is crippling and dangerous. A whole new way of organising our economic life is now *latent* in the top-heavy, obstructed system. This, *when we see it*, becomes the starting point for reorganising society, as Marx teaches, without a financial dictatorship of the owners of capital. If this is achieved, we find ourselves on a higher plane than the old society, just as the creation of capitalism itself, an exactly similar process, created a new and more productive society than pre-capitalist society.

But nothing happens until *thinking* begins to criticise the old ways, old institutions, ideas, habits and, above all, *theories*—economic theories, political theories, sociological theories of human nature, ethical theories. Nothing happens automatically.

Whether we think in this way in the simplest *reciprocal* changes of our daily lives, in the daily improvements in a business, or a school or a hospital, or on the large scale of reorganising industry and politics, *this* is dialectical thinking. And if it is objected: "Don't we all of us, all the time, think like this?" the answer is, "Certainly not. Economic laws, political systems, philosophies, views of human nature, are frequently regarded as static, as 'according to nature', conforming to 'natural right'; basically unalterable." That is why we need to loosen up our thinking dialectically.

In making clear the importance of thinking dialectically and not statically, *reciprocally* rather than considering different aspects in isolation, Marx is not propounding a philosophical system, though his method of dialectical thought can of course be systematically discussed. He is explaining how men *think* whenever they think effectively, and by thought he does not mean cogitation, the meditative turning over of ideas, the construction by reason of a philosophical theory, he means simply *effective thinking;* and again not "contemplative thinking", merely seeking to know by observation, but thinking whose aim is to *change* the environment, to modify what is known; or to change our *methods* and systems of organisation with a view to getting things moving. Effective thinking is problem-solving thinking; not just solving puzzles, but overcoming obstacles.

Effective thinking Marx contrasts with *crippled* thinking, and paralysed thinking. There are many forms of futile, wasteful, ineffective thought: for instance, finding explanatory theories for the universe, speculative metaphysics, mythological or religious thinking; but also thinking which merely observes the facts as they are, regarding the mind as no more than a mirror to reflect objective reality. If the first kind of ineffective thinking is typically idealist, the second, Marx says, is the kind of materialist approach which he also rejects.

Real thinking is proper only to man and not to animals. Animals simply react to their environment, seek immediate satisfaction, fulfil instinctive needs. Animals are acted upon by their environment and simply respond automatically to it. They are pushed about by instinct and circumstances. Man forsees the end, devises the end, and plans to attain his goal by intelligently conceived means, notably tools, instruments. *This is an activity in which the mind never ceases to be engaged.*

Marx criticises non-dialectical thinking as basically an erroneous theory of knowledge, as artificially separating mind and the object thought about. In the *First Thesis on Feuerbach* he says:

"The chief defect of all previous materialism (including that of Feuerbach) is that things, reality, the sensible world, are conceived only in the form of object of observation, but not as human sense activity, not as practical activity."[1]

He then points out, as Lenin was to do also, that this fatal flaw in thinking was corrected by idealist philosophy, in spite of its errors in other directions. Marx, as himself the inheritor of that tradition, regards the indissoluble unity of knowledge and reality as fundamental. The materialists of his day were guilty of the grave error of creating an unbridgeable gulf between the knowing mind and the material reality it knows.[2] Marx sees this dualism as precluding effective action, as an *empiricism* which only observes things as they are, and sees no way of really altering them.

In Hegel's *Phenomenology* Marx finds and welcomes the approach which sees every form of knowledge as obtained in working upon and changing the material world; and since this is how *our knowledge* grows, it is how we ourselves, as Hegel says, create ourselves, our persons, our habits, our experience, in such action. This whole approach Marx accepted, and proceeded from this starting point to develop his own social and economic theories.

His first published work written in collaboration with Engels, *The Holy Family*, systematically criticised the materialist conception of knowledge at great length, and *The German Ideology* contains a thorough and extended account of man in action, altering, using, cultivating his world, and creating and enlarging his own consciousness. It is here that Marx adds to the basic conception of active knowledge, his historical theory, the sequence of technological stages and systems of economic production corresponding to them, the succession of economico-social orders of society. Here the dialectical principle of change is again the knowledge that perceives discrepancy between the technology and the organisational form, the economy, operating it, and instigates a drastic reorganisation of society; thus bringing into existence:

"in the whole evolution of history a coherent sense of forms of economic intercourse, the coherence of which consists in this: that in the place of an earlier form, which has become a fetter, a new one is put, corresponding to the more developed productive forces and hence to the advanced mode of the self-activity of individuals—

[1] Marx, *The First Thesis on Feuerbach*, and Marx and Engels, *The Holy Family*.
[2] Just as the same widely prevalent dualism separates fact and value, reality and phenomena as experienced.

a form which in its turn becomes a fetter and is then replaced by another. It shows that in history at each stage there is found a material result: a sum of productive forces and a historically created relation of individuals to nature and one another. . . . It shows that circumstances make men just as much as men make circumstances."[1]

Here is the paradigm of Marx's theory of history, further elaborated in the Grundrisse. It appears again in the Preface to the Critique of Political Economy in 1859, and is then worked out in Capital in relation to the "fetters" which a developed capitalism imposes on production.

Marx is arguing all the time that knowledge as a passive observation of reality can effect nothing, it can only reflect and be determined by what impresses itself upon the senses. Only active, critical, handling and manipulation, constantly altering, improving and reconstructing both facts and ideas, can create and re-create the world, direct, and then alter by re-direction, the operation of organised production and social institutions.

Marx's theory of knowing in action is not a logical or philosophical theory that can be examined and described and discussed in itself, it is a description of the only form of effective thinking that there is. Marx is not offering a theory, he is talking about real thinking, and criticising defective thinking. Real thinking is dialectical because it involves continuous and unbroken reciprocity between provisional, pragmatic knowing for action, under existing conditions, and the action it calls for, initiates and directs.

Action immediately changes the object and the conditions, and so creates for our probing eyes and mind and grappling hands a new reality with its own demands, problems, difficulties and opportunities. These tax the searching, exploratory mind to find the right thing to do. Thinking enquiringly, critically, constructively, it attempts what the reasoning imagination offers as the course likely to succeed; and this again alters the objective world.

Thus, as Marx says,

"The whole thing can be shown in its totality and therefore, too, the reciprocal action of these various sides on one another. . . . It does not explain practice from the idea, but explain the formation of idea from material practice."[2]

---

[1] Marx and Engels, The German Ideology, Part I.   [2] Ibid.

6

MATERIALISM

The first influence in Marx's intellectual development, as we have seen, was German philosophy, especially that of Kant, Fichte and Hegel: the second main influence was French Materialism, which he discusses in a brilliant historical sketch in *The Holy Family*.[1] Marx never described his philosophy as "Dialectical Materialism"—that was Plekhanov's term[2]—nor did he ever think of himself as a "materialist" in the metaphysical sense.[3] On the contrary he launched the severest criticism of "all previous materialism", and bitterly opposed the current materialisms of Büchner, Vogt, Molescholt, and Lamettrie (*Man, a Machine*). This Cartesian conception of the material world gave rise to mechanistic materialism which Marx was strongly opposed to. The idea of *l'homme machine* of Lamettrie he regarded as a simplification stultifying the development of materialism.

There was a more significant materialist trend, derived not from Descartes but from the English empiricists Bacon, Hobbes and Locke,[4] which culminated in the philosophy of Holbach and Helvetius (1771). Marx was deeply impressed by their recognition of the immense influence of the social environment on human character. The reform

---

[1] Compiled jointly with Engels and originally published in 1845. It only became available in an English translation in 1956.

[2] The term was first used in Plekhanov's *Zu Hegel's Sechzigsten Todestag*, published in *Neue Zeit* in 1891; and then in his Foreword to the Russian translation of Engel's *Feuerbach* in 1892. Lenin used the term for the first time in *What the Friends of the People Are*, in 1894. Engels never used the term, he always spoke of "modern materialism". (The chapter heading "Dialectical Materialism" in *Feuerbach* is by the editor.)

[3] Materialism has been defined as the view that only matter is real; that matter is the fundamental constituent of the universe; that only sensible entities, processes, or content are existent or real; that the universe is not governed by intelligence, purpose or final causes; that everything is strictly caused by material, inanimate, non-mental processes or entities; that mental processes are caused solely by material entities or processes and themselves have no causal effect; that nothing supernatural or mental exists; that all qualitative differences are reducible to quantitative differences and everything is explainable in terms of matter in motion; that the only objects which science can investigate are physical or material. (*The Dictionary of Philosophy*, ed. Dagobert Runes.)

[4] Marx recognised the importance of these philosophers as the inspiration of the French Enlightenment, and for their criticism of the superstition of religious orthodoxy. Their attack on all speculative thinking and metaphysics was also very much to Marx's liking.

of society, they believed, required the reform of the environment; and that is why Marx saw the mere preaching of a better mode of social life as "so much worthless earnestness". If man derives all his ideas, his habits and his values from the environment, the only way in which he can be helped is by placing him in an environment which elevates instead of corrupting him. As Marx reminds us, the whole development of socialism down to St. Simon and Robert Owen depends on this idea.

This theory led, however, to a dilemma which Helvetius and the other materialists never overcame: if man passively receives sensations derived from the material world, and if he is the passive object of the corrupting influences of his environment, of society, who is going to educate the educators? If man becomes what he is because he receives the impress of his environment, how can he alter that environment, for he himself is its product? But Marx held that just as man had once created that very environment, possibly in the teeth of old traditions and set ideas, so, when new possibilities appear and new dangers threaten, he can make it again. Man is a living, active, integral part of his world. Impress and reaction are continuously reciprocal.

Now we can see who or what educates the educators. The subject is all the time educating and changing himself, because his activity is at one and the same time making the object of his knowledge, his world, and remaking it, making himself and remaking that too.[1] Marx's insistence on man's capacity to modify the environment which, after all, man himself was responsible for, again illustrates his rejection of the earlier forms of materialism which regarded man as simply determined by his environment and wholly subject to natural law.

But Marx had a second criticism of the materialism of his time. The first thesis on Feuerbach declares that

"The chief defect of all previous materialism (including that of Feuerbach) is that things, reality, the sensible world, are conceived only in the form of *objects of observation*, but not as human sense activity, not as practical activity, not subjectively. Hence in opposition to materialism, the *active* side was developed abstractly by idealism, which of course does not know real sense activity as such."[2]

[1] See an important section of The German Ideology on the alteration of men "on a mass scale".

[2] Marx, Theses on Feuerbach (Bottomore's translation). Pascal, in his notes to the Theses, says that Anschauung, usually translated as "contemplation", should be understood as "sense perception". Bottomore uses the phrase "objects of observation".

Marx repudiated the notion that knowledge was derived from the mere reception of impressions from the material environment.[1] No-one who knew Kant as Marx did, and recognised the close relationship of the subjective and objective in knowledge, could ever rest content with the naive realism of the empiricist and rationalist philosophy which in effect separated the perceiver and the perceived object so that the sensations in the mind were mental events supposed to "correspond" to or "copy" the physical object. Marx rejected this view in the *First Thesis on Feuerbach* as attempting to understand the object only through sense-perception and not from the standpoint of the perceiver's active handling and utilising of the object. It is this *active* side of perception, says Marx, that was developed by idealism.[2] Lenin makes the same point in the *Philosophical Notebooks*, pointing out that philosophical idealism maintains "one of the characteristic aspects of knowledge".[3] This is not a side issue but the very essence of Marx's whole position; both his understanding of the material world, his understanding of society, and his dialectics depend on this. Its neglect must involve a failure to understand what Marxism is all about.

Marx rejects this form of materialism, then, for ignoring the creative role of the mind in shaping the world of experience, and points out the constitutive role of conscious activity in man's knowledge of the external world.

Knowledge cannot be obtained by a simple reflection of facts. *Are there any "facts"* which can thus be perceived? Surely knowledge is always interest-directed, selective, conditioned, value-controlled; it actively integrates, interprets, builds. Suppose a number of men are looking at a meadow: a farmer thinks in terms of hay, or putting it down to plough: a botanist in terms of the thirty or forty species of plants found in that situation, these being different from the ecology of heath or bog or chalk or down or woodland: an artist in terms of colour, sky, hedgerows, and form: a sportsman in terms of a golf-course, or football pitch. The old-fashioned materialism of 1690[4] had

---

[1] The view, which Engels also sometimes appeared to adopt, and Lenin propounded in some passages of his *Materialism and Empirio-Criticism*, but subsequently repudiated after reading Hegel (see the *Philosophical Notebooks*).

[2] Of course, Marx was fully aware of what was erroneous in this form of philosophy; but to reject its permanent achievement because of its errors would be disastrous, and was for Marx impossible.

[3] Lenin, *Philosophical Notebooks, Collected Works*, Vol. 38, p. 363.

[4] John Locke, *Essay Concerning Human Understanding* (1690); Thomas Hobbes, *Human Nature* (1650).

long ago, after entangling itself hopelessly in its metaphysical theory of perception, which made the sensations (sense data) in the mind all that was directly known, given way to the critical philosophy which wrestled with the puzzling consequences of this theory, and overcame them by a more accurate theory of knowledge. No instructed thinker after that could ever go back to the naive metaphysics of "representative perception"—that the sensation represented a reality which itself never appeared. That was why it was impossible for Marx to accept this position. Nevertheless, some of his followers, who had little or no philosophical training, fell headlong into the pit and involved themselves in endless difficulty and confusion.

It is important to understand that man does not require a theory of representative perception to understand that he is a living person in the world, along with other people, a part of nature, an intelligent part, a creative part (*homo faber*). This for Marx, the trained philosopher, was the indisputable premise of his work.[1] It was those who adopted the "theory of reflection", trying to be more philosophical than Marx, and going back to Locke and Hume, who got into a hopeless muddle which still clouds the issue for many people.

In *The Holy Family*, therefore, Marx draws a sharp distinction between the two materialisms. But although he recognises the great social importance of the English version, he rejects its theory of passive reception of sensations which merely reflect the material world. This, he says, was the fault of *all* previous materialisms, and one which Marx avoided by what he called "consistent naturalism or humanism", which he distinguishes from both idealism and materialism, claiming that this way of putting it unites what is essential to both. "Here we see how consistent naturalism or humanism distinguishes itself both from idealism and materialism, constituting at the same time the unifying fruits of both. We see also how only naturalism is capable of comprehending the act of world history".[2] Engels calls this Marx's "new materialism", and he himself uses the expression "modern materialism".[3]

The rejection of the supernatural was of course another reason for regarding the whole materialist development of immense importance.

[1] Marx, *Economic and Philosophic Manuscripts*, p. 156 (Milligan translation).
[2] See *Economic and Philosophic Manuscripts*, pp. 102, 109 etc. (Milligan translation). And McLellan, *Marx before Marxism*; "The Paris Manuscripts", p. 199.
[3] Engels, *Ludwig Feuerbach*.

But this is a position that is just as emphatically held by naturalism in our time. The basic premise of this naturalism leaves no place for spirit or mind as a disembodied force. It does not imply the denial of thinking, but only the existence of "mind" without material substance. Its advantage is that it is a more comprehensive concept than matter. It includes the physical basis but also the undeniable phenomena of life and thought, including the highest creations of the artistic powers of man.

Materialism, however, has assumed forms hostile to the *humanism* which was the teaching of Marx's own materialism (and that of Helvetius and his school), and Marx never concealed his hostility to what both he and Engels repudiated as "bourgeois materialism—a dry, gloomy and melancholy doctrine". Marx directed equally severe criticism against the individualistic materialism of John Locke, who was by no means a protagonist of socialism.

Thus if Marx is a materialist it is only when he can equate his materialism with the "humanism" and "socialism" with which, under his treatment, it coincides; but not if materialism remains in the mechanistic and reductionist form which is incompatible with his conception of man.

The emphasis on "materialism" makes it clear that the world with its inhabitants is not a derivation from, or in Hegelian terms a 'manifestation" of a world of pure spirit; though Lenin was perhaps a little too worried by the possibility of subjectivism in knowledge seriously implying this. However, it became the habit to insist on the "reflection" theory of knowledge as a way of making it clear that mind in itself does not give rise to the material world; but on the contrary the world in the course of its development produces mind, and all mentality is consciousness of the world we live in.

So far so good; but this must not become the theory of knowledge which Marx repudiated. Knowledge is certainly of the material world, but it is not a passive reception of sense data; and further, thinking is not merely a *product* of matter which does not rise higher than its source; nor are ideas merely an *effect*; on the contrary they can and often must question, criticise and overthrow the facts they comprehend, substituting new conceptual patterns. This is by no means a mere product of reflection of the world that is thought about. There is a further, closely related, aspect of Marx's naturalism and humanism to be mentioned. A strong feature of Cartesian materialism was its recognition of the importance of the scientific understanding of natural law for the control of nature.[1] The materialists were eager to show the relationship between progress and the rule of reason by stressing the role of scientific and technical development in history. This shows man as increasingly linked with nature, while nature is progressively receiving the stamp of man's knowledge and purpose. Marx fully recognised the truth and importance of this side of the materialist tradition. Inconsistently, the same philosophic trend progressively widened the gap between the human *mind* and nature, since consciousness was never, for these philosophers, in direct touch with material reality, but was only conscious of mental images. Why should the latter really represent the material world? In fact no-one has ever pretended to answer that question. Those who hold this view have only to hope that no-one will raise it! It is a pure act of faith.[2]

We turn now to the materialism which after the death of Marx came very generally to be regarded as part of Marxism—dialectical materialism. This takes a different form from the theory which states that the ultimate reality of all things, including man and his mental life, is material—that matter is all there is. On the contrary Marx described his own standpoint "as fully-developed naturalism, equals humanism, and as fully developed humanism equals naturalism".[3] In society man and nature are *united*. Man does not stand over against the material world knowing it by sensation; he knows it by altering it, by making it over in pursuit of his ends.

The first view, which reduces everything to matter, goes beyond experience itself, which includes much that is certainly not *matter*. It is easy to see that Menuhin's violin is material, but is the Bach Partita? *Dependent* upon matter it certainly is, but dependence is not identity. A painting consists of, and is dependent upon, the chemical substances of the paint, but is that what the painting *really is*? Nor are we helped by being told that the spiritual[4] experience of man, the colours and sounds he sees are "forms of motion", an attempt to establish the

[1] Descartes, *Discourse on Method* (1637). "For by it I perceived it to be possible to arrive at knowledge highly useful to man . . . and thus render ourselves the lords and possessors of nature."
[2] See below, "Digression on Epistemological Materialism", p. 85.
[3] Marx, *Economic and Philosophic Manuscripts*.
[4] Materialists must not baulk at this word. It is used in this sense by Stalin in his *Historical and Dialectical Materialism* and also in *The Fundamentals of Marxism*: "Spiritual, mental phenomena can, of course, be the object of cognition as well as material things."

identity of physical and mental facts. The idea of "motion" cannot be extended to mean something wholly and qualitatively different, different not merely on the physical plane, but because we are now beyond it altogether.

Reality exists on more than one level. Beyond the physico-chemical is the biological, and beyond the biological the mental and spiritual— which does not imply, of course, the existence of a mental world parallel with and independent of the material world. This is not a dualism of mind and matter, but *naturalism*, which recognises the full value and significance of the highest levels of evolutionary development and does not reduce them to "matter in motion".

Engels made a considerable contribution to materialist philosophy by propounding many years before Lloyd Morgan, Samuel Alexander and others, the theory of *emergence*, that is to say the distinctive qualitative levels in the evolution of matter, each however containing as its material basis the elements and laws of the previous stage and depending upon them, though operating with its own laws at a higher level.

If the phenomena on the higher levels are *real*, their difference from the primitive form of matter from which they evolved must preclude their being described as mere matter. To do so would be to extend the notion of matter so far as to include everything, and it becomes meaningless. If we mean to say that particles in motion, electrons, electro-magnetic waves, energy, are the *only* real reality, then let us not pretend at the same time that a Chopin Nocturne is a Chopin Nocturne—that the spiritual life of man has any real existence.

The theory of emergence[1] is admirably dealt with by Shirokov of Leningrad in his *Textbook of Marxist Philosophy*.[2] He points out that if we think that by reducing the activities of a living or thinking organism to its chemical and physical elements we are being scientific, on the contrary we destroy the reality of the complex living organism which we set out to study. Of course the more complex quality includes in itself elements of the simpler; but the elements of the old, by being subordinated to the new system, themselves become something new.

---

[1] The theory of emergence now generally accepted by biologists, does not of course imply any "vital force" or directive agency at work (as it did in its earliest forms when propounded by Morgan and Alexander). Its operations are wholly within the sphere of scientifically ascertained causal sequences.

[2] Translated by Moseley and Lewis. Originally prepared by the Leningrad Institute of Philosophy as a textbook for institutions of higher education. (London, 1967.)

"Wholeness is a qualitatively unique form of existence which includes in itself elements of the old, refashioning them in a new system". Engels takes up the same argument. Describing biology as the science of "albuminous bodies" (proteins), he says that he wishes to stress both the connection with and the dependence on the pre-living condition and its laws, "but also on the distinction, the *break* between the two fields. Biology does not in this way amount to chemistry".[1] The chemical processes associated with life are not now simply chemical, they manifest a qualitatively new and higher level of being, which we call life.

The older conception conveyed the impression that whatever is evolved is composed of, and therefore in reality *is*, the more primitive thing out of which it came. To the emergent evolutionist, each new level of being is an arrival, to whose advent the whole surrounding figure of events has contributed. It is not derived from any pre-existent pattern and cannot be reduced to the elements from whose re-patterning it emerges. The "nothing but" phase ceases to be appropriate without our in any way abandoning the conception of a lawful universe. The world is capable of giving birth to novelty, and, in a sense, of stepping upward.

Whether we are speaking in biological, in economic, or in sociological terms we must recognise that the key concept is neither quantitative increase as giving rise to the leap or an evolutionary "Life Force," but *change of pattern*. It is the new type of *organisation* that gives rise to novelty, not a miracle, not the injection of something from the super-natural world, and not mere quantitative increase, but a change of pattern. Organising patterns are not immune from scientific grasp and understanding; but their laws are not reducible to the laws governing the behaviour of substances at lower levels of complexity. Laws of this higher organisation only operate in the new level.

The whole matter has been clearly stated by the Russian biologist Zavadowsky:[2]

"The true task of scientific research is not the identification of the biological and the physical, but the discovery of the qualitatively specific controlling principles which characterize the main features

---

[1] Engels, *Second Note to Anti-Dühring. Dialectics of Nature* (C. P. Dutt translation), Appendix I.
[2] Article, "The Physical and the Biological in Organic Evolution" in *Science at the Cross Roads*.

of every phenomenon. It is necessary to renounce the simplified reduction of some sciences to others . . . Biological phenomena are not reducible to physico-chemical or mechanical laws but display different and qualitatively distinct laws."

Hegel was one of the first to point out the importance of evolutionary succession in history. Here he finds a succession of civilisations or social orders, each derived from its predecessor by rational evolution and yet different qualitatively, and each one a step towards greater complexity, rationality and freedom. But Hegel never discovered the principle of progressive social change. He saw it as the unfolding of the Absolute Idea. Marx saw it it in terms somewhat analogous to (but by no means identical with) biological evolution. Here if the form of an organism is not adapted to its function it perishes. Function changes because the environment changes, or because the animal seeks a new one. Marx and Darwin hold in common that nature is in process of evolution, that the forms of nature are changing, and that these forms are determined by the modes of activity or behaviour of natural entities in interaction with other entities and environmental conditions. Form is the result of function, although when acquired it of course determines further changes in the environment in turn— a perfect example of dialectics. In society, if owing to the development of economic powers and resources the enveloping economic form proves inappropriate to those forces in their advanced condition it must give way to a new one, as the developed bird emerges from the very conditions within the shell that fostered and completed its development. Thus what is called "dialectical materialism" is a philosophy with a theory of development which recognises discontinuities as well as continuities in society as well as in nature. But social change differs from biological change in the tremendously greater importance of the internal conditions of society—technology, the existence of classes, the rational behaviour of man—as compared with the physical environment. This difference derives from the underlying difference between man and the other animals.

The question now arises as to whether naturalism in the sense used by Marx, and in contemporary thought, is identical with scientism or positivism, that is to say the philosophy which holds that the sciences in their totality are capable of comprehensively including everything that can be known. This would reduce philosophy to formal logic and the laws or principles of dialectic; "everything else is merged in the positive science of nature and history".[1]

Needless to say Marx himself made no such claims, which are inconsistent with his philosophical position. We tend to think that the rigid tests and logical inferences of scientific method and its control by observation and experiment make its findings the only valid ones, and that its findings are exhaustive and concrete. On the contrary its exactness and definiteness is only obtained by rigorous abstraction—by ignoring the independent variables and separating the measurable aspects from the complex whole. Each science abstracts a selected aspect for its own purposes. If we combine all the sciences, not even the sum of these abstractions can give us the whole. Physics, plus chemistry, plus any other physical science, does not attempt to describe, measure, explain, in fact deliberately excludes, the *whole* of reality. Concrete reality includes far more than all that. It is the entire sphere of human experience in all its richness and complexity. *That* is the concrete. The human significance of a beloved child, or the subtle beauty of a painting or a poem—science abstracts from this; not because the scientist doesn't believe in these things, but because it is not his purpose to deal with them, any more than the weighing machine is concerned with anything but one's weight. Human life itself is wholly beyond the material entities involved in its material basis. The musician and the hearer of music are in fact totally uninterested in and unaware of the sound of the vibrating air, and rightly so. The beloved is not so many pounds avoirdupois or carbon, hydrogen, oxygen, nitrogen, sulphur and phosphorus, but something richer because really the concrete person.

Epistemological Materialism: a digression[2]

For some materialists the fundamental argument for their position is that nothing else is given to us in perception but material objects, and only that which is perceived is real. 'Matter' then is the philosophical category designating the objective reality which is given to man by sensation and which is copied, photographed, and reflected by these sensations, while existing independently of them.

The difficulty with this theory is that we can never demonstrate that the images in the mind, that are all we are directly aware

[1] Engels, *Anti-Dühring*, Introduction, I.
[2] This brief critique may be of interest to those who wish to discuss this rather specialised aspect of the philosophy of materialism.

of, really represent the material objects which cause them. Effects by no means resemble their causes—if you press a switch the *effect* is that the light comes on. That gives us no copy or image of the cause.

We cannot compare the image with the reality which is its source by jumping out of our bodies and running round to have a *real* look. Nor does practice help, because all that happens as a result only appears in our minds as more images. This cannot prove anything at all about the correspondence of the images to what is their origin. *That* we never reach. Thus all that epistemological realism assures us of is the contents of our minds; for it constantly assures us that that is where the images are—"in consciousness", and that they are mental, immaterial.[1] This extraordinary dualism between mind and matter, image and reality, consciousness and the actual world, is a cliff-hanger, likely to precipitate us into phenomenalism: the view that we never actually *know* directly anything but mental experiences, which is all that sense-data are. Is this, could this be, materialism?

If sense impressions are caused by stimuli from physical objects which are not directly perceived, this postulates two worlds, between which there is no real bridge: the world of nature, and the world of mind. If all we have to go on directly, all we have access to, are images in the mind, then we never touch reality itself. This is what Whitehead calls "the bifurcation of nature" into a reality that never appears (it is only known as what we *hope* are copies), and appearances that are not real (that are *not* the thing itself, but reflections). The sense data are not part of the natural world. The natural world is their cause and cannot itself be perceived. This view deprives nature of what we experience and relegates it to the unknown and unknowable cause of our sensations. From this difficulty we can only escape by the unproveable assertion that the sensations are copies, photographs, of what caused them. But why should the waves stimulating the sense organs, from which chemo-electric impulses reach the brain, in which the nerve cells break into chemical activity, produce a *picture* of the object? The physico-organic circuit is not a television set linked to a transmitter. We simply require this assumption to satisfy our theory.

Moreover the whole theory depends on our objective knowledge,

---

[1] *Fundamentals of Marxism* (Moscow, 1961), p. 116.
"They are mental images" . . . this theory of perception "makes a distinction between consciousness and matter".

in advance of the theory, of the material source of the sensation, of the waves, of the microscopes and scientific apparatus, the nerves, the cells, and the brain and its structure. We assume the existence of these *as we know them* and describe them—which is exactly what the theory has to prove! Therefore to prove the theory we begin by assuming that it is already true, and we cannot prove it otherwise.

But is belief in the objectivity of the world given us in perception what is meant by materialism? Who denies it? Berkeley never denied it; not did any idealist philosopher; nor do other non-idealist philosophers who are not materialists, but realists of one sort or another. All these believe that the object of knowledge exists independently of our knowing it. But the argument for epistemological materialism makes it appear that the belief in the objectivity of knowledge is an argument for materialism; and that if we reject the theory that there are no independent objects of knowledge, we have established materialism. Clearly this is not a view that any philosopher or any ordinary person either, can accept for a moment. It is entirely gratuitous.

It is sound philosophy and sound common sense to say that we know the real world directly, and not at second hand. What we know is the real world, and our knowledge of the world around us is not a phantasmagoria of mental images. What is equally important is that we know it relative to conditions, to our present knowledge, to our interests and values; but relativity must not be confused with subjectivity; for real knowledge can always be tested in practice and checked by the experience of others. Testing our *direct* knowledge of the real world in practice is totally different from trying to test whether the images in our minds correspond to the objects which, it is assumed, cause them.

What we know is the real world. Nature is all that we experience, except what can be shown to be illusion. But in it there is always an element of selection and interpretation, nor can it be otherwise. Nothing is *known* independently of the conditions under which it is known.

We come back to the philosophical position which Marx adopted, never discarded, but enriched and developed to become the core of his whole position. This is expounded most fully in *The German Ideology*, where Marx explains how "the sensuous world around (man) is not a thing given direct . . . but the product of industry and the state of society".[1] Man makes the world, and what he knows is the material world made over by his work. Marx thus maintains the world as a unitary reality, not divided into "appearances which are not real, and a reality which does not appear", which is the consequence of every dualistic theory of knowledge which sets the mind and sensations over against the material world which is their cause.

The *priority* of external nature is accepted by many non-materialist thinkers. It is certainly not peculiar to materialists, though it is of course part of their theory. But "priority" must not be allowed to imply "primacy", which is what it does mean for the materialist in the sense that the material basis is held to be more real and more important than the phenomena it gives rise to. This is the fallacy of origins which discovers the final nature of a thing in its beginnings. A chicken originates in an egg but it is not a curious kind of egg. Man has evolved from a unicellular organism, but that throws no light on his human nature—nor does his ape-like ancestry limit that nature of man, who in any case evolved for 30 million years along a totally different line (the *hominidae*,) from the apes, who for all that length of time were evolving in the direction of the *pongidae*.[2]

The assertion of qualitative differences, and higher levels, establishes what is the defining characteristic of existence at that level—i.e. what *man* really is, as distinguished from other mammals. This qualitative uniqueness in no way ignores or denies the persistence of the lower levels, their own characteristic entities and laws in man. A man has weight, and is subject to the law of gravity; he is also a biological organism which feeds and breathes. In each case, at each level, the complex quality includes in itself elements of the simpler.

"Social man cannot exist without the physiological process of respiration and metabolism, just as also there is no life without determined physico-chemical process. But here is the point: the elements of the old, by being subordinated to the new system, by entering into the new synthesis, themselves become something new. ... Wholeness is a qualitatively unique form of movement which, since it proceeds from previous stages of the development of matter, includes in itself elements of the old and refashions them in a new system".[3]

---

[1] Marx and Engels, *The German Ideology*, Part I.
[2] The *pongidae* comprise the line terminating in chimpanzees, gorillas and orang-utangs.
[3] Shirokov, *Textbook of Marxist Philosophy* (Leningrad Institute of Philosophy).

Engels makes the same point in his second note to *Anti-Dühring*. He wishes to express the transition of each of these sciences into the other, and therefore the connection, but "also the distinction, the break between the two fields. Biology does not in this way amount to chemistry yet at the same time is not something absolutely separated from it".[1]

The same rule holds in social development. The levels are qualitatively new. It is a matter of great importance to trace the historical development of institutions, of ethics, of art, of law, and supremely of social systems, but it does not eliminate the uniqueness and the *higher* quality of the level to discover its origins. Because socialism has developed from capitalism, that does not mean that it is only another and later form of capitalism. Nor can the morals, institutions, human qualities and ideological characteristics of socialism be understood wholly in terms of their origins; for the essence of socialism is the *negation* of these, even though the old is carried forward and appears again on the higher level, for on this level it is transformed, and the old is genuinely negated. Of the first importance is the emergence of new law systems on this level, so that the old laws (e.g. economic laws) no longer hold. The whole point of the dialectical development through negation lies in the emergence of new law systems.

The essence of evolution is its dialectic of *continuity* and *difference*. If only the distinct *differences* are accepted, it is not evolution, but an arbitrary sequence of systems—"historical specificity". If only *continuity* is stressed, there is no evolution, but only a series of modifications of that from which later stages are derived—*one* system of laws, only, prevailing. Yet for some materialists, "priority" always tends to *reduce* that which arises later in biological and human evolution to its origins and to its material basis.

This is why Marxists have felt compelled to describe the materialism of the Cartesian Enlightenment as "the ideological form of the bourgeois revolution." This is a materialist conception of nature which is still not the materialist conception of history. This is clearly seen in the view which finds in *laissez faire* the continuation for man of the evolutionary process and thereby its justification. As Engels said,

"What a bitter satire (Darwin) wrote on mankind, and especially on his countrymen, when he showed that free competition, the

---

[1] Engels, *The Dialectics of Nature* (Clemens Dutt translation), Appendix 1. Notes to Anti-Dühring (b) on the *Mechanical Conception of Nature*.

struggle for existence, which the economists celebrate as the highest historical achievement, is the normal state of the animal kingdom."[1]

The essential difference between man and the pre-human world of nature is the capacity of man to create and recreate the world of technology and society; and it is here that Marx's conception of dialectics comes in. The previous stages of development were described by Engels as themselves brought about by a "dialectics of nature", which he explained in terms of quantity changing into quality; the negation involved in contradiction bringing about a new and higher form of motion and so forth. But this is clearly extracted from the *Logic* of the arch-idealist Hegel. In thus reverting to Hegel, Engels revived the Romantic project of Nature conceived as a developing organism moved forward by a teleological principle —almost a growing "person" realising his potentialities.

But the processes of evolutionary development in physical nature— cosmological, geological and biological—are all being systematically explained in terms of testable natural laws in which intelligence and consciousness play no part, We may use the term "dialectical" for all these changes including those leading up to man; but we are not then using the term as Marx used it. For Marx it necessarily involved the understanding of history as man's self-creation by the discovery of new methods of production, so that in changing his world he changes himself. Intelligence is the *sine qua non* of this form of development; and it is peculiar to man.[2]

In this process cognition is not the reception of stimuli from the external world, simply giving a mirror-image. This is the view emphatically rejected by Marx. For him sensation, cognition, and action are the result of interaction between the environment and an active and sensitive individual, responding with intelligence to the pressure and challenge of the external world. Marx, following Hegel, calls this an object-constituting activity, and he regards it as the primary datum of philosophy, emphasising the active attitude of the new as compared with the contemplative attitude of the old materialism.

That man is a part of nature does not mean that he is limited by pre-human natural conditions, but that he is produced by them and continues to make use of them; but in him nature rises to a new level, with unique processes and laws involving intelligence and

¹ Engels, *Dialectics of Nature* (Clemens Dutt translation), p. 19.
² See Chapter 5, *The Dialectic*.

valuation. Man is a part of nature carried on by its forces to work the works of intelligence. In him it reaches sustained consciousness of its own evolution, producing in man knowledge of its processes, estimation of the goals to be striven for. Man is not added as some extraneous figure, for he has grown out of nature's own stuff and been wrought in nature's workshop. He is the supreme instance where nature has evaluated itself and become clearly conscious of its own processes.

Marx speaks of man's perception as taking place through the humanised character of the senses, as knowledge develops through social activity; human sensibility coming into existence only through "humanised nature".[1] Thus man in society, through his work achieves

"the naturalism of man and the humanism of nature both brought to fulfilment".[2]

Marx's materialism is an understanding of the real world as the sensed natural and social environment into which man is born and where his consciousness and ideas have their origin. His successful attempt to widen the scope of natural phenomena is perhaps Marx's most important contribution to philosophy. "All events are equally natural; in particular, social, moral, and spiritual life, all that is truly creative and powerful in man, belongs to the natural order of things, as much as man's biological life".[3]

Marx himself takes up this question of evolutionary origins in the General Introduction to the *Grundrisse*. This developmental concept of bourgeois social science, as he regards it, starts from the illusionary character of that "so called historical evolution", according to which "the last stage regards the preceding stages as being only preliminary to itself".[4] He reverses the whole conception and thus destroys what he regards as its metaphysical character. While bourgeois evolutionists imagine with Spencer that they can explain the more complex organisation of the higher forms, both in animal evolution, leading to man, and in the evolution of society, by reference to the simpler organisation of the lower, Marx ridicules this view with the statement that, on the contrary, "the anatomy of *man* is a key to

---

[1] Marx, *Economic and Philosophic Manuscripts* (Milligan translation), p. 108.
[2] *ibid.*, p. 104.
[3] Jordan, Z. A., *The Evolution of Dialectical Materialism*, p. 61.
[4] *Grundrisse*, General Introduction, pp. 38–9 (McLellan's edition).

the anatomy of the ape".[1] The economic and social categories of capitalism are not explained by those of feudal society, which must be thought as an independent historical formation with its own categories. On the other hand Marx refrains from providing a detailed picture of future stages of development; going no farther than indicating the main tendencies of further development leading up first to the transitional stage after political victory, in which many features retain their bourgeois characteristics, and ultimately to what he calls the developed communist society.

Throughout his notion of social evolution Marx lays stress on the conscious human-social act, which for the first time knows what future it is trying to make, a theory which involves the "total destruction of bourgeois evolutionary metaphysics".[2]

There are always two implications in traditional materialist thought that are difficult to escape even if one is anxious to do justice to the richness of life in our world. The first is to think in terms of "nothing but", a reductionist attitude: "The symphony on the record can be reduced to grooves on a disc", "human behaviour can be explained without the mind as a system of stimulus and response", "man is only a naked ape", and so on. To this we must continue to reply that "We are unable to deduce the world of nature and human experience with its richness of directly observable qualities from an indeterminate primordial matter and mechanical motion".[3]

The second, which follows inevitably, is to regard man as subject to the whole system of natural laws, which are entirely independent of man himself. Therefore we become limited to its inexorable objectivity. Either we simply observe[4] the facts and laws, and learn to conform to the laws of nature; or perhaps we see an imminent law of development and change in society, which again we simply register and willy-nilly acquiesce in as its agents. But in that case the concern

[1] op. cit.
[2] Karl Korsch, "Leading Principles of Marxism" "Marxist Quarterly", October–December 1937.
[3] Jordan, The Evolution of Dialectical Materialism, p. 155.
[4] To observe the facts. The empiricist sees facts as given, as self-evident and to be accepted. All we can do with them is to summarise and generalise on the basis of the data. This raises the whole problem of whether facts are ever independent of our activity in knowing, selecting, and interpreting. The tendency of empiricism is to subdue us to the tyranny of things as they are, as ultimate and unalterable. Scientific thinking whether in natural science or sociology always goes beyond the facts to understand them, to see that they are strictly relative to certain conditions—therefore, above all, alterable.

with the evolution of man in society, which was Marx's chief concern, and the unique contribution of man's intelligent re-direction of the social structure, have been pushed into the background, and the human, moral and sociological aspect of Marxian philosophy has been subordinated to an abstruse metaphysic, appearing under the guise of science. This has been put forward as the principle of the development of nature, history and thought, asserting itself everywhere and determining all change, motion, growth, and evolutionary advance. Is not this simply the re-appearance of the Hegelian dialectic in nature and history? It is certainly not what Marx meant by dialectic, which is first and last the interaction of human consciousness with the world and with society.

Natural law, unless it is endued with magical or metaphysical properties, is quite incapable of bringing about social progress. The reduction of all reality to the physical, to the observable and to the calculable effects of the interaction of such entities, subjects all existence, from matter to man, to the rule of inviolable law. It is on this basis that determinism is extended to human behaviour and to historical development. This is precisely what happens in the world of economics, where the interaction of "economic men", each individual driven only by his own financial profit, brings into existence the law system of capitalist economics and "the tendencies which work out with an iron necessity towards an inevitable goal".[1] Marx is talking of "the natural laws of capitalist production". This, however, when man rises to the level of comprehending the situation, gives rise to the human understanding and intervention which deals with the disastrous effects of economic determinism, which negates these laws, and subjects production to rational control where they no longer operate.

We thus see that a philosophy, whether materialist or whatever, which subjects man wholly to natural law reflects the mechanistic and non-human reactions of capitalism. What Marxism seeks to do is to transcend this subjugation of the individual to economic law, which Marx calls alienation and the fetishism of commodities, to "go beyond" the impersonal and irresistible laws of an unconscious economic progress, and thus to escape alienation and to achieve emancipation.

Any philosophy which sees man standing over against an automatic and impersonal system of objective law can do no more than observe the interaction of natural objects and forces. It may see man making

[1] *Capital*, Preface to First Edition.

use of this knowledge, but only by acceptance of the laws of things as they are. This materialism, which Marx rejected, was the philosophy of capitalist individualism—the "possessive individualism" of Locke, Bentham, Adam Smith and Mill. The only freedom left within this system is to accept the existing law system and use it *as the system requires*. That subjects our freedom to the limits imposed by the law system of capitalism: which is the situation that all reformists, liberal or labour, whole-heartedly accept, but which Marxism rejects.[1]

Marxist dialectics transcends the capitalist world and its laws. Creation by man himself passes through and transcends the stages which are inhuman. Alienation and the laws of commodity deny living men. But men in their turn deny the laws of commodity. By knowledge and by action they transcend the conditions which inevitably gave rise to it. Economic reality, as we see it, is not the only reality. It is relative, an historical phase, to be transcended once men have become aware of the possibilities of capitalism—which capitalism itself cannot realise. This transcending process will be the essential creative act of our age.

This leaves one question still to be settled: who is to be the agent of this change? One view is that it will be a new élite; a highly trained, carefully selected minority, which alone knows what is for the good of humanity, and will liberate and lead their suffering fellow men.

This was not Marx's view at all. We shall only be able to overthrow "those conditions in which man is an abased, enslaved, abandoned, contemptible being", when the workers *as a class* become aware of their situation. It is not a minority, but a majority that must become enlightened that it may be emancipated.

---

[1] It is beyond our present scope, although it is most significant, that this whole ideology extends, as we might suppose, beyond economics to society and human nature. Man is explained in terms of stimulus and response, eliminating consciousness as unobservable. What we know about him is only what he *does*, his *behaviour*, and this is all the man there is. Hence the behaviourism of Eysenck and others regarding man as comprehended and controlled much as a laboratory rat—the ratomorphic view of man! Beyond man we have men in society, also conceived as operating the fixed structural system described by sociology. Here again the system as it stands is accepted *empirically* as just what is and has to be, and man must make the most of it.

7

WHAT IS MAN?

Every philosophy, every political system, every form of society represents at bottom a theory of the nature of man. Our own society is perfectly satisfied that it knows exactly what human nature really is. Human nature being what it is, we say, *this* policy is utopian, or *that* quite inevitable. We assert without hesitation that human behaviour is bound to be—*as it is*. Those who long for a better world, who are indignant and distressed at the evils of society, and plead for more humane ways, are regarded as sentimental, and their ideal society more to be wished than hoped for.

And so, in the press, in our newspapers, on the radio and television, we have competent men of affairs and exponents of social principles roundly affirming that man is inherently competitive and aggressive; that he is driven by a "territorial imperative" to grab the earth and get as much as he can hold; that man's object is and ought to be "success in making money".[1]

While this life aim is very commonly accepted both here and especially in America, what is significant is the strong support afforded to it by what purports to be scientific opinion. This naturally weighs with editors, critics and broadcasters, who have an almost superstitious reverence for anything claiming to be scientific. Recently we have had a stream of books, all claiming to speak in the name of anthropology, genetics and sociology, declaring that man having descended from predatory carnivores is himself predatory and a killer, that these traits are established genetically by the survival of the fittest and cannot be eradicated by education. Anthony Storr takes the same line in his *Human Aggression:* "We possess the same instinctive equipment which served to ensure the survival of men for whom existence was a perpetual struggle." Reviews unanimously endorsed these views and concluded, for the most part, that "any idea of progress which ignores these ape-like qualities is doomed. . . . Man, and consequently his

[1] B.B.C. *Any Questions*, January 30, 1970, Lord Thompson, an opinion not questioned by Lord Watkinson or Mr. Roy Jenkins, also members of the panel.

society, is immutable. The old adage, 'you can't change human nature' becomes true once more".[1]

The considerable weight of really expert opinion which rejects this whole position and argues that cultural development on the basis of intelligent control of the environment has, for man, superseded genetical mutation as the determinant of cultural and ethical process, is simply ignored.[2] This is almost certainly because the theory of man's innate possessiveness does reflect the dominant ideology of a capitalist society.

Another form of the theory of human nature which sees man as incapable of cooperation for the common good is the Freudian idea of man as driven by basic instincts. Freud regarded the basic human instinct of aggression and destruction as "the greatest obstacle to civilisation". "The truth is that men are not gentle, friendly creatures wishing for love, but that a powerful measure of desire for aggression has to be reckoned with as part of their instinctual endowment."[3]

From quite another angle man's nature is again reduced to something mechanical and less than human. This is the behaviourist conception of the reflex pattern of stimulus and response (SR) extended by the notion of automatic conditioning.[4] Man thus becomes no more than the product of the external forces impinging upon him. The economist sees these, of course, as economic. For him, man is controlled from without by the pressure of economic forces, which arise automatically and mechanically from the laws of supply and demand, and from monetary cause and effect.

Koestler has labelled this behaviourist psychology "the ratomorphic view of man", since the laws applied to man are precisely those derived from the conditioning of laboratory rats. Clearly the danger of this reduction of human nature to instinctive drives, conditioned reflexes, and mechanical reactions to uncontrollable external stimuli and pressures, is to lapse altogether into a sub-human world of thought and action. It was when humans regard other humans as

[1] Nicholas Tomalin, New Statesman, September 15, 1967.
[2] The scientific evidence counter to the Ardrey-Morris scholo of thought has been set down in Naked Ape or Homo Sapiens? by Lewis and Towers.
[3] Freud, Civilisation and its Discontents.
[4] Conditioning as Pavlov originally saw it was not the pressure of education, propaganda, custom and the mass media, but a totally different conception of extending the range of the automatic reflex by replacing the inherited stimulus with another one by frequently associating the two. It is this process that the behaviourists are concerned with, not the former.

"animals" or "vermin" that the Nazi concentration camps became possible.

There is little doubt that these theories do fairly represent a very widespread conception of man, which might be said to be part of the basic philosophy of our society. But that does not mean that every society is of this kind, or is inspired by such a philosophy. There are today, and have been in the past, very different conceptions of man, and very different social systems. We are at liberty to ask whether the society gave rise to the philosophy, or the philosophy to the society. Perhaps however this will turn out to be a "hen or the egg" question, and the real question will be: what brought the society *and* its philosophy into being? And we may further ask whether this would appear to be a very desirable or endurable society. Is "the war of all against all" the only conceivable principle for humanity?

This is the ideological form of what has been called our own "acquisitive society". Ever since the appearance of class in the earliest slave civilisations society has been dominated by one form or the other of an exploiting class, each with its own philosophy and system of values, each dominating by one form or the other of a ruling class. We are concerned however with the special ideological defence and theoretical armoury of our developed capitalist society, with its consciously wrought individualistic philosophy.

It is surprising that this picture of our civilisation meets with such ready acceptance. Clearly it does reflect a very fundamental trend in our society, because we live in a particular period, with its own fairly recent and most influential philosophy: the competitive individualism which was not conceived as a philosophy before Hobbes and Locke in the 17th century, or as a system of economy before Adam Smith in the 18th century. This philosophy and this economy do characterise our society, but only as an historical epoch, only as a controlling social trend that works in and upon a more fundamental pattern of society, which also recognises quite other principles and human characteristics. There is, and must be, in every human society enough mutual responsibility, recognition of social obligation, of service of the community and common decency, to maintain its collective being. To state, off hand, and with some dogmatism, that we are all basically antagonistic to one another, "predatory animals", or, in Anthony Storr's phrase, are under the sway of "those same savage impulses which lead to murder, torture and to war", is not only a libel on the human race, but incredibly

D

foolish. Those who say this, don't believe it of themselves, or their friends, their wives and children—but only of the rest of us, of the world in general, excluding themselves. We cannot simply ignore or deny the immense amount of responsibility, affection, pity and comradeship in the world, in spite of all the inhumanity. If that were not the case, could mankind maintain its existence?

We shall find then, if we are objective, that while this ideology of "every man for himself" is certainly characteristic of our capitalist society, and above all of its economy—that is to say of the basic method of producing our means of existence—there is a deeper counter-ideology, persistent through all civilisation and all ages, working in the opposite direction. What is significant is that the structure and rule of our organised system of social life constantly obstructs and denies the more fundamental humanism. It would seem then that the theory of man as 'a beast of prey', and innately antagonistic to his neighbour, is not so much basic to human nature as an integral part of the present phase of social development we call capitalism. It is not men whose nature is like this, but capitalist men; and even they, only in part—though a very important and often determining part. But it is no more permanent than capitalism itself. It was not the philosophy of any society prior to capitalism, and if socialism succeeds capitalism it will not continue to characterise, or to inspire and guide, society in the future. We may yet see the emergence of a community no longer dominated by money values, and no longer ready to acknowledge the supremacy of the fittest who survive in the competitive strife for mastery.

The immediate question, of course, is whether such a hope is mere wishful thinking, a sentimental yearning for what is quite impossible—contrary to the possibilities of human nature. Marxism does assert the superiority of human values. But it does not believe that they are to be established merely by ethical propaganda. The title of the most widely read book on Marxist theory was *Socialism, Utopian and Scientific*, which lifted the criticism of capitalism and the methods of working for socialism from the utopian, moralistic, and idealistic level, to the scientific. It would be a profound mistake, however, a mistake sometimes made by those moving from idealistic to scientific socialism, to imagine that Marx and Engels dismissed the moral element as "ideological" or a form of subjectivism or idealism. They were both of them, through their whole careers, men deeply imbued with the traditional ideals of socialism, with a profound pity and a severe condemnation of the inhumanity of capitalism and its indifference to human personality and spiritual values. They did not lose this, they were continuously inspired by it, in the whole course of their analysis of the historical process which brought capitalism into existence, as a necessary phase in man's development, but then transcended its individualistic and inhuman economy and ideology.

The first step in seeing society as by no means fixed in the pattern of possessive individualism and the money economy, or represented by economic man, the predator, is to widen our perspective to see that man has organised himself into many other patterns of society, each with a type of man not in the least resembling the supposed unalterable "human nature" of our very recent creation of a capitalist society. Going back into history we find a whole sequence of societies from primitive communism to small farming and fishing communities, pastoral economies, and peasant communities like those still to be found all over the world.

Let us take the pattern which preceded capitalism and from which our capitalist society developed. As we see from the *Communist Manifesto*, Marx is perfectly well aware of the exploitation of the feudal age, of its barbarities, its hypocrisies, its privileges, and ruthless class rule and exploitation; but he also sees the rise of capitalism as an altogether more inhumane and mechanised affair then feudalism which has

"put an end to all feudal, patriarchial, idyllic relations. It has pitylessly torn assunder the motley feudal ties that bound man to his 'natural superiors', and has left remaining no other nexus between man and man than naked self-interest. . . . It has resolved personal worth into exchange value, and in place of the numberless indefeasible chartered freedoms, has set up that single, unconscionable freedom—free trade. In one word, for exploitation, veiled by religious and political illusions it has substituted naked, shameless, direct, brutal exploitation."

Nowhere has the profound difference between medieval society with its network of recognised social relations and responsibilities, however distorted by feudal exploitation and the total dissolution of all social bands in the war of all against all, been so ruthlessly and powerfully set forth as in the *Manifesto*.

From the Middle Ages through the Renaissance up to the 17th

century, we find a society which saw its basis as the corporate body of citizens, often organised in the Trade Guilds. There were money and commerce and manufacture, but the fluid, unrestricted operations of the market had not arrived. For centuries usury was condemned, as was the monopoly which deliberately cornered the market to put up prices. The basic economic principle was not supply and demand but "the just price". There was exploitation, but the wage labour of propertyless men had not taken over the life of the poor man. The Church, also corporate, a fellowship in which men stood related by bonds of duty and respect to others, was also the pattern for society. No man could live as a man, as a person, out of fellowship. Human life was corporate. To be out of the community was to be ex-communicated, cut off and lost. This is the picture of man we find in medieval literature like Dante's *Divine Comedy*, and in moral theology, and social theory.[1]

The tremendous rupture of the whole moral and social structure of this society and of its ideological foundation is described in Weber's *The Protestant Ethic and the Spirit of Capitalism*, and in Tawney's *Religion and the Rise of Capitalism*. The contrast between these two types of human society and thinking has nowhere been better shown in our time than by Tawney, who contrasts the medieval pattern in whose social philosophy labour was declared to be necessary and honourable, trade necessary but perilous to the soul, and finance sordid and disreputable, with the new commercial spirit which found expression in the Protestant ethic, which reversed the principle that economic advantage must be subordinated to moral consideration and that society was held together by mutual obligations, to the new conception that business should follow its own laws, unhampered by the intrusions of an antiquated morality, and the belief that by a kind of happy, pre-established harmony, the self-interest of the individual would automatically secure the welfare of society. As one Protestant preacher told his flock, "Prudence and Piety were always very good friends. You may gain enough of both worlds if you mind each in its own place".

New men and new morals. A commercial oligarchy will produce, as morally acceptable and to be highly regarded, the man who succeeds in unrestrained competition, and will regard as immoral and obviously deprived of God's blessing the worker struggling to secure better conditions.

---

[1] We find a picture of it in William Morris' *Dream of John Ball*.

Tawney shows how the whole Catholic social ethic broke up and was superseded by the individualistic profit-for-the-individual system of competitive capitalism and the disappearance of the corporate patterns of human society held together by a system of mutual obligation, which was now replaced by "a congeries of possessors and pursuers", motivated by self interest, a society in which *gain* was accepted as the driving force of men. This would have appeared "as irrational to a pre-capitalist man as making the instincts of pugnacity or sex and their unrestrained operation the basis of social theory".[1] The old feudal morality differs from modern bourgeois morality as does knightly chivalry from business solvency.

This is one example out of very many, and a brief glance, no more, simply to disabuse the mind of a too easy acceptance of our own society and its structure as something in the nature of things, eternal, above all "natural". Of course one could also find communities today, and viable ones too, already working on entirely different principles, though they have only entered on the first experimental stages of a new order. These are the established socialist societies where, if we can rid our minds of total unbelief, there exist stable communities which have escaped altogether the kind of economic crisis that threatens Western capitalism, and are looking towards the accomplishment in the near future of a practicable non-capitalist, socialist society.

It is difficult for us to imagine any social order whether medieval or modern, working on a fundamentally different plan from our own. But it is the first pre-requisite of historical understanding to loosen the fixed categories of the mind which prevent us from seeing anything other than the possibility of our own evanescent and rather rickety economic order. "There are also people beyond the mountains".

We have said enough to refute the idea of human nature as somethings invariable and therefore determining only one form of society, and that our own competitive and gain-seeking individualism. If human nature, of this unchangeable type, were really the ultimate determinant, would this not require that all societies, in all ages, and all communities large and small, everywhere in our modern world, should manifest the same type of basically aggressive, anti-social social life and habit? But is this so? How is this able to explain the immense variety and fluctuations in the history of mankind? We cannot explain by any such theory the profound changes in the types of civilisation

[1] Tawney, *op. cit.*

and social life, or the profound differences between for instance, peaceful agricultural communities, and aggressive militaristic peoples, between well organised hard working and efficient industrial societies, and predatory gangs, tribes, and societies.

If that is so, a paradoxical situation reveals itself; how can a type whose character is determined by the social structure, by the pattern of social customs and pressures, himself alter that structure to a totally new one, bringing with it a different type of man?

"If human nature is invariable, how then can it serve to explain the course of intellectual or social development of mankind? If the course of social development is essentially variable how can it be explained by something that is invariable, that is fixed once for all? Is the reason why a variable magnitude changes, that a constant magnitude is its cause?"[1]

Both history and anthropology bear witness to the extraordinary capacity of human nature to change. The fierce pirates who raided our shores in the time of the Saxon kings are now peaceful pig farmers; the brilliant Arabian civilisation and its cultured human type strangely deteriorated within the space of a few centuries. Margaret Mead describes the complete reversal of character in the Manus of New Guinea within twenty-five years. Originally a quarrelsome and ill-disposed tribe, many observers came to regard them as permanently cast into this mould, and deeply inbred with a rather unpleasant kind of original sin. But changes in the social and political organisation, and in religious and ethical beliefs, resulted in a striking change; from the appearance of the villages to changes of customs, ceremonial, marriage relationships and personality. They became friendly instead of harshly competitive, relaxed and unworried instead of anxious, irascible, bad-tempered and aggressive.[2]

It would appear then that, so far from showing a fixed character type, man is extraordinarily variable, and that his character appears to be not genetically determined or instinctual, but largely formed by his social environment.

To point out that primitive communities are often stable and cooperative is not to argue that they are uniformly model societies, but simply that they are not, as those who believe in original sin (whether theological or genetical) make out, uniformly bad. Anthropologists who

[1] Plekhanov, *In Defence of Materialism.*   [2] Margaret Mead, *New Lives for Old* (1956).

have lived for many years in such communities invariably have a good opinion of them. Theories as to the ineradicable beastliness of human nature are not found among those who know the primitive at first hand.

It would appear then that if we are to understand the real basis and origin of our society, we must see how it came into existence to replace the society that preceded it. That takes us back farther still to discover, if we can, the reasons for the appearance of the medieval world, and of the classical age of the Graeco-Roman world which preceded *it*. Is there a rationale of social development, something that explains not only a simple organic growth of continuous change, but a series of transformations, of mutations, like those characteristic of organic evolution?

The Marxist doctrine of man goes back to the very roots of Marx's philosophy. Man appears as the creature who learns to understand, manipulate and alter his environment, instead of, like the animal, adapting itself to its pressures. Man is the tool maker and user, who conceives distant ends and pursues them through intermediate devices, he is the first creature to produce his own means of subsistence—to plant and reap, to herd and breed his cattle. As he makes his environment conform to his needs, so he makes his world. He knows and understands in terms of what he does and what he achieves. He and *his* world—the world as he sees it and knows it—evolve together. He is therefore neither created in the image of God, nor is he nothing more than the purely instinct-driven animal he evolved from; but creates himself as he makes his history, becoming a new man with every significant leap in the mastery of his environment, and every time that advance requires a new pattern of social relationships.

It is by going back to the origin of society that Marx, working in anthropological terms, seeks to demonstrate how society appears, what man's relation to it is, and how both man and society are in constant change of a progressive character. "The whole of history is nothing but a continual transformation of human nature", says Marx.[1] "By acting on the world and changing it, he at the same time changes his own nature. He develops his slumbering powers and compels them to act in obedience to his sway".[2]

From man's first beginnings we see his existence as essentially the mastery and control of nature so that he may satisfy his primary needs, develop the wider and richer needs of a civilised community,

[1] Marx, *The Poverty of Philosophy* (Quelch translation), p. 160.
[2] Marx, *Capital*, Vol. I, Chapter 7.

and fulfil them. Marx endeavours to show that men can only complete the development of society, and reach the point at which *all* men's needs are supplied in rational association with others, in mutual aid and development of social forms, by the achievement of a cooperative commonwealth, of socialism.

Let us at once point out that, contrary to what some critics suppose, Marx is not attempting to explain this historical process as the unfolding of some vast principle of historical evolution, or by the operation of some immanent dialectic of development through *thesis-antithesis and synthesis*—ideas which Marx contemptuously and emphatically rejects. What he is doing is to show, in strictly anthropological terms, how society arises, develops, changes, and how in the social control of natural forces and the building of civilisation man realises his own potentialities.

Men, unlike animals, create their own means of subsistence and do not simply wander about looking for food and consuming it. They cultivate the soil, they herd cattle, they fabricate pottery and woven material, they forge iron, and make ships and wheeled carts. And all this from the first is social activity, and means the accumulation of valuable techniques and other forms of knowledge which can be taught in society by society to its younger members, "a partnership with the dead", as Burke described it. In these ways men alter their environment, and themselves. The animal, on the other hand, constantly *adapts itself* to a relatively stable environment, and remains through centuries and millenia virtually the same animal, with the same instincts and habits.

Human labour, as Engels says, is "premeditated, planned action directed towards definite ends known in advance, and the character of the change effected on the environment is accordingly different and far more extensive".[1] The animal destroys the vegetation of a locality without realising what it is doing. Man destroys it in order to sow field crops on the soil thus released, which he knows will yield many times the amount sown. Consciousness and intelligence have taken the place of instinct. Man's constructions are planned in the imagination before he constructs them in reality. When he so acts "he actualises in the world outside himself his own purposes, the purposes which give the law to his activities and to which he subordinates his own will".[2] Intelligence enables man not only to use nature but to change it to serve ends.

[1] Engels, *Dialectics of Nature*.   [2] Engels, *Anti-Dühring*.

All this he does not carry out in a loose association of separate individuals. Sociality is the defining characteristic of human nature. The fulfilment of man's needs cannot be achieved in a war of all against all, but only in close and friendly association. The human community is not a pack or herd, but is organised to carry out planned activities, using long-term schemes to achieve in stages the desired ends. Man cannot do what he wants to do alone. He is unfree as a solitary individual. He attains his freedom only by cooperation with his fellows. Economic production is social. It is because of economic production that man is free: it means organised agriculture, road building, car construction, lighting, heating, and engineering.

"In production men not only act on nature but also on one another. They produce only by cooperating in a certain way and mutually exchanging their activities. In order to produce, they enter into definite connections and relations with one another, and only within and through the medium of these social connections and relations does their action on nature, does production, take place".[1]

"Activity and consumption both in their content and their mode of existence, are social: social activity and social consumption. The human significance of nature first exists only for social man for only here does nature exist for him as a bond between men—as his existence for the other, as the life-element of the human world. . . . The naturalism of man and the humanism of nature both brought to fulfilment".[2]

In his productive labours not only has man built cities, dug canals, created lakes, cut down forests, drained swamps, but he has transformed the surface of the earth by covering it with his plantations and crops. By thus creating, and then re-creating his own conditions of life, he creates himself and his own history. We have long realised that the conditions in any society make the type of man within it. We have not always realised that men themselves *make* those conditions, and are thus the creators of their own nature. Since man never ceases to alter that environment and those conditions, he is constantly changing himself. Where then is the unchanging inherited "human nature" which cannot allow men to behave differently from the way they now behave?

[1] Marx, *Wage Labour and Capital.*
[2] Marx, *Economic and Philosophic Manuscripts of 1844* (Milligan translation), p. 103.

But it is not, of course, only the means of production and the physical environment that are altered, but the whole pattern of social life necessary to carry out the activities demanded by a world that has been changed in a particular way, as, for instance, by agriculture when it was first invented. This means that one form of society, with its customs, rules, type of behaviour, technical skills, and type of character appears in the early years of agriculture round the great river basins: but quite another when metals are discovered and other techniques devised, and when ores have to be fetched from abroad and trade is organised. Yet another pattern of life, and another type of man appears with the machine age. This gives us distinct types of human nature: the farmer is not the cloth weaver in a power driven mill, and *he* is not the maintenance engineer in a modern factory. Again, there is one type of man, of mentality, of customary life, for the member of the closely knit trade guild of the Middle Ages, and quite another for the new industrial society deliberately created on the basis of competition and money values, with the commodity and the market as the overriding forces in the new world of commerce. "The handmill gives you society with the feudal lord; the steam mill society with the industrial capitalist".[1]

This understanding of human nature is basic to Marx's way of thinking. He sees man as simultaneously shaping history and adapting himself to the world that he himself has changed. This process makes man into man, differentiates him from the animals, and lies at the bottom of his ability to create and change the conditions of his life.

Since man is essentially social, it is his relation to the members of his species, quite as much as his relation to the material world, that gives man his objective being, his "nature" at any one period. Marx says that man is essentially "species man". What does he mean by that? Does he hold that there is a hidden essence of man, in a Platonic or Hegelian sense, that is gradually unfolding itself? On the contrary, "the essence of man is no abstraction inherent in each individual. In its reality it is the ensemble of social relations".[2] Marx means by this that man reflects the sytem of relationships he builds up at any stage in his history. It means that man is not a complete man until we find him in a developed society.

This was the principle first worked out by Aristotle, who saw that

---

[1] Marx, *The Poverty of Philosophy* (Quelch translation), p. 119.
[2] Marx, *Theses on Feuerbach*, No. VI.

man in the small family unit is only on the first step towards his manhood, in the village he is more of a man, but he is only a real man when he creates the *polis*, the city, where his responsibilities, his complex relationships, his culture, for the first time are on the level of real humanity. This is what Aristotle meant when he said that man was a "political animal" he is a man only when we find him playing his full part in a civic relationship.

This requires a society organised for the common good: at any lower stage men are only on the way to becoming men. A horde atomised into warring hostile units is not a *polis;* and its individuals are not yet fully men. Nor is any class society in which the privileged use other men as instruments, as means to their own ends, as is the case under slavery, under feudalism, and under capitalism. At the present state of social development true man has not yet appeared; he is still in the making. As Engels put it, German philosophy's discovery that "God is man" called for a rearrangement of the world that would make it possible for man to experience himself in it as a godlike being. While Marx in *The Holy Family* declares that "The empirical world must be arranged so that man experiences and assimilates there what is really human, that he experiences himself as man".[1]

Man is continuously improving both the machines, the organisation of industry, the methods of work, and so on. Although he is himself adapted in habits and outlooks to his present system that does not prevent him from continuously modifying it and changing it; and, as he does so, even within the capitalist system, he finds that he has to adapt himself to his new machines, industrial processes and organisational methods.

It is when, in the highest stage of capitalism, the advance in technology and the new problems of markets, trade and the financing of industry which this brings with it, begin to create insuperable difficulties, contradictions and anomalies, that what is required is seen to be more drastic reorganisation of industrial society, involving the radical change of structure demanded by socialism.

At this time men begin to question the whole economic pattern and the system of social relations up to then regarded as inevitable as if it were determined by natural law. It is now that the science of economics itself is called in question. At the same time the associ-

[1] Marx, *The Holy Family*, p. 176, using Bottomore's translation in *Karl Marx, Selected Writings*.

ated forms of thought and life, the ethics of capitalism, its legal expression, the subordination of politics to high finance, are questioned. Finally, in the field of culture, the ideology of a society rent with paradoxes and involving so many in unnecessary deprivation, now comes under criticism.

Thus men come to see the necessity in our time of pushing home drastic changes of the economic system to get things moving again, to break the deadlock, to overcome the contradictions and frustations of capitalism at this stage of its development. If this means challenging vested interests they will have to be challenged; if this means getting political power to carry such changes through, then political power must be won.

It is thus that each new form of society has been brought into existence, and in due course capitalism gives way to socialism.

In our society we are approaching, and in some parts of the world have already begun to build, the next form of society which, unlike those which have hitherto taken place, does not begin by creating a new economic system that still leaves large groups existing only as the means to the ends of the masters and rulers of the economy. Capitalism can only be replaced by social ownership and by a rational organisation, not for private gain but for the satisfaction of human needs.

There is about this progress from stage to stage not an atom of mechanical or logical necessity. It is the activity of human intelligence meeting the series of opportunities and obstructions which its own improvements and adjustments bring about. It is at this point that we leave the technological development and consider the psychological phases, the ways of thinking and feeling, that guide, motivate and control the periodic reconstructions of society. Each step forward, as we see, requires a new pattern of social organisation, for instance when the first great step from hunting and food-gathering to a settled agricultural community was taken; and we can see at once the changes in the mind that must occur as the discovery is made and exploited, and as the new pattern of living is established. We can also see that the mentality of the farming group will be very different from that of the wandering hunters. In other words, human nature has changed. It was the same kind of change which we saw when the pre-capitalist economy, its values and customs, its institutions and ideology, gave way to the capitalist order of things, habits of thinking, and competitive ethic. Again human nature was re-made.

We see then a parallel development of the economy of society and its psychology, as two interacting and never separable sides of the same process. Considering for a moment the psychology of man in any one phase of social development, we can see that the success of his efforts in devising new machines, new discoveries in science, new sources of power, brings into being a productive apparatus to which the original patterns of life are no longer appropriate. The old idea and habits are even obstructive and hampering. A radical change in mentality begins. Once again this is not the *effect* of mechanical pressure, or the evolutionary life force, it is simply ordinary human intelligence seeing that certain ideas and ways of working are out of date and getting its thinking geared to the new situation. Of course this may well mean vigorous arguments, the conflict of old and new ways of thought—as we saw so well exemplified in Tawney's study of the rise of capitalism. A similar struggle of ideas is today taking place between the ideology of orthodox capitalism and that of a nascent socialism.

It is when a whole era is in process of transformation that the steady, piecemeal changes that take place all the time—in technology, in organisation and in ideas—enter a critical phase of more radical transformation, involving the appearance and growing influence of a new and important group closely associated with the rapidly developing economy.

Capitalism was established when the groups associated with developing machine industry, with their new demands, new ideas and values, obtained political power and began the reconstruction of legislation and institutions. As they succeeded, and their influence spread, as their new methods were applied and their new rules and habits and ideals took over, so the mind of the period was re-made in the new pattern. We can see quite plainly this happening in the formation of capitalism, and with it the appearance of the pervading capitalist ideology and of the "human nature" now regarded as "natural", as the only kind of human nature there is.

If such a transformation has taken place so recently, why should it not take place again? It is not in the nature of things impossible. Man is infinitely malleable, and has demonstrated this again and again in his own history. He will begin the process of re-making himself and his economic thought, not under the impulse of a utopian dream of a perfect society, but when the highly developed forms of modern capitalism find the current economic system hampering, obstructive and inappropriate—its ideas out of date. Then begins the dawn of new and challenging ideas, the drastic criticism of the old psychology, the formulation of new patterns of social organisation in keeping with the new forces and able to deploy their full potentialities. This is the coming of socialist ideas, types of economic organisation, institutions, attitudes of mind, ethics and values, the new psychology, the first steps towards a socialist mentality, and socialist human nature.

8

ALIENATION

The term "alienation" is often used so vaguely and loosely that it has become little more than a catch phrase in some quarters. This is unfortunate because it does refer to a form of human experience of great significance. The experience, one of distress, confusion, bewilderment and intense loneliness is an inescapable fact—the term comes later; and should it be misused, what it represents still remains.

It is not a modern phenomenon, still less a concept peculiar to Marxist ideology. In our own times it goes back to religious roots. It is also a psychological condition very much the theme of literature and poetry. And thirdly it is a philosophical concept, found first in Hegel and Kierkegaard, then in Heidegger, and emerging as central in Existentialism. The most familiar, and indeed prevalent form of alienation is that familiar to us as "the human condition", or "the human predicament". Here it is taken as a fact of life for which no explanation, religious or philosophical, need be sought. It is the experience well described in the words of A. E. Housman:

> "I a stranger and afraid
> In a world I never made".

It is a profound malaise, a feeling of impending disaster, a sense of spiritual exhaustion and a yearning for a return of life, of confidence and of conviction. It appears in some of the best works of modern art, in which the dissolution of our world is pictured with masterly fidelity. Beckett's plays, and Pinter's, and a good many of our most significant films are eloquent witness of a generation whose disillusion and confusion of spirit has touched bottom.

In Existentialist terms, it takes on a more philosophical dimension as the feeling of being abandoned, forgotten, caught up in the purposeless stream of life, left rudderless on tempestuous seas, bewildered and empty—*Waiting for Godot*.

A recent study of alienation by Melvin Richter[1] distinguishes four

[1] *Archives Européens de Sociologie*, 1967.

principal meanings: estrangement from one's fellows; from one's work or profession and its products; from oneself, the loss of identity; and from the values and institutions of one's political society. As such, alienation is seen in the social and political context of society, and reflecting its profound inner contradictions.

In seeking for some explanation one is not inventing the experience as a necessary concomitant of the theory. Quite the contrary: the experience is present, an unhappy, inescapable and distressing fear of life and society. Explanation is offered from various quarters: religious thinkers attribute it to estrangement from God, the sceptic to the total absence of meaning in the universe, the sheer cussedness of things, the existentialist to the inescapable fact of man's aloneness in a world into which he comes from darkness and goes out into that darkness, a world without purpose and without values, direction, or any valid standards of right and wrong where he *has* to make his own meaning, and the validity of his value judgments rests on no more than his arbitrary, but responsible choice.

In the 19th century when all thinking men, at any rate in Germany, were philosophers, and all philosophers were Hegelians, alienation had its philosophical interpretation. Hegel considers every objectification, especially of nature and the world of objects, as a kind of alienation, as though in creating something we lose ourselves in what we have made. For Hegel,[1] if it could be overcome, it would only be by rising to a higher level of consciousness where the unity of creator and object is recovered. We need not linger over a phase of philosophy long past except to notice one important fact—Hegel declares that man creates his object and himself at the same time, by *labour*. And it is the product of *labour* that confronts him in hostile form and seems to have taken away from his something of his essential humanity.

Hegel considered this an inevitable phase in the development

---

[1] For Hegel, the development of society, which is the mode of self-development of the Absolute Idea, occurs through the projection of mind into matter, the self-estrangement of mind in a material form alien to its true nature. Through the struggle between mind and its estranged form, higher forms are produced. The process of self-estrangement is the very form of existence of mind, leading to the final stage of absolute knowledge. At the higher level of consciousness the mind recognises itself in the object and overcomes the feeling of duality and antagonism. Feuerbach and the Young Hegelians saw self-estrangement or alienation, as the loss of man's true essence, his deprivation of a full life, of freedom and the satisfaction of the potentialities of his nature.

of man in relation to the objective world and society. He explains society as an "estranged" institution because of the historical form of "bourgeois property" which distorts even the most private and personal relations between man. Thus man has come to live in a world that, though moulded by his own knowledge and labour, is no longer his, but stands opposed to his inner needs—a strange world governed by inexorable laws, a "dead" world in which human life is frustrated.

Feuerbach, a philosopher who greatly influenced Marx, explained it differently, and in terms of religion; people projected the best of human nature upon their conception of the deity, thus stripping themselves of their humanity. Religious self-denial, discipline, other-worldliness, is man humbling himself before God. He transcends this alienation, said Feuerbach, by getting rid of the idea of God and taking the attributes he ascribes to the deity back to himself, so that "man becomes a god for man", as he ought to be.

We have to note then that a universal problem for thinking men in the eighteen-twenties and thirties was the unhappy fact of the human condition, and Hegel's attempt to explain it from *above*, from the Idea, from the self-realisation of Spirit. Feuerbach steps on the scene to reverse the explanation. It is not the Absolute (or God, to consider the phenomenon of alienation in religious terms) that creates alienated man. It is man who creates his gods, and his absolutes. Being *always* precedes thought. You can have no "thought" in itself. It is *men* who think, and they think about their world and themselves. They can indeed create an objectification of their own thought, which however is purely *subjective*, a *projection* of their own minds. They *create* the image of God; they are no longer the object created by God the great Subject. To get rid of their alienation they have only to *see* this, and the illusion disappears, and they regain the strength, and goodness and other divine attributes they stripped of to characterise their deity.

Marx at once accepted the fact that being, and above all social being, is the source of all consciousness, all ideas: but he rejected the notion that the gods, the Absolute, the transcendental, were only intellectual errors, to be dispelled by a whiff of rationalism. There was a *reason* for the condition of being deprived, of being rejected, considered a mere object. And Hegel suggested why when he said that it was the product of man's *labour* that alienated him. What kind of labour dehumanises a man, treats him as a mere purchaseable factor in the economic process, buys, uses and exploits his *labour?* What if not wage-labour under capitalism?

Thus when Marx first raises the question of alienation it is by no means in an idealist or utopian or Hegelian spirit, but as an *economic* phenomenon. Hegel *had* seen it philosophically, even though he related it to "moving life of the dead" which, in his view, characterised modern industrialism; but Marx, in the first six essays in the group of papers in which he expounds the basis of his dialectic[1], shows the worker as a commodity, caught up as a cog in the mechanism of the capitalist economic machine. This he considers the alienated condition of wage labour. There Marxism begins. And it ends in the transition to socialism, as described in *Capital*, where Marx sees this "fragment of man" recovering his humanity in the classless society to become a "fully developed human being" achieving "the self-realisation of the person", "realising all his potentialities".

Marx therefore comes forward with a double-barrelled theory. The same work by which man makes his world, subdues it, satisfies his needs, both builds civilisation and develops his potentialities, at the same time, at this advanced stage of social development, capitalism, uses him as a means to the ends of an owning and dominant class.

Marx finds the cause of the deep hunger for consolation, for a power to depend on and to save, where Freud found it, in the suffering and privations of social life. It is the evils of human society itself which give religion its power. It arises, says Freud, from "the oldest, strongest, and most consistent wishes of mankind" for solace, reassurance, help. The secret of religion's strength is the strength of these wishes, and the depth of this need. Therefore it is a shallow rationalism that seeks to dispose of religion by refuting the philosophical grounds for the existence of God. "The call to abandon their illusions about their condition is a call to abandon the condition which requires the illusion".[2]

Marx does not expect these conditions to disappear until man has achieved genuine cooperative fellowship in labour; and that is not something to secure even by a political victory, but only by the long, slow process of social and economic change that follows victory;

[1] *Economic and Philosophic Manuscripts of 1844.*
[2] Marx, *Introduction to Critique of Hegel's Philosophy of Right* (Bottomore's translation), p. 44.

though that process *begins* when the political power of the capitalist class is brought to and end.

It is important to see this form of alienation not as part of an abstract theory, reflecting or attempting to explain certain economic phenomena; but as a solid fact of social-economic life, ramifying in every department of life, affecting all classes and representing a disease of the body politic. Primarily Marx relates it to the fundamental aspect of social life, man's basic creative activity, that which makes him a man, as it takes form in a class divided society. His increasing and effective control of the world through technological invention and social organisation in order that human needs may be satisfied and man's life goals fulfilled, involves the subjugation of the many to the few. This is how civilisation makes itself and men become men, but since the days of slavery the immense increase in production and wealth has been purchased at the heavy price of exploitation.

Class society is effective, it is progressive, and it is inevitable. It is now marked by two features—on the one hand its immense potentiality, and on the other its fundamental contradictions, involving alienation. This brings us to the second aspect of Marx's position. From the condition of alienation we reach the stage of "going beyond" class exploitation, and therefore of transcending alienation. This becomes necessary in order to escape the dangers and disasters of an enormously developed economy crippled by a totally inadequate economic system to operate it.

We then have the whole structure of Marxism as built around social labour

(a) producing man himself and his world,
(b) proceeding by exploitation and creating alienation,
(c) transcending class society to release the forces of production, overcome alienation, and achieve fully social labour and fully developed man.

It is surprising to find certain forms of Marxism which wish to eliminate from Marxist theory these three basic conceptions of Marxism:[1] man's self-creation as a social being, alienation, and transcendence.

This would be to reform Marxism by abolishing it. The difference between this emasculated Marxism and Marx's Marxism is that the first becomes a system of economic concepts abstracted from the rich

[1] Althusser's *For Marx*, pp. 197, 199, 217.

concreteness of *Capital;* whereas Marx's is not any such theory, but the substance of the actual world in process of change as this is understood by those who on the basis of their understanding are changing society from its capitalist to its socialist form.

Let us, before proceeding to the more detailed description of alienation as Marx sees it and as we experience it, briefly review the development of alienation *theory*. For Marx is it not a religious phenomena, for this has to be unmasked to reveal its secular and economic form before we can see it as it is. Secondly, alienation is not a tension or contradiction inherent in existence. It is not just "the human condition". It is an historical phase and one that hastens to its own supersession as it increases, as it becomes more intolerable and dangerous. It is not part of the accidents and inevitable frustrations of life, for these cannot be overcome, while alienation can be overcome; it is a removable evil; and one that it is necessary, and not merely desirable, to overcome.

Nor is it a *philosophical phenomenon*, spirit estranged from itself as an event within the realm of mind. Marx rejects Hegel's view that "my real human existence is my philosophical existence". His concern is not with a process within an abstract conceptual system, but with the actual and concrete conditions of life which produce alienation.

Passing to the overcoming of alienation, Marx shows that alienation cannot be overcome within the system of using labour as a purchaseable commodity; firstly because that is essentially a dehumanisation that men will not eternally endure, and secondly because what is economically possible or even inevitable in the earlier period of self-righting crises, is no longer possible in the period of international monopolies, automation, international inter-dependence, and bank finance. Escape at this stage can only be through the replacement of the uncontrollable mechanism of the market by the controlled economy of human cooperative labour. Finally, transcendence is not just a moral *"ought"*. Some of its critics think that to construe Marxism in terms of overcoming alienation is to rely simply on an ethical demand for overcoming the alienation of man. Marx on the other hand regards the change as the only way to create the condition within which it is possible to live a genuinely ethical, that is a genuinely human existence.

There is one other fundamental element in Marx's theory of alienation; it is the key to *all* forms of alienation and dehumanisation. A society the very basis of which is commercial, where the market rules, buying and selling prevail, production is not for ultimate use but ultimately to create new investment capital, will involve itself in institutions, legal systems, degenerate forms of luxury living, a commercialised press and entertainment industry, and areas of profound social decay and criminality. Nor can any of these symptoms of the debasement of social life to the money level be removed by tinkering with symptoms or by preaching sermons.

The very first writings of Marx are concerned with alienation. Critics have sometimes seen this as the expression of immaturity, utopianism, philosophical idealism: the later Marx abandoning alienation, humanism and other idealist lumber for a calculating economism, elaborated in a theoretical system. Such a position betrays a distressing ignorance of the persistence of the idea of alienation right through Marx's works: *The German Ideology*, *The Holy Family*, the *Grundrisse*, and *Capital* itself, as the basis of Marx's thought.

Marx began his enquiry in 1844[1] with his examination of alienation, and after stating the result of his analysis and the prospect of the transcendence of alienation, for the rest of his life's work he deals with nothing else. He does not see mankind simply finding out how to raise wages, or abolish unemployment, nor is he trying to set up a more moral, a utopian alternative to capitalism. He is showing men how they have to transcend *all* these forms of alienation, and that this is not merely desirable but more and more urgently *necessary*, because in its final stages of development capitalism becomes menacingly unstable and violent, threatening mankind with rapid decline and catastrophic breakdown. Marx offers no instant remedy but only the possibility of turning a dangerously increasing trend of alienation into a decreasing one, which therefore points to the possibility of its ultimate elimination.

Alienation is seen in its place in a dialectical process, whereby experiencing it and revolting against it man creates his own self and thus fulfils himself. For Marx it is the *negation* inherent in reality which becomes its moving and creative principle. This is because alienation bears witness to the incompleteness of the development begun by capitalism, to the intolerable status of millions of people necessarily treated as *things*, since their role in the pure mechanism subjects them to the automatic laws of the system which reveal themselves as destructive.

---

[1] In the *Economic and Philosophic Manuscripts of 1844*.

This was worked out in the *Economic and Philosophic Manuscripts of 1844* in opposition on the one hand to Hegel's theory of the self-estrangement of the Absolute Mind, and on the other to Feuerbach's notion of the religious projection of the human essence onto God. Marx saw the human condition under capitalism as the distorted expression of the division of society into classes, of the exploitation of the wage-earner when he sells his labour to the owner of the machines. He concludes that to abolish alienation you must abolish the class monopoly of the means of production, the private ownership of the machines.

Certain critics of the early Marx have suggested that the *Manuscripts* represent the high-water mark of Marx's Hegelianism. This is surely a mistake. The first four essays are purely economic and concerned with man as a wage labourer under the economic system as described by the classical economists of Marx's time, such as Ricardo and Maculloch. Marx, in these essays, rejects both Hegel and Feuerbach, showing that the real cause of alienation is the capitalist wage system, and not a stage in self-consciousness, as Hegel believed, or religion.

Under the economic laws of capitalism the product of labour, the commodity, is there for sale and not primarily for use. It is the "object for sale" which now determines the nature and end of human activity, so that the materials that should serve life come to rule over its content and goal, and the consciousness of man is made victim to the relationships of material production. Even worse, once the new laws begin to operate, they do so independently of human intention and control, and this uncontrolled economy now legislates over all human relations, over the disposition of economic resources, and above all over its distribution and consumption. As soon as this mystifying character of the system is penetrated, it is no longer seen as an unalterable law of nature, the economic conditions appear for what they are, the complete negation of humanity.

Under such a system no man's faculties can develop. He cannot become a true man, that is a sound man. His faculties can only be fulfilled if he *with other men*, in fellowship and mutual intercourse and labour, makes the best use of the developed wealth of human resources for the common good.

Individualist society is a caricature of a true human society, since man has become so isolated that his separateness from other men is accepted as his natural form of existence and the human bond is believed to be unessential, and social obligations even of a positive and cooperative nature are unwelcome. Man becomes only a means to the ends of others, and thus, used as a mere commodity, finds himself the "plaything of alien forces".

From the economic point of view, when a manufactured object is only a commodity for sale its use value is separated from its exchange value, and is only considered, and made and sold and distributed, in conformity with that feature of its existence. In consequence we all become no more than buyers or sellers. Exchange value, money, becomes the supreme value and the moulding force of our lives. Every man is constrained to face the world in an acquisitive spirit, and to aim solely at possessing for himself all he can. But as Marx says: There is no fulfilment in mere possession, whether of object or money or people. A world in which the acquisition of property or money is the dominant motive denies the fulfilment of man's being.[1]

This is inseparable from estrangement from other lives and also from one's true, human, self—a condition of spiritual desolation and dread.

The modern economist is today sometimes found emerging from his own tunnel into the daylight—a rare but refreshing occasion. Professor Galbraith confesses that "the values of a society totally pre-occupied with making money are not altogether reassuring". Nor is this merely a moral judgment, for the system itself becomes every year more menacing. "An angry God has endowed capitalism with inherent contradictions." Professor MacPherson has also seen the inevitable deprivation that necessarily follows from economic indi-vidualism: "if we leave men free to appropriate and to gain control of the means of production, leaving the mass of men propertyless, we deny full humanity to a substantial part of mankind."[2]

Nor can the Welfare State prevent or reverse this, because it would kill capitalist enterprise upon which the Welfare State relies to main-tain the productive work of society; nor can society conceive of any other way of getting any utility produced, whether food, clothes, houses or anything else, unless it be a profitable enterprise for some investor. When most people are involved in this delusion we all become grovelling worshippers of the same fetish as our masters.

The fundamental irrationality of this situation is the picture of man at the summit of his technological advance, but halting on the threshold of a new world, confronted with unlimited potential resources,

---

[1] *Economic and Philosophic Manuscripts of 1844*, Private Property and Communism.
[2] MacPherson, *The Political Theory of Possessive Individualism*.

and a vast mass of misery, helpless and baffled. The effect on all our thinking and feeling, the inevitable frustration and conviction of the irrationality of existence, can be seen in contemporary literature and philosophy and in the prevalent condition of neurosis in all classes of society.

Central to Marx's position on alienation is, of course, his theory of the nature of man. *Capital* opens with the recapitulation of the view first enunciated in 1844, that in controlling nature and satisfying his needs through co-operative labour man builds his own personality. The alienation of capitalism, while it carries the process of control of nature forward, goes backward in its depersonalisation of man. But if alienation is transcended man can begin the process of diminishing (rather than increasing) alienation, and so move nearer the realisation of all his human potentialities.

This is what Marx calls "humanism", and in our day we can call "Marxist" humanism. It is bitterly attacked by Althusser on grounds that it is idealist in principle, that it postulates a metaphysical essence Man, from which men derive their being. Therefore Althusser calls for a Marxist *anti-humanism*, and for the philosophical myth of man which we find in Marx's writings to be "reduced to ashes".

The Marxist conception of man is said to be the acceptance of an abstraction, the reification of the general idea as a pre-existent Platonic absolute, a real transcendent, extra-terrestrial entity— MAN, dwelling in the sphere of Mind. But Marx himself was careful to say, when elaborating the ideas which Althusser so strongly objects to, that he totally rejected the notion of an abstract entity embodying itself in individual men, and that by "man" he always meant flesh and blood people existing by the sweat of their brows and the labour of their hands. What he said was that it is of the nature of man to live a communal life of cooperation, to unite with, work with, and live in fellowship, and only in so far as he does this is he man at all. This is what he meant when he said that man is "the ensemble of social relations". Since in a class society, and especially a capitalist society, he is placed in a non-human relationship with others as a purchaseable commodity, he must in these circumstances be *less* than a real man, for he is alienated. Marx held that man's true nature is not realised (actually established) until he attains a fully social being in a classless society.

The aim of socialism is to pass beyond the class society to a classless society, by which Marx means not a society without differences and distinctions, but one in which it is no longer the case that a minority enrich and fulfil their lives by depriving the majority of the possibility of doing so. In passing beyond the buying of men's labour (and thus the man himself) as a commodity, we enter the realm of full cooperation and mutuality in which the *conditions* for fulfilment are established. This is the process of *transcendence*, of superseding a less than fully human society. And the transition to socialism is just that. It is how man becomes completely human.

Man, unlike some solitary predators, is essentially a social animal who becomes himself in society by accepting its obligations and receiving the social benefits, following the acceptance by others of those obligations to create, serve and maintain the human fellowship. In a capitalist society man is still "the ensemble of social relations", but the co-operative relations are contradicted and in part nullified by competitive relations. Man becomes himself only in the pattern of social relations found in common ownership and social control of production for the common good. This is what Marx means by "the concept of the human species brought down from the sky of abstraction to the real ground of earth; what else is it if not the concept of society?"[1]

Now the critics of alienation, and of human fulfilment, of humanism, are also strongly opposed to the idea of *transcendence*, and also to the notion of the *historical process* which Marx sees as deriving from man's earliest beginnings and now seen in our capitalist society which itself is passing over into socialism. This too seems to them ideological, Hegelian and idealist, and Marx's own summary of it in the Preface to the *Critique of Political Economy*[2] is described as Hegelianism and evolutionism which have caused havoc in the history of the working-class movement.[3]

It may well be asked how it is possible to conceive of Marxism with all this cast out? Althusser's reply would be that while something like this does characterise the young Marx down to 1845, at that date he broke completely with all these ideas, and they never occur again except as an occasional and unfortunate hang-over here and there, after that date, and that they are really confined to the

---

[1] Marx, *Werke*, Vol. 27, p. 425.

[2] This is the well-known passage covering some three pages beginning:
"At a certain stage of their development, the material forces of production come in conflict with the existing relations of production", etc. etc.
The whole passage is quoted *in extenso* by Lenin in two of his publications (Lenin's *Collected Works* (1930 edition), Vol. XVIII, p. 25; Lenin on *Karl Marx* and again in *What the Friends of the People Are*, of course with approval. Althusser nevertheless says: "Never for a moment did Lenin succumb to the influence of these pages!"

[3] Althusser's Preface to *Capital*.

unpublished *Economic and Philosophic Manuscripts of 1844* and some
earlier writings, all of which we must reject out of hand.

Unfortunately for this view, the theme of alienation and its transcendence runs through the whole of Marx's writing. It is prominent
in *The German Ideology*, at the very point at which Marx is said to
manifest his total rejection of the idea. It appears again and again in
Capital itself, not always in the form of the German word *Einfremden*,
but in the exact meaning of the deprivation and frustration of humanity caught in the toils of capitalist economic law. Marx writes here of

"the character of independence and estrangement which the capitalist modes of production as a whole gives to the instruments of
labour and to the product, as against the workman, is developed by
means of machinery into a thorough antagonism".[1]

Capital shows how the growing contradictions involve the negation of
alienation itself (the negation of what itself was a negation of humanity), so that the capitalist order is transcended and "human potentialities" are at last capable of being fulfilled.

Far from leaving behind him the conception of the historical
process by which this is achieved Marx is describing how it is the
fundamental role of man to be the initiator and controller of the
historical process; how this has been frustrated and alienated though
the economic laws of capitalism and the "fetishism of commodities". But when capitalism is transcended man at last is set free to
develop "his own natural and acquired powers".[2]

We can only conclude that the extrusion of these concepts from
Marxism totally destroys it. "The concept of alienation is seen to
be central to Marx's whole thought, including Capital".[3]

Careful thought must be given to the problem of *how* man is
going to effect this transcendence. If it is not the power of pure idea,
or of his moral enthusiasm, what is it? Is it the mechanical operation

[1] Marx's *Capital*, Vol. I, Ch. 15, Section 5.
[2] We have mentioned elsewhere that in Marx's most important unpublished work, the
Grundrisse, the work of his maturity in which he outlines the whole future course of the
theories he is to embody in *Capital* and many other works, *alienation* is a central concept,
being specifically mentioned some 300 times; and the historical process briefly outlined
above is elaborated as the scheme of his ensuing volumes. The date of the *Grundrisse* is
1857, twelve years after he is supposed to have broken completely with this whole
sequence of ideas.
[3] David McLellan, Introduction to *Karl Marx, Early Texts*. We are greatly indebted to
McLellan and to Istvan Meszaros, for the re-enforcement their recent studies have brought
to the full understanding of this fundamental aspect of Marx's thought.

of the economic law which brings capitalism to its final crisis, and operating through a multitude of independent wills, eventually creates a socialist economy; man acquiescing and irresistibly participating as he is swept forward on the tide of history?

This is not Marx's idea at all. Marx does not see history operating except as controlled by the conscious acts of man. Man confronts nature, "acting on the external world and changing it", as Marx says, and the product is one of *social* labour, "the direct outcome of cooperation", in which "he transcends his individual limitations and develops the capabilities that belong to him as a member of a species", the species *Homo sapiens*. Man *is* a communal animal. (If he were no more than an individual, he would be autistic, an "idiot".) This is what Marx means by "species man". It is man's social action and reaction in the world that is both the making of history *and* changes the world and man himself. It is "a continual transformation of human nature". Yet these critics, who passionately declare themselves to be the true Marxists, call for the rejection of this whole historical process.

What then do they put in its place? The economic theory elicited from *Capital*, built into an authoritative system? But is not such an authoritative system itself a special form of alienation? For Marx calls all separate *theories of explanation* examples of alienation. The essence of dialectic is the living unity of understanding an actual situation while we are grappling with it, what Marx called *praxis*. Marx nowhere creates a system, an explanatory theory, which thereby becomes a kind of theology, a network of abstractions fabricated by the mind, and like all systems necessarily inadequate for life. As Kierkegaard said, "You can have a purely logical system but you cannot have a system of existence."

Marx sees this dichotomy of theory and practice as the same kind of separation you have when intellectual labour is separated from manual labour, theory from practice (even if you subsequently apply your abstract theory to reality), *explaining* the world from *changing* the world, mind from matter. All are examples of alienation. All are of the same pattern as the opposition of owner and worker, the dualism of a class society or the opposition between man and the economic law which dehumanises him. This is why Marx finds forms of alienation in religion, in philosophy, in the family, and in political economy, as well as in human deprivation. All of them do violence to the unity in which alone man is really man.

The most obvious and menacing form of alienation is the creation of a system of economic laws which are created only by the economic system they have brought into being, and are then accepted as a form of natural law, like the law of gravity. Under its rule man becomes the helpless victim of this complex system and its operations, which appear as something objective, self-existent, and unalterable. As Marx says, "the productions of the human brain appear as independent beings endowed with life".

This reification, or transformation of an idea into a *thing*, can also be described as *the hypostatisation of abstraction*, which occurs when we first invent a general term (an abstraction, therefore—a sign) for a number of allied things, such as "fruit" for apples, pears and plums or "mammal" for dogs, elephants, cows, and wolves; and then give the "idea" a superior and originating actuality, eventually declaring that the "eternal and transcendental fruit" manifests itself as apples and pears.[1] Now this is how *Ideas*, principles, law systems, moral ideals, come to have a being and an authority of their own as if they *preceded* the real things which gave rise to the general term embracing them. This is how Hegel came to derive all existence from the Idea; whereas Feuerbach and Marx pointed out that all ideas are ideas about existing things, situations, events. Thus the authority, and presumed *existence* and independent truth, of a theory, a philosophical system, the economic laws of capitalism, the doctrinal system of Catholic theology, come to rule over actuality—a complete inversion of the truth. Moreover every such system develops an elaboration and development of itself into a complex of doctrines, endlessly debated, and used as legislation for ruling men.

This tyranny of the reified law system we see in economics, in theology, in law, and in philosophy; and each system comes into existence not merely as an intellectual mistake, but as an aspect of the dichotomy of experience, as seen most plainly in class society in the separation of owning class and working class, in the workers' subordination to the economic law and class rule which arises from his propertyless condition in industry.

Now the surprising thing is that "Marxism" can itself be reified, its laws or theories can be hypostatised, it can develop into an authoritative system of dogma imposed on man. But this can only be the case so long as there still remains, even under some forms of socialism, a dichotomy between governors and governed, an alienation at the

[1] Marx and Engels, *The Holy Family* (Moscow edition, 1956), p. 79.

social level, which translates itself into an alienation on the ideological level; for any system of Marxism of such a final and authoritative form is still "ideological"; and there are such systems.

Wherever such ideologies are found, wherever the dichotomy of mental and manual labour, mind and matter, theory and practice, God and man, ruler and ruled persist, or class of one sort or another is not finally eliminated, alienation continues.

Is it not very much the same thing when we are offered a new total system of economic theory extracted from *Capital*, constituting another kind of alienated ideology, of reified abstractions and *hypostatised* conceptual doctrines? Clearly this has no sanction in anything in Marx's writings. Indeed, he fought implacably against all total theories of that kind. What is interesting is that the exponents of the new doctrinal orthodoxy with its final authority over practice are vehement in their rejection of the hypostatisation of the Idea as we find it in Hegel; yet just as Hegel derives history and its practice as issuing from the Absolute Idea, so the new dogmatists see historical practice issuing from the Absolute Economic System. Two perfect examples of ideologies deriving from and perpetuating alienation.

One last word needs to be said. It is often objected that in some existing socialist societies both alienation, rule by a privileged and authoritative political group, and a rigorous doctrinal system, can persist. How is this? Marx clearly foresaw this himself. He never said more than that the disappearance of an *owning* class (and that has gone in socialist societies) created the *conditions* which made possible the beginning of a process of emancipation, education, reconstruction of the state apparatus, and democratisation, the aim of which would be the free man. In the *Critique of the Gotha Programme* he points out that in the transition period with its *differential* wages, a period in which the ideal of distribution "to every man according to his needs" does *not yet* prevail, "right can never be higher than the economic structure and the cultural development of society conditioned by it". Only in the society of the future, the obstacles to its attainment now overcome, but with much still to do, "will people *gradually* become accustomed to the observation of the elementary rules of social life that have been known for centuries and repeated for thousands of years."[1]

Marx, after the completion of his fundamental theoretical works, never anticipated or prophesied an instantaneous transition to com-

[1] Lenin, *The State and Revolution.*

munism, or even an imminent revolution. The point of change he saw as a long way off, *after* the political victory that establishes the *conditions* for the ending of alienation. Socialisation is not the end of alienation. It survives but in a different and more controllable form; no longer increasing, as it does towards the end of capitalism, but now ever diminishing as society develops towards the fully socialist society and communism.

9

THE ECONOMIC IMPASSE

PART I

"An angry God has endowed capitalism with inherent contradictions", says Professor J. K. Galbraith of Harvard—and he is no Marxist! It is time to face these contradictions, whose seriousness we can no longer minimise, rather than to go on saying we don't believe in ghosts while one is breathing down our necks.

We now live in an era of potential plenty. The excuse of scarcity, which was credibly the underlying truth of 19th century economics, weakens as a developed technology creates the means for fulfilling human needs. Yet we are faced with an economic dilemma which affects those who suffer unnecessary poverty, whether in the heart of an affluent society or in distant lands, and racks the affluent society itself with financial and economic crisis—with uncontrollable inflation, stagnation of economic growth, and financial panic.

As long ago as 1844 Marx was aware of the flaw in the economic system of capitalist society. In the same year that he wrote the *Economic and Philosophic Manuscripts* there was published Engels' *Outlines of a Critique of Political Economy*, which analysed the trade crises through which, strangely enough, economic law asserted itself periodically, and concluded that the struggle of capital against capital "drives production to a fever pitch at which production turns all natural and rational relations upside-down." Of course Marx and Engels had a great deal to learn of the complex processes which resulted in this disequilibrium; and it was Marx's task to unravel this problem. This was the task he sought to accomplish in *Capital*.

It was by no means merely an economic exercise. Marx was concerned with human degradation and emancipation, but from the first he saw this as more than a hortatory task. He never proclaimed a utopian solution. He saw the development of capitalism to the conditions of almost permanent crisis as creating the conditions of huge potential productivity, of monopoly organisation, of the separation of management from ownership which were the necessary preconditions to socialism, and presaged it—required it.

Against the French socialist Proudhon who thought that you could retain capitalism but remove its evils—a view generally held today—Marx argued that they were as ineradicable as the fact that when you pull your rope down over a pulley the bucket goes up. The contradiction is inherent; but it is not simply a blot, a fatal flaw.

"It is the bad side that produces the movement which makes history, by constituting the struggle . . . . In order for the oppressed class to be emancipated it is necessary that the productive powers already acquired and the existing social relations should no longer be able to exist side by side. The organisation of the revolutionary elements as a class supposes the existence of all the productive forces which can be engendered in the bosom of the old society."[1]

The volume in which Marx works out his analysis of the contradictions of capitalism is the practical exposition of his philosophy of alienation and its overcoming. It is a philosophy shown as operative in the real world, not a theory merely in the mind. Man as he makes his world and changes it must become aware of what is happening in society and to himself, for it is not merely a tale of suffering but of promise, and not merely of promise but a call to action. The time is approaching for the realisation, the actualisation of the philosophic dream.

"As history develops and with it the struggle of the proletariat becomes more clearly defined, they have no longer any need for such a science in their own minds, they have only to give an account of what passes before their eyes and to make of that their medium."[2]

We are now to see what it is in our day that passes before our eyes—the crisis of capitalism which is both its condemnation and the promise of the future.

Students of Marx sometimes wish to restrict their enquiries to the generalisation and necessary abstractions in his more theoretical work, and we are a little put out by his deliberate turning towards the concrete, and spending more than forty years of his life on *Capital* and in the practical problems of the international working-class movement. But to be put off by this is to miss the essential point

[1] Marx, *The Poverty of Philosophy*, 1847 (Quelch translation, p. 132).
[2] Marx, *The Poverty of Philosophy*, *loc. cit.*, p. 136.

of his philosophy. All his ideas are related to the actual movement of economics and politics of his time, to the concrete developments of historical forces. Marxism is in the facts or nowhere.

As Marx himself said, "It is man, real living man that possesses and fights; 'history' is not a person apart, using man as means for its own particular aims; history is nothing but the activity of man pursuing his aims."[1]

The essential thing about the philosophy of history developed by Marx is that it always proceeds from social reality, not from abstract categories: from 'the simple material production of life,' not from intellectual constructs: from practice, not from a set of self-generating, self-developing, self-resolving ideas.

We shall proceed to state some—a very small part of course—of the facts of poverty in a world of potential plenty, not simply to blame "the system" and declare "socialism" to be the answer, but in order to invite a critical probe into the precise reason for this halt in progress. No Marxist attributes this to personal or class ill-will or hardness of heart (in which case the answer would be sermons and divine grace!), nor, as I have just said, is a blanket condemnation of "the system" enough. We want to know what exactly in its actual working is the cause of this economic impasse, so that people can say, even with all our modern resources at our disposal, "Well, that's the way things are". We want to know just how the operations of the laws proper to this particular "game" work inevitably to fetter rather than release the immense resources at our disposal.

If we are to understand this let us remember the theory of Adam Smith (1776) which reflected the vigorous individualism and scientific rationalism of the capitalism of the 18th century.

He taught that if free rein were given to the economic interests of capitalists, the maximum freedom of competitive individuals will produce as a resultant of the free play of forces the greatest social good. There is a pre-established harmony which operates through the economic laws of *laissez faire* to achieve the benefit of society. Pope seems to have had the same idea when he told us that it was Providence "who bade self-love and social be the same".

We now see that whatever may be said of it as the philosophy of a necessary phase of economic history, *laissez faire* was clearly appropriate enough as an effective method of creating a surplus in the hands of

---

[1] Marx, *The Holy Family*, Ch. VI (Moscow edition, 1956), p. 125.

E

capitalists for reinvestment and so fostering the rapid growth of industrial capital.

However, the process was a painful one for many; ruthless competition forced the weakest to the wall and kept wages as low as possible. And, as Marx and Engels saw, the operation of these economic laws created periodic conditions of disequilibrium resulting in falling prices, a contraction of production, unemployment and reduced wages. These phenomena had the effect of restoring equilibrium, and the cycle is repeated.

Even with the mitigation of the worst consequences by social insurance and the lessening of the crisis by monetary and fiscal control, dislocation still continues on a distressing scale and capitalist production potential is never utilised to the full in spite of desperate human need. We are exhorted to put up with these evils because the effective working of the system necessarily involves hardships, irrationalities and what will be felt as injustices. But, argues Professor Hayek, it is foolish to resist:

"the individual, in participating in the social processes, must be ready and willing to adjust himself to changes, and to submit himself to conventions which are not the result of intelligent design, whose justification may not be recognisable, and which will appear to him unintelligible and irrational."[1]

Hayek strongly deprecates any unwillingness "to bow before any moral rules whose utility is not rationally demonstrated." This is not a voice from the past. Professor Hayek spoke as Professor of Economic Science in the University of London, in 1946.

However, we *have* resisted and we have *not* bowed before irrationality and injustice. Beginning with the Factory Acts and continuing with Social Insurance we have achieved a Welfare State in which some of the worst evils of capitalism have been considerably alleviated, but by no means removed. But the *philosophy* remains the same, as the Business Supplements of *The Times*, the *Guardian* and the weeklies testify. Mitigation runs parallel with it or is the countervailing power, it has not changed the basic motive of capitalism which remains, disastrously, under the complete control, as ever, of *the market*. The claims of labour still seem a menace and wage demands and strikes present a serious threat to the economy.

[1] Professor F. A. Hayek, *Individualism: True and False* (1946).

Marx is concerned precisely with the market and its threat to human values. His indictment was supported through the 19th century by prophets and reformers like Carlyle and Ruskin; and in our time has been supported not only by evidence confirming the damning chapters in *Capital* on the social consequences of industrialism, but by the sociological analysis of men like Dr. Polanyi and Professor Macpherson, who while not communists yet support Marx in his philosophical judgment on the alienating tendencies of the capitalist economy. Marx never preached "the iron law of wages"—that was the doctrine of his opponents. He insisted that trade union efforts and political pressure could and should raise the standard of working-class life; but he insisted that the basic disequilibrium could never be finally overcome within the structure of capitalism.

It may be useful to look at the conclusions of Polanyi and Macpherson because they take the enquiry beyond the description of social evils to the underlying forces responsible for them; and that too is Marx's contention. Polanyi[1] draws attention to the fact that the basic principle of capitalist economics was and is that all men seek the maximum money gain and seek the greatest possible freedom from government interference in its pursuit. The development of the socio-economic philosophy of "possessive individualism" from Hobbes and Locke to the present time has been ably discussed in Professor Macpherson's *Political Theory of Possessive Individualism*.[2]

Polanyi in his documented history of the period shows that the unregulated operation of economic law threatened the workers with extinction just as boundless wealth appeared. The doctrine of Harmony, as Hayek continues to affirm, requires submission of the individual even if it destroys him, but of course humanity and common sense took in hand the series of ameliorative reforms which satisfied the elementary requirements of organised social life in order that society should not be annihilated by the operations of the self-regulating market. Polanyi insists, however, that it is not economics as such that threatens society (*every* society is based on economics), but economics controlled basically by the motive of self-interest. Polanyi sees the economics of industry working against society—involving a clash between economic power and political power. But the necessary regulation does not reverse or modify the economic principle as such— it works to counteract it. Polanyi concludes:

[1] Karl Polanyi, *Origins of Our Time* (1945).
[2] Macpherson, *op. cit.* See also his *The Real World of Democracy*.

"Neither Engels nor Blake nor Carlyle was mistaken in believing that the very image of man had been defied by some terrible catastrophe. And more impressive even than the outburst of pain and anger that came from poets and philanthropists was the icy silence with which Malthus and Ricardo passed over the scenes out of which their philosophy of secular perdition was born."[1]

Of course it will at once be said that all this was true enough of the 19th century but things are very different now. In his book *The End of Ideology* Daniel Bell has argued that the fundamental problems of the industrial revolution have been solved and the need for ideologies or utopias to motivate men to social action has disappeared. We have already achieved

"the egalitarian society—which the intellectuals associated with the Marxist tradition have been calling for during the last hundred years. Technical experts will have no difficulty in coming to grips with the few problems that remain".

To this Noam Chomsky replies that

"It seems fairly obvious that the classical problems are very much with us; one might plausibly argue that they have even been enhanced in severity and scale. For example, the classical paradox of poverty in the midst of plenty is now an ever-increasing problem on an international scale."[2]

We shall return to the question of the unsolved problems of poverty and economic crisis, but even if things were a great deal better than in fact they are the fundamental Marxist criticisms remain. Even in prosperous times labour is still a commodity, "productive units" as an industrial magnate recently described his men; the determining force is still the blind drive of the market, not human welfare; the real god of our time is still gold. Human welfare has got to be the by-product of an economic process the single drive of which is a return on invested capital. The notion of controls refers not to social objectives but to centralised monetary and market direction, and the coordination and financial assistance of constituent concerns of large associations.

[1] Karl Polanyi, *Origins of Our Time.*
[2] Noam Chomsky, *American Power and the New Mandarins.*

As Harrington points out,[1] the difference from the classical period of laissez-faire is that the theory of individual free competition automatically producing the social good has gone. It was originally an attempt to secure a moral end by the most effective means. This has been exploded, unregulated competition proved disastrous and has been scrapped for monopolies and controls, but for what end? Not, of course, for a deliberate planning for social benefit, but for a surer profit. But there is no longer any philosophical or scientific claim, as there was for the original theory, that the automatic result of a planned economy aiming at profitable investment will necessarily secure the highest good of society. That was the purpose of free competition. It is not the purpose of monopoly and government control of money and trade etc. It is merely hoped or expected to be the by-product. But whether the aim remain the same or has now become solely the interests of the business community, it seems unlikely that there is any mysterious alchemy to bring golden results in social welfare out of the leaden instincts of possessive individualism and the forces behind the market. Can anyone reading the pages of any Business Supplement see a glimmer of regard for human need, or the slightest hint of an ethical motive in the analysis of business trends, dividends and commercial prospects? And no suggestion now of any "unseen hand"; that faith has long ago evaporated.

Marx is convinced that just these motives and economic forces, and the "entities" that now have mysteriously appeared: what he calls the "money fetish", the commodity, the market forces, the economic laws, the reduction of employed humanity to an expended factor in production, deliver man to an unconscious mechanism that is destructive of human values in all sections of society among the rich, the not so rich, and the poor, in the trade unions and among the employers; for all are driven by the same motive.

It remains to be seen what the consequences in 1971 actually are. Granted that trade unions, political pressure, and social feeling have ameliorated conditions in the advanced democracies, if nowhere else, after 300 years of the new system and its philosophy has the expected end been attained? Have the unexpected contradictions really been overcome? Is there among economists and business experts any confidence that there will be a solution of the pressing problems of the economic system, any hint of a solution of its baffling dilemmas? In September 1970, the National Institute of Social Research

[1] Harrington, The Accidental Century.

confronted us with the only manifest alternatives: mounting wage claims and soaring inflation on the one hand, sagging production, dwindling investment and a stagnant economy on the other. Does this indicate the end of our problems, "the technical experts having no difficulty in coming to grips with them", as Daniel Bell so confidently affirms?

The market rules absolutely, and what government does is to take its own measures to get the best results from the operation of economic laws—not to replace them. Whatever control and modification government and trade unions have achieved the contradictions remain, their consequences are more extensive and cruel than we are sometimes willing to admit, and there is little promise of their being overcome in the near future. In fact these anomalies have once again taken a menacing form and threaten at any time a recurrence of the great slump of 1929.

In the words of the Leader Writer in the *Business Observer* (May 1970):

> It may well be that the summer of 1929 was the last time in which the capitalist world as a whole might reasonably look forward to the future without foreboding of war, revolution or economic collapse; it was the last time, perhaps, in which men and women in the Western world could still hold to that belief in the inevitability of progress and the rationality of the social and political order to which most of them had subscribed since the eighteenth century."

We can no longer evade the fact that poverty is widespread in the world today, not only of that two-thirds of the impoverished third world whose people live permanently below subsistence level, but the stagnant pools of poverty in the United States, the persistence of depression, of slums, of unemployment in Britain, the large areas of miserable poverty in Italy, Spain and Portugal. And these are but examples.

"Three successive American Presidents have launched a War against Poverty in the United States and then for economic reasons have been compelled to call it off—a disaster, and one of the most miserable failures in American history".[1]

[1] From the recently issued *Citizens Board of Inquiry into Hunger and Nutrition* (1970).

There are in the United States today at least 10 million undernourished people.

"No Western country permits such a large proportion of its people to endure the lives we press on our poor. While four-fifths are affluent, one-fifth are unmercifully degraded and slow starvation has become a way of life."[1]

(Twenty-five per cent of the poor in the U.S. are coloured. The poor whites are still in a majority. The unemployed now number some five millions, about 4 per cent of the labour force.)

America has some of the worst slums in the world and large areas of impoverished people in many widely separated districts, as illustrated by a moving C.B.S. television programme, displaying child malnutrition, sickness, bad housing and an abysmal standard of sub-human existence in some widely separated districts of the United States; and by no means only in the Negro communities.

Recent studies in Britain show nothing as bad as this, but recent investigations have shown that two-thirds of a million children are living below the poverty line, as measured by the basic National Assistance Scale of relief. One in eight live in extreme poverty. The gap between the rich and the poor is widening, and property incomes are rising faster than earned incomes. This means that the abundance, the comforts, the opportunities the poor see all around them are beyond their grasp. Is keeping people alive good enough?[2] Lord Beaumont, a leading figure in the Liberal Party, has recently stated that 18 per cent of all households in Britain live below the minimum standard of the National Assistance Board. Nine million people live in sub-standard houses, 1,800,000 of these being condemned as unfit for human habitation: 750,000 old people are living below the minimum.

Britain is one of the most wealthy and highly developed countries in the world, yet here is a state of poverty and squalor which should be unthinkable in the light of the resources we have available.

There is no shortage of manpower or materials, indeed there is much unused capacity. Private enterprise cannot build houses at rents that the worker can afford to pay. Even those built by local authorities have long waiting lists, and are let at rents well beyond the pockets of

[1] *Loc. cit.*
[2] See John Hughes (Ruskin College), "The Increase in Inequality", *New Statesman*, November 8, 1968; Ken Coates, *Poverty: The Forgotten Englishman*, 1970.

many workers. Things are worst in the great cities like Liverpool and Manchester. The London waiting list for rehousing is 170,000.

We are all concerned about this poverty and squalor in one of the three wealthiest countries in the world, about large sections of the population left behind in what appears to be a general advance towards prosperity, but what are we to do about it? The whole purpose of Marx's *Capital* is to show that capitalism does not represent the final, finished and absolute structure of an industrial economy; that its mechanism, its set of rules, represent only one, formerly useful but passing, economic system; that what is impossible in that particular "game"[1] is possible if you change the rules; and the appearance of plenty allows us to shift the economic system from the field of *scarcity*, where Rule Book A holds, to the field of plenty, where Rule Book B, representing a quite different economic system, can be applied. Of course all institutions like to think that their concepts reflect final reality.[2] This is never so. All conceptual systems are relative, historical and passing.

What inhibits the maximum utilisation and deployment of our resources is the monetary mechanism. It seems natural and proper to us that everything connected with producing and exchanging the necessities of life, all employment of labour and resources, should be conducted in terms of money, of prices, of a fair return on capital, on the basis of competitive costs, interest-bearing loans, and so forth. But consider the fact that you could have people with no homes on the one hand, and on the other raw materials and labour available and yet it would be *financially* impossible to get the houses built because the *final* cost of the £3,000 house after paying the interest on the loan would be £9,000, and the low-income family could not afford either the economic rent or the mortgage rate if purchased. People on a desert island beginning to build huts and dig for yams and fish might be stopped by an economist among the survivors and told that since they had no money they couldn't do it. If they then created some money and used it they might find in a week or two that they had too many coconuts for the people to be able to buy, several able-bodied men unemployed, and a banker with a lot of coins he didn't know what to do with!

---

[1] We use the term "game" in conformity with recent logical studies which analyse the valid inferences granted this or that or the other assumed "rules of the game".
[2] That is to say they are *ideological* forms and therefore assumed to be unalterable systems of the order of nature.

Marx has an interesting comparison between what he calls *transparent* modes of production, Robinson Crusoe's situation, or what we would find in a simple farming subsistence economy, on the one hand, and *opaque* modes of production where economic realities are presented only in terms of money, and *money itself* dictates possibilities and necessities rather than the actual resources and manpower available, on the other.[1]

The point is that money and its laws come to take the place of the real relationships of working for use to satisfy basic needs, and are regarded as realities endowed with inherent power in themselves. The world of powerful tools, useful objects, employable men, is represented by tokens and laws made up about them, *once useful*, but now inhibiting their full use. This Marx called the dominance over man of his products, and the illusory sway over man of his own organising scheme and artefacts. Like the imaginary forces of the witch-doctor, they are accepted implicitly as the ultimate forces which must be yielded to.

Haldane objected to the use of the word "law" in science. He preferred to speak of the "uniformities of nature", and do away with the possible implication of a lawgiver or a legislative body. "If a piece of matter does not obey a law of nature it is not punished. On the contrary we say that the law has been incorrectly stated. It is quite probable that every law of nature so far stated has been stated incorrectly".[2] No laws are absolute, not even Newton's laws, which were found to hold only under certain conditions. There appears, however, to be no reason for saying that there are no regularities in nature to which our statements of natural law correspond. "One might as well say", wrote Haldane, "that because no maps of England give its shape exactly, it has no shape."[3]

PART II

In science, at each stage of its development, forces and laws were imagined which came to *limit absolutely* what man could conceive possible, in chemistry, physics and medicine. There had to be a "paradigm shift" before at a higher level of explanation, using new concepts, entirely new possibilities appeared.

[1] Marx, *Capital*, Vol. I.
[2] J. B. S. Haldane, *The Sciences and Philosophy*.
[3] *Ibid.*

So in economics. A new consciousness is needed to unmask the witch-doctors. We have to transcend the social structure which subordinates us all not only to a man-made law, but to a privileged group who maintain the necessity of themselves continuing to operate the economic system primarily in their interests. But every economic system (including socialism itself) is relative and provisional, and is destined to be transcended once men have become aware of the immense range of possibilities opened for them by a radical change of concepts, by a revolution of the mind.[1]

What we have to see is that it is impossible to show these possibilities as practicable in terms of the old conceptual patterns, terms and laws, just as radio-telegraphy is impossible if electricity is thought of as "a fluid". You *have* to grasp the theory of electro-magnetic waves. It is the appearance of such vast and obvious possibilities in contrast to actual impoverishment, and failure to utilise the power and material all around us, that eventually shatters the original model and liberates the mind. That was what Marx meant when he said that man does not merely adapt himself to a given pre-existing environment—that is not what is meant by knowledge. He reshapes and modifies the external world. If it isn't open to rational cognition *in this way*, it has to be made over to a new pattern, and new laws discovered.

We pass to the second form the economic crisis takes, which clearly demonstrates the hypnosis of the money fetish. This is the financial tangle of our present unhappy condition. A cabinet minister recently declared in the House of Commons:

"No free democratic society has solved the problem of achieving simultaneously four basic economic objectives:
First, a rapidly expanding economy;
Secondly, full employment;
Thirdly, reasonable price stability;
Fourthly, equilibrium in the balance of its national payment".[2]

Our economic difficulties are intensified by the class conflict between

---

[1] According to Marx *Socialism* would in turn be replaced by *Communism*. (See the *Critique of the Gotha Programme*.)

[2] A few years ago (and even now occasionally) we were informed—never by economists, usually by writers in the weeklies—that Keynes had long ago shown us the way out of the economic difficulties of capitalism. This is manifestly not the case. Government is exercising controls everywhere, but in our *inflationary* dilemma the economists (Keynes or whoever) have no unanimous and considered course to recommend. They themselves are at loggerheads.

trade unions and employers. It is strange that while on every hand we hear that the class war is an outdated conception, in fact it has reached menacing proportions. The whole production process, always out of gear in any case, has been and can be at any time completely stopped by massive strikes. Export trade has been damaged on many occasions by stoppages, and a handful of specialised workers producing an essential component can hold up a whole branch of industry. If the strike succeeds the increased wages are often given as a reason for increased costs and export prices, or the next step in general inflation, according to the rules of the game. Why not change them?

Yet organised labour is more determined than ever before to secure a regular increase in its real wages, and is not deterred by the pleas even of a Labour Government, let alone by the arguments of economists, bankers and employers' associations.

This is an excellent example of the basic principles of a capitalist economy working, as in so many other cases, self-destructively. It is absurd to tell the workers to subordinate their interests to those of the community, firstly because this means not only the community but basically the interests of the investors; secondly because capitalist economics is based on the principle that the economic parties concerned *are* to pursue *their own* interests, and that is the only way the interests of the community can be served. That is what business does when it buys and sells. It buys in the cheapest market and sells in the dearest. It keeps costs down and puts prices as high as the market will stand. No manufacturing firm is asked to sell a car at less than an economic price, as a matter of principle, "for the good of the community". Why should workers alone be asked to sell their labour for less than the market price for the good of the community? You cannot ask the employers to follow the good old rule of capitalist economics, and the workers to follow the rule which capitalist economics has rejected for itself and for every capitalist society.

If the right course is to accept the welfare of the community as the over-riding law, well and good, apply it not only to the trade unions but to the employers, and run industry as a public service, the whole affair owned and operated on the basis of planned production for consumption. But that, of course, is socialism!

One more example, this time of the influence of purely financial considerations on farming. In the United States the small homesteads are falling into hopeless poverty and disappearing: they now comprise only 8 per cent of American farms. About a million and a-half of these small farms are marked for extinction. The peasant population is breaking up and the large farms employ troops of seasonal migrant workers under appalling conditions, inhabiting primitive camps where health conditions are bad. The agricultural product of American farms is unsaleable at an economic price. The Government buys the surplus to the tune of $4,700,000,000 a year, and subsidises the cotton fields at the rate of $650,000 for each of 13 big farms, and $2,000,000 for still larger farms, and the smaller farms at a proportionate rate.

The grain and farm surpluses are stored in warehouses and the volume is such that it would give the 480 million people in India all the calories they need for a year, or provide all the people of Asia with an extra 200 calories a day.

In the summer of 1969 it was announced by the principal wheat exporters that there was a surplus of 700,000,000 bushels for the year. This was regarded as an appalling disaster, since to release it onto the market would result in a catastrophic fall in price and the ruin of the farmers. An agricultural journal concludes its leading article with these words, "An unusually good crop spells ruin to the agricultural producer."

Discussing this with a lecturer in economics from one of the Midland universities, I mentioned the suggestion that had been advanced to destroy the surplus to maintain the price of wheat, since a serious price collapse would spell disaster for the producers. I suggested that in a hungry world that would be insane. "Well," he replied, "it's a pity, but what else can you do?"

This is only one example of the hopeless paradox of poverty in plenty in the prosperous and highly industrialised West, where the operations of the market place the potential sufficiency out of reach of the hungry millions. As one critic of this economy well put it, "Would a maggot starve because the apple was too big?"

The rule of the Market is a strange one. Every blessing becomes a curse. An increase in the food supply is a disaster. America stores its surplus while a million citizens suffer hunger. The decline in infant mortality in India reducing the figure from 146 to 120 threatens efforts to reduce the population increase and avert famine.[1] And now automation, especially in the United States, is so rapidly reducing the demand for unskilled labour as to create growing unemployment. Thus with declining demand everywhere owing to a surplus of some

[1] Though the rate of increase of population in India is no greater than it is in the United States.

six million workers the increased output at reduced prices cannot be purchased and production is cut to prevent a crisis.

At the other end of the situation the Market leaves a number of human needs untouched, notably in housing, where economic demand ceases long before need is satisfied owing to high costs, and rents. The Market has no mechanism designed to link production to the actual needs of society.

It has frequently been said that Marx argued in terms of the capitalism of the 19th century, before the days of automation and cybernetics; and that the immense productivity of modern industry has completely transformed the situation, making high incomes and full employment possible wherever modern economic methods have been introduced. This is why Daniel Bell and others speak of "the end of ideology", meaning the end of any justification for a socialist criticism of capitalism.

But in the last few years we have found that Marx, in a really prophetic fashion, anticipated just this situation, and believed that automation would destroy the very basis of the capitalist system itself. This forecast of the development of capitalism appears in his *Outline of the Critique of Political Economy* (the *Grundrisse*)[1] written in 1857–8 and setting forth Marx's system in its fullest scope. On its basis he intended to write a whole series of treatises, but only got as far as the first volume in the economic study which was to precede the whole series (*Capital*). The importance of this thousand-page *Critique*, is that it contains much more than an economic critique. It accepts and develops the principles first laid down in the *Manuscripts* of 1844 and in *The German Ideology*, and expands and discusses at greater length than in the earlier writings the principle of alienation. But we are not concerned here with his remarks on alienation, but with the light which the *Grundrisse* throws, and so disconcertingly, on the new situation in industrialism which we now, for the first time, have to face.

Marx points out that in modern industry "the creation of real wealth depends less and less upon labour time . . . the powerful effectiveness of these machines bears no relationship to the labour time which it cost to produce them". This changes the very char-

---

[1] At present, untranslated as a whole, the *Grundrisse* is available in English only in a relatively small portion (see Chapter 1). The *Introduction* published as an Appendix to the *Critique of Political Economy* of 1859, is really the Introduction to the *Grundrisse*. D. McLellan has translated a few selected passages of the whole work. This was published in 1971.

acter of work. "Man's labour no longer appears as incorporated in the production process. Rather the worker relates himself to production as a supervisor and regulator". This development, Marx continues, means that the very basis of wealth has been transformed. Now, "neither the actual labour power expended by man, nor the length of time during which he works, is the great pillar of production and wealth. That pillar is now the appropriation of man's own universal productivity."

We have thus, argues Marx, passed altogether beyond the period in which the forced maintenance of low wages was necessary to secure the capital for expanding industry, which led to a consumer demand so restricted as not to be able to purchase all that industry wanted to sell. *Today it is economically possible to expand the productive apparatus without having to impose sacrifices on the workers.* But at the same time technology demonstrates itself capable of restricting employment by massive reduction of employment while creating abundance. At this point the system breaks down as a rational enterprise.

To expand production, says Marx, there must be a vast expansion of consumption. But this cannot take place unless the organisation of industry is directed *primarily* to the satisfaction of consumer demand rather than the accumulation of surplus value by restricting consumer demand, wages and employment. This restriction is no longer required for the maintenance and multiplication of the machines. In this new phase as Engels said in 1844,

"The community will have to calculate what it can produce with the means at its disposal; and in the light of the relationship of this productive power to the mass of the consumers it will determine how far it is to raise or lower production."[1]

Marx himself in the Third Volume of *Capital* points to the time when society in the proper sense will be formed, when the class war will end and history proper will begin; for then, at last, men will really control their destinies.

"There can be freedom in this sphere only to the extent that men in society, the associated producers, govern rationally the material given them by nature, and bring it under their common control, instead of being governed as by a blind force; develop it with the

[1] Engels, *Outlines of a Critique of Political Economy*, 1844.

least expenditure of energy and under conditions worthy of and adequate to their human nature".[1]

This is the real freedom which only becomes possible when the economics of scarcity has been transcended by the development of capitalism itself, to the point at which, in Lenin's words, "Socialism looks out at us through all the windows of capitalism".[2]

Lenin means by this that in the course of its development, within capitalism itself, "the outline of socialism appears before us. . . . It emerges from every large scale measure forming a step forward on the basis of modern capitalism." This is what Marx calls "the constant revolutionising of production", even though the basic social structure is not radically altered. These steps towards socialism, its appearing outline, are seen, says Lenin, "with every step towards regulating the economic life as a whole." Thus, the final transition to socialism is a "realisation", an actualisation of the germs and beginnings, the outlines and tendencies, already seen within capitalism.

This leads us to the second major area of evidence for the irremediable contradictions of modern capitalism. We have dealt with the paradox of poverty in the highly industrialised affluent countries, the United States and Britain. We turn now to the poverty of two relatively backward areas, South America and India. Here it is necessary to point out that it is a mistake to imagine that these and other similar areas, notably Africa, have simply been left behind by some accident of history, and are now in the position of catching up, or as Rostow phrases it, "just taking off". Not so, they are and always have been an integral part of Western capitalist development and present prosperity.

They are at once suppliers of raw materials, markets for consumer goods, and areas for capitalist investment. It is capitalist development on a world scale which produces progress at one end of the world, and backwardness at the other. Foreign investment is still very important for advanced capitalist countries. Over 80 per cent of Indian industry is in the hands of British and American investors, and the United States is the economic master of South America.

Since this is the case, loans and grants through the various plans for economic aid do not lead to the development expected and desired. This is seen when we find that the total sum advanced in this way is wiped out by the fall in prices of what they have exported, leaving a

[1] *Capital*, Vol. III, Chapter 48 (A. D. Lindsay's translation).
[2] Lenin, *The Threatening Catastrophe*, 1917. In Collected Works, Vol. XXI.

net loss of $2,000,000,000.[1] America today receives a higher rate of dividends from overseas investments in South America, Africa and Asia, than from its investments in Europe.

I propose to take two examples out of the very many cases which could be considered to show the perpetuation of poverty in two countries. Two centuries ago there was no rural poverty in either country. Today we find in India failure to achieve economic growth and to develop agriculture to the extent required to deliver millions of poverty-stricken people from their unnecessary misery, and in Peru the immense increase in the wealth of the few, considerable economic advance, but associated with it the increasing misery of the poor. This is what Marx means when he said that "from forms of development of the forces of production, these [capitalist] relations turn into their fetters",[2] imposing the conditions of scarcity and impoverishment of past ages on society in the modern world of potentially unlimited affluence.

The question before our world is this—can a state of civilisation be reasonably envisaged in which human needs are fulfilled in such a manner and to such an extent that the enforced poverty of two-thirds of the human race can be eliminated? Marx believed that the obstacle to advance results from a social structure based on private ownership which alone is responsible for the failure to utilise resources cooperatively on a world scale; but institutions now inadequate for the social tasks required by human need and made possible by modern technology and agricultural science are preserved because they serve the interests of the dominant social group.

This is demonstrated with cruel urgency in any South American state. Let us take for our witness an impartial and non-political writer and traveller James Morris. This is what he writes of Lima the capital city of Peru:

"Immediately at your feet, however, clustered on the hillside like some nightmare belvedere, there lies a quarter very different: magnificently sited upon that eminence, ironically surveying the grandeur of the prospect, squats a slum so festering, so filthy, so toad-like, so bestially congested, so utterly devoid of water, light, health, or comfort, so deep in garbage and excrement, so swarming

[1] Dr. Eugen Staley, *The Future of Undeveloped Countries* (Royal Institute of International Affairs).
[2] Marx, Preface to *The Critique of Political Economy*.

with scabbed ragged barefoot children, so reeking with squalor that just to wander through its alleys makes you retch into your handkerchief. From these unspeakable stews the stench of degradation rises, veiling the City of the Kings in a kind of haze, and even eddying around the cross on top of the hill.

". . . nowhere in the world have I experienced quite so distressingly the gulf between the immensely rich and the unbelievably poor. Away in the Andean Sierra millions of Indians are on the verge of starvation and 70 per cent of Peru's Indian babies, poor little unfortunates, are said to die before their second birthday.

"Peru presents all the stock symptoms of reaction: absentee landlords, enormous semi-feudal estates, widespread illiteracy, political irresponsibility, intricate meshworks of financial interest, snobbery, sophistry, indulgence and ostentation."

Now let us turn to India. While since 1946 the government has pushed through three economic plans, agriculture still lags behind and here capital investment is out of the question because it could not pay dividends. The gap between food supply and subsistence level is still about 25 per cent. This is partly because the landlord system is untouched, but also because the whole of the Indian peasantry are in debt to local money lenders. Illiteracy is considerable (75 per cent) and religion and superstitition, for example cow-worship, hold back progress. The remarkable way in which these very conditions have been overcome in China indicates that difficulties are not insuperable but they appear to be so where the government is determined to maintain a basically feudal structure of society in the country and capitalist structure in the towns.

Today infant mortality in India is 120 per 1,000, four times that of the United States. "The grinding poverty of the masses, their unvarying and insufficient diet, often still at the mercy of the landlord or village usurer, all enveloped in a decaying caste system", presents a disturbing sight.

Let us, for the situation in the big cities, turn to the witness of Alistair Cooke after his recent visit to Calcutta:

". . . you brace yourself when you come to Asia for the thud of certain heavy abstractions: poverty, illiteracy, disease, heat, tribalism, rampant nationalism, the bondage of a single crop, the groaning birth trauma of self government.

"It is the point of this series to make vivid the humbling fact that nobody can be prepared for the sight and sound of these abstractions.

"But of all the big familiar abstract nouns, poverty is the one that in Asia assumes a wholly new scale and immediately. For your own sanity you very soon learn to accept, and to pass by, the nightly bundles of rags, shored up against dark tree-trunks in the country and the buildings of the cities, which occasionally stir and stretch and turn into prostrate human beings.

"There is no reliable count of the people who sleep in the streets of Calcutta. A quarter of the people live in slum huts, and almost eighty per cent of these house five families with a common privy and a water tap (where they are lucky enough to have either), and living room for each human of about seven feet by five.

"Every night the ambulances clatter round the rough streets, and when a body with thighs like bamboo poles refuses to be kicked into protest, it is turned over and found to be dead and hauled off to the mortuary. Two to three hundred a night of such corpses is the grudging figure."

India, South America, Malaysia and Africa remain firmly linked to Great Britain and the United States, which have provided almost the whole of the investment capital and receive a considerable tribute in dividends for executing what help is sent. In addition the fall in the prices of primary products during the first two plans meant a loss in export prices greater than all the benefit received from grants in aid.[1]

When it is realised that India, Egypt, South Africa and South America are integral and essential parts of Western capitalism, the overwhelming proportions of their capital investment being American and British (the dividends from India at 14 per cent are the highest of all American overseas investment), and also provide considerable quantities of raw material and food products, we have to consider on the basis of exact statistical evidence whether those countries under

---

[1] The very slow economic development in India in spite of the tremendous efforts of the Government in its three successive plans is sympathetically discussed in Alan Mountjoy's *Industrialisation and under-developed countries* (1966). In spite of massive investment in industry by 1966, industrial unemployment still amounted to 4,000,000 and the average income per head did not rise more than £2 per annum, over the fifteen years of the three plans, from £24 to £26.

capitalism will ever escape from this poverty and economic subordination to Western industrial society.

We must draw this discussion of the basic contradictions of modern capitalism to a close. We do so by propounding four fundamental questions raised by Marx, which Professor Murray Wolfson of Oregon State University discusses in his *Reappraisal of Marxian Economics* (1969), a balanced and critical estimation by a non-Marxist expert.

1. Can there be full employment and real wages without at the same time eliminating the profit incentive (for invested capital)?
2. Can depression be controlled and a reasonable degree of full employment maintained along with control of inflation?
3. Can the concentration of economic power be controlled and the public protected from the economic and political evils of monopoly?[1]
4. Can the developed nations assist the other areas of the world to progress economically, or must the relationship be one of colonialism and exploitation?

Does this look as though all our major problems were well in hand and remaining difficulties well within the grip of the economic expert, as Daniel Bell and many others profess to be the case?

Socialists believe that not only do the problems appear to be more intractable than the economists aticipated, but that the human reality is more profoundly dissassociated than ever before; that the world of products, of tools, techniques and money is turned against man, even while he uses it. Hoping for liberation in the future he obeys the destiny laid down for him by these transcendent powers whose laws he dare not question.

One thing we must now be quite clear about; whether we experience deprivation, economic frustration, poverty, inadequate provision of houses, health, education and care for the aged—and all these spell one thing—the failure depends not on the lack of available resources, nor on the fact that we are an undeveloped economy, but on the fact that the operation of the economic system does not allow the full use of man-power and machines.

The result has not only the gravest economic consequences but

[1] We have felt it necessary to omit the discussion of monopoly for reasons of space, important though it is. There is an immense amount of material on this question prepared by both non-communist economists and by Marxist economists.

profoundly affects the whole working class, and just as harmfully, the owning class itself.

"Labour's product confronts it as something alien, as a power independent of the producer . . . this appears as loss of reality for the workers, objectification as loss of the object and object bondage—appropriation as estrangement, as alienation. . . . The alienation of the worker in his product means not only that his labour becomes an object, an external existence, but that it exists outside him, independently, as something alien to him, and that it becomes a power on its own confronting him; it means that the life which he has conferred on the object confronts him as something hostile and alien.[1]

Consequently the worker does not fulfil himself in his work but denies himself and does not freely develop his mental and physical energies. The relation of the worker to his own activity sees the transformation of strength into powerlessness, creation into emasculation, and man is moreover not only alienated from himself but from other men.

We thus have a threefold breakdown in the Market economy. A failure to utilise available resources even when the need is desperate; a failure to guarantee employment and a living wage, even in our most affluent societies; resulting in a profound and permanent sense o in security affecting those whose lives fluctuate above and below the poverty line, almost as much as those who live permanently below it. This means the loss of a meaningful existence for millions. Not only are men reduced to what the efficiency experts describe as "productive units", completely depersonalised purveyors of working power put up for sale, but that working power cannot be used. As Marx insisted both in his *Manuscripts* of 1844 and right through *Capital*, man is reduced to an object, and knows it, feels it:

"The instruments of labour confront the worker as a mere mechanism, that dominates and pumps dry his living power. For all economic and commercial relations have been transformed from personal relations into impersonal operation of the market. Thus the social forms of capitalism have become antagonistic to a true society and to the self-achievement of the individual".[2]

But even for those of the new technological strata, the highly-

---

[1] Marx, *Economic and Philosophic Manuscripts* (Milligan translation), p. 70.
[2] Marx, *Economic and Philosophic Manuscripts*.

paid skilled workers who enjoy some affluence, there is a discontent situated deeper than the level of consumption and income, another malaise, more vague but more general—a maladjustment of the human structure to a social reality which does not allow it to express itself and to develop.

The problem becomes one of awakening a consciousness of their exclusion from genuine participation in industrial affairs, that is to say at the level of assuming responsibility for decisions.

This whole enquiry into the problems and contradictions of capitalism, so far from contradicting Marx's critique, confirms it. The basic condition is one of alienation, and alienation arises from the class ownership of capital and the economic system geared to its expansion. This, argues Marx, results in *reification*, the fetishism of the market, where all human relations are expressed in terms of the buying and selling of commodities. The workers, even when they sell their labour, are not valued as men, not asked for responsibility or initiative above the level of the machine they mind or efficiency on the shop floor.

What Marx is demanding is a rational understanding of what has hitherto been only an impersonal mechanism whose laws we recognise and in a measure regulate, though we are still ultimately dependent upon their relentless operation. For Marx the economy and the history it gives rise to must come to have a human meaning and not continue as merely part of the general processes of blind natural forces. Marx believed that at this point in history it ceases to control us; we begin to control it; and the realisation of the possibility and necessity of taking control of the whole economy and transforming its automatism into conscious regulation in the terms of human need becomes at the same time the direct and conscious participation of man in the making of their own history and in the business of putting a human meaning into existence.

To realise and achieve this historical destiny is not the loss but the achievement of freedom; for its indispensable condition is not simply the awareness of something happening to us, but a total revolution in human thinking, a paradigm shift, which for the first time in history shows us what we have to do to emancipate ourselves and make our world.

Note on Economic Disequilibrium in 1970.

The dilemmas, as our economists and financial experts in London and New York (June 1970) see it are these:

1. *We cannot both restore the balance of payments and maintain a desirable rate of growth.*

Therefore the Chancellor restricts credit and limits growth at 2 per cent or 3 per cent although he knows, and himself states, that to raise wages and carry out desirable welfare improvements a growth rate of 5 per cent is essential.

But such a growth rate would cause a rapid price rise, tremendous demand by consumers for foreign goods, and high costs for exports. The Government would then have 'to take the heat out of the system', by reversing this policy and once more restricting credit, raising the Bank rate and the price at which money could be borrowed and thus reducing expansion.

2. *How then should he deal with inflation?*

To do this, says Professor Galbraith, he must reduce or hold down wages, curtail the social services, raise the bank rate and restrict credit. These measures will double the figures for unemployment which will rise from 3 per cent to 6 per cent. He doubts whether any government would dare to carry through such an unpopular series of measures.

This is not the judgment of a communist economist, but a brief summary of the analysis of the situation (May–June 1970) in the financial press. I quote from the Business Supplement of the *Sunday Times* for May 30, 1970:

"The United States is at present in the grip of that ominous phenomenon: stagnation and rising unemployment combined with an apparently uncontrollable wage and price inflation. The situation is now so serious that some senior American statesmen are now talking of the need for official control of wages—and possibly even prices—right there in the home-land of free enterprise.

"This is a serious indictment, but as America drifts closer to anarchy it does not seem exaggerated. All segments of society are at bitter war with each other, and each in its own way has contributed to the general malaise.

"The economy is breaking down because business lacks confidence in the basic stability of the country."

In the United States there is a radical division of opinion as to whether to continue credit restriction in spite of rising unemployment and a slowing of growth, since nothing else will hold inflation in check, or to expand credit, absorb the unemployed and hope that inflation won't go to such lengths as to bring about a dangerous stock exchange boom and the inevitable crash which must follow.

The dependence of the whole economy, and of the economy of the whole capitalist world on the wild vagaries of stock exchange boom and slump, which is entirely independent of the actual possibilities of production, illustrates the domination of the forces of pure finance.

No other aspect of Marxism has occasioned so much misunderstanding and indeed misrepresentation as its anticipation of the consequences of the basic contradictions of capitalism. It has been declared that Marx believed that the "iron law of wages" made the improvement of working-class conditions impossible and that nothing could prevent the worsening of wages and conditions. This is false. Marx along with other economists in his time saw that there was a tendency for the rate of profit to fall; but they did not regard this as necessarily disastrous. There would be counteractive measures, one of which would certainly be a higher rate of exploitation. There would also be a tendency to reduce wages to subsistence level. But Marx pointed out that trade union and political pressure working against the normal pressure to reduce wages could increase wages and improve conditions. That was what trade unions were for. Marx fiercely combated the views of those (particularly the French Socialists) who talked about the "iron law of wages", and the uselessness of trade unions. Even if there was strong economic pressure to keep wages as near the level of subsistence as possible we must remember that Marx meant by subsistence level the normal level for a particular trade, that is to say its customary differential in an upward direction. This will vary in different trades.

In 1865 Marx debated the "iron law of wages" in the International, and his lectures were published as the well-known work *Value, Price and Profit* in which he vigorously combated this theory and showed that his opponents were really advocating passivity and submission to capitalist pressure.[1]

We turn to the theory of "increasing misery". Marx said that with the growing concentration of capital "the mass of misery, oppression, slavery, degradation, exploitation" also grows, but, he immediately added, with it the organisation of the workers and their growth in political consciousness. He also spoke of the appearance of a "reserve

[1] Lichtheim asserts that given fairly full employment and trade unions with adequate bargaining power, according to Marx's own theories real wages *must rise*. See his *Marxism*, p. 189.

army" of unemployed as a necessary phenomenon under developing capitalism.[1] But this does not mean the progressive decline into misery of the whole working class. The point of the argument is firstly that real wages cannot rise permanently much above an economic level, and secondly that capitalism spreads its exploitation over the whole world and especially into colonial areas and here poverty becomes far worse than it was before economic imperialism established its control. This as we have already shown has indubitably been the case. But where Marxists have concluded that steadily worsening conditions for the organised workers in advanced capitalist countries are inevitable, the facts show them to have been wrong.

Suppose there does appear in some countries at the bottom of the social pyramid a class of the permanently impoverished and ill-housed. Marx placed no hope at all in the revolutionary possibilities of such a class, and never confused them with the reserve army of the unemployed or with those plunged into destitution by economic crisis. What he was on the look out for was an historic bloc largely composed of those organised workers capable of envisaging the next step.

In Western Europe it is the organised Labour Movement with its trade unions and mass political parties which has enormously improved wages and conditions in England, France, Italy and Germany and is vigorously demanding further benefits. Ken Coates in his study of working-class conditions in Nottingham found that it was the better-paid workers organised in their unions who were asking for more and were dissatisfied, while it was the poorly paid, who were not organised, who displayed "feelings of hopelessness and despair which develop from the realisation of the improbability of achieving success".[2]

It is the better off and the technicians and managers who are likely to be disturbed by the fundamental irrationality of capitalism when in its ups and downs they are suddenly jolted into awareness of how easily their standard of living could be swept from under their feet. And in this connection we should remember that the white collar workers associated with the T.U.C. have increased their numbers by 70 per cent since 1948 and this does not include the teachers not in the N.U.T., the nurses and the doctors.

[1] The Governor of the Bank of England has recently (1970) urged that this must be allowed to rise to something like one-and-a-half millions if the economy is to be kept stable.

[2] The wave of strikes and successful wage claims in Britain 1969–70 bears this out, and contradicts the pessimistic outlook of Marcuse, who speaks from American experience.

The third misunderstanding of Marx's attitude to capitalist crisis we have already dealt with: the capitalist system does not inevitably break down; on the contrary economic crisis represents the mechanism whereby the system restores its equilibrium, at the expense of the small man, the weaker concerns, the workers, and the unemployed. John Strachey, criticising the hopeful gradualism of Labour in the pre-crisis years (1925–1929), and the effect of the crisis of 1929 and the inevitability of further crises, spoke of "gradualism in reverse gear",[1] a gradual loss of earlier gains under the stress of adverse economic conditions. This is certainly a possibility.

The question that arises is: What change of attitude is likely to take place among the better-off workers, and large sections of the new class of blue-collar workers, when faced with redundancy, rising prices, and evidences of a dangerous threat to their relatively high standard of life?

Should the present economic difficulties continue or worsen and unemployment increase, a growing number of technicians, managers, research men and executives may also find themselves unemployed, with no hope being offered of a return to full employment.[2]

The question is, at what point will the sheer irrationality of continuing economic dead-lock produce the mental jerk which recognises the absurdity of the modern paradox? If it is not reached at all, and the heavy conditioning of opinion by press, radio and television, which has already reduced millions to acquiescence and passivity in the face of the inexorable laws of capitalist economics, cannot be overcome, we may expect to see a long, slow period of social and cultural decline, punctuated by sporadic uprisings of the more desperate sections of the poor. Meanwhile advance will proceed in those areas where the revolution in economic thinking has been achieved.

The most difficult thing in the world is to see the obvious. But there comes a point of no return, when blindness becomes incurable and history transfers the leadership of progress to some new area of the world. It has happened before. The old order is indignant and incredulous, of course; but this is a destiny with which it is useless to quarrel.

In retrospect, the crisis year of 1970 saw little increase in optimism as it drew to its end. Anthony Harris of the *Guardian* Business Section

---

[1] John Strachey, *The Menace of Fascism.*
[2] From the United States come reports of unemployment of precisely this sort among high-level research scientists and corporation executives (January 1971).

(November 9, 1970) produced a list of fifteen proposed remedies for inflation; all from distinguished experts and leading statesmen[1]— all offering different policies. His own solution was a wage freeze. The *Guardian's* leader for this issue headed *Can we beat Karl Marx?* asked whether we were "doomed to provide Karl Marx with posthumous proof of his theories. Must our capitalist economy perish from its own inner contradictions?" The answer of the economics editor seemed to the leader-writer only likely to succeed if wage restraint was coupled with a guarantee against price rises and a return to economic growth—conditions which he was compelled to admit do "not exist today".

We see the facts not by simple perception but always in terms of our categories, our world view, our presuppositions; but the irrationality of the economic impasse in the West must surely reach the moment of truth before long. At this point then we might expect the realisation of the possibility of its rejection.

Marx believed "no social order ever perishes before all the production forces for which there is room in it have been developed."[2] How is this statement to be interpreted? Not, I think, as a complete halt in economic growth. Capitalism possesses considerable staying power and adaptability. It fails not by total paralysis but by failure to use its available resources to satisfy the needs of millions of people dependent upon it. In modern terms: no social order ever disappears until its economic growth is unable to proceed to the full utilisation of resources to satisfy the basic needs of mankind. When capitalism cannot develop world resources to fill the gap between starvation and subsistence for two-thirds of the human race, then we might suppose that its limits are being reached, and the paradox would become apparent, since, as Marx goes on to say, "the material conditions for its solution already exist or are at least in the process of formation".

Its efficiency is called in question by its failure to use its resources, to secure full employment as the normal condition of the economy. Can it secure the indefinite continuation of prosperity, of the rate of progress demanded by trade unions, teachers, doctors? Can it absorb and assimilate the permanent revolution in technology? Can it keep pace with socialist economics in technical innovation, in the replace-

---

[1] The Chancellor, Sir Roy Harrod, the Cabinet, The Confederation of British Industries, Mr. Aubrey Jones, Lord Balogh, Lord Stokes and others.
[2] Preface to the *Critique of Political Economy*.

ment of obsolescent capital equipment? Above all can it find the long term resources for massive investment in expensive development offering little financial returns for many years? Can it afford at the same time the educational advance, the developments and modernisation of the health service, the end of the housing shortage, expected of a successful economic system having at its disposal the resources of our modern world?

Under the proud system of a fully developed capitalism why is it that poverty keeps appearing for unexpected reasons? There seems to be some mysterious process at work continually creating poverty and inequality, a process endemic in our industrialised society. There are always prompt excuses: if it were not for this event or that, for the follies of the government, for the trade unions, for the foreigners, for people, everything would be all right. There is always something very simple that will do the trick. But no-one ever pulls it off. Not one of the last four Presidents of the United States succeeded, though they all tried. Is it possible that we are witnessing the decline of a whole civilisation because although "the material conditions" for the solution of all these problems exist, there is no likelihood of the productive forces meeting this demand? The system has "no room in it" for that kind of expansion. Its limits have been reached.

At this juncture Marxists believe that socialism represents the only rational exit from the impasse into which capitalism has driven mankind.

Reason and common sense insist on overriding the theoretical objections of current economic theory with the limits it imposes on the possibility of making full use of available resources. But when reason directs its assault upon the old Ptolemaic astronomy of capitalist economics, philosophies begin to appear that question the whole conception of rational investigation, and the very possibility of any critical analysis of society and its structure is questioned. In our time irrationality is being explained as something in the nature of things: poverty and war are accounted for as part of "the human predicament". Instead of rejoicing at the potential plenty of our advanced industrialism civilisation feels called upon to defend itself against the spectre of a world which could be free. A new hostility to reasoned investigation spreads over late industrial civilisation wherever the interests of ownership and investment prevail. Critical analysis is precluded by a new ideology of negativism, even nihilism, finding support in Freudian psychology, and in theories asserting the persistence of animal instincts in man against which education and reason are powerless, and which insist that since man is "a beast of prey" appeals to cooperate and be sane are futile. Mr. Desmond Morris, whose best seller *The Naked Ape* has reached millions of readers, cannot have failed to persuade many of them that when we expect to "remould our way of life, control our aggressive and territorial feelings and dominate our basic urges this is rubbish. Our raw animal nature will never permit this".[1] The reviewer in the *New Statesman* agrees: "Any idea of progress in politics is doomed. The truth must make of us all if not reactionaries, at least revisionists".[2]

On a more sophisticated level the impossibility of passing beyond existing categories, structures, laws and conceptual patterns is based on the empiricism which takes the immediate facts of present experience as all we have to go on, and precludes any radical alteration or re-contruction as utopian, or mystical, or metaphysical. This is the grand philosophy of "things as they are" and no nonesense about historical progress and radical change. Talcott Parsons, the American sociologist says, "a general theory of the processes of change of social systems is not possible in the present state of knowledge. . . . The only type of empirical generalisation which can be validated is correlational and probabilistic".[3] Bienstedt supports this, "sociology simply does not possess a solution to the vast and complex problem of social change".[4]

We shall return to the philosophical basis of a positivist sociology when we consider the question of ideology; for the present can we not cut the Gordian knot rather than untie it by pointing out that radical changes in social structure certainly have taken place? The whole history of society bears witness to it. Consider the transforma-tion of ancient society into the medieval world after the fall of Rome, or again the break up of the medieval synthesis with the appearance of the new ideas, philosophies, institutions, concepts and values of the Renaissance. This is followed by the beginnings and development of the scientific revolution of Bacon, Copernicus, Galileo, and Newton. Within the space of a century and a half a revolution had occurred in the way men regarded the universe. This was not only a change in astronomical and physical ideas; with the new thinking and the new technology a new economic, social and political world came into being, which had its culmination in the Reformation and

[1] Desmond Morris, *The Naked Ape*.
[2] Nicholas Tomalin, *New Statesman*, September 15, 1967.
[3] In Becker's *Modern Sociological Theory* (1957).
[4] Bienstedt, *Modern Social Science* (1960).

158   THE MARXISM OF MARX

the English Revolution of 1640. The new world of morals, social patterns, economic organisation and political thinking has been the theme of many volumes.[1] Our present society is less than 200 years old; and the profound technological, ideological and conceptual revolutions involved in its establishment have been discussed over and over again.[2]

Insistence on the impossibility of change has characterised the reactionary opposition to all scientific progress, to the discoveries of Galileo, Lavoisier, Harvey and Darwin. The contemporary conceptual framework of thought does not allow for the operation of concepts involving new postulates. But when sectional economic interests bar the way to change, the opposition is not merely intellectual but involves class interests, though we are not always ready to admit this.

Even so, when overriding interests demand it, even today we may find the very economic principles usually declared to be sacrosanct set at naught. There are many examples of huge diversions of resources and money to uses which are quite other than economic, and un-motivated by consideration of a financial return. One can instance as the most spectacular and expensive, the Moonshot, which cost the United States some $30,000,000,000 dollars. Of course the firms concerned in the Moonshot did well, but the massive expenditure itself brought no return to those who were willing to sink the nation's resources in it; yet it turned out to be feasible.

Will the time arrive when in a great burst of common sense we come to realise that the feeding and housing of the population may be as important as getting to the moon? We already understand that education and health are such priorities. Whenever we do that, or when we spend vast sums on space travel partly for reasons of national prestige, we transcend purely economic considerations. The question that the future poses is: when will a sufficiently large section of in-formed and deeply involved opinion see the inevitability of the over-all control of our economic resources and of the great consortiums and monopolies?

Every year the concentration of economic power in fewer and fewer hands increases. In 1960 as much as 92 per cent of the income from property went to the richest 5 per cent. In the United States the share

---

[1] Notably Lawrence Stone's *Social Change and Revolution in England*, 1540–1640.
[2] Knowles, *Industrial and Commercial Revolutions in Great Britain during the Nineteenth Century*. Karl Polanyi, *The Origins of Our Time*. Macpherson, *The Political Theory of Possessive Individualism*.

assets of the largest 200 corporations increased from 49 per cent in 1950 to 57 per cent in 1965. And some 68 per cent of the total profits of American capitalism fell to the share of this 57 per cent.

The situation is very much the same in this country: 192 companies owned in 1960 65 per cent of the assets. The process of concentration is increasing. In six years, for instance, the percentage of the total assets held by the top 20 per cent of companies in the car industries increased from 76 per cent to 86 per cent and has increased even more sharply since then. The same increase in concentration is to be found in textiles, in engineering and in the retail trades.

The much popularised idea of a "property-owning democracy"; of an increased proportion of small shareholders securing effective control of the economy, finds no support in the light of these statistics. In fact the leading people in the various groups form a closely-knit body and are in effect a powerful oligarchy influencing all major political and economic decisions of government as well as having a profound effect on business policy throughout the economy.[1]

The possibility of securing full democratic ownership of this enormous concentration of economic power at present guided solely by the criterion of investment policy depends upon a democratic populace capable and desirous of determining its needs and making them the guiding principle of the economy and of society.

Is this quite as utopian and beyond the bounds of economic possibility as those who are hypnotised by our economic and financial system believe?

It is some of our own leading economists who, in an economic situation that has compelled them to be far more frank about the present financial crisis and the dilemmas of inflation, credit, interest rates, and economic growth than the politicians, are now considering in terms of suggestive experiment in this direction the economy of the socialist countries. I refer to Andrew Schonfeld's articles in the *Observer*, and a lecture recently delivered by Professor Peter Wiles (Fellow of New College, Oxford), to the Congress of Cultural Freedom. Professor Wiles is politically somewhat to the right of the Conservative Party and declares that his remarks "connote no political sympathy with communism whatever". Andrew Schonfeld too is a vigorous exponent of capitalist economics with no tendencies in his thinking in the direction of socialism.

[1] See Maurice Dobb, *Argument on Socialism*; J. R. Campbell on "Marxist Theory and its Application Today" in *The Challenge of Marxism*.

Wiles, basing his remarks not on official Soviet figures, but on statistics from the United Nations and other foreign sources, comes to the following conclusions:

"Perhaps the most important fact in all modern economics is that the rate of growth of productivity is higher in the Soviet Union than in any important free country at the period of its maximum development let alone now. That is, whether we take roughly comparable circumstances or the present circumstances, the Soviet superiority remains. The best performance by a large non-communist economy for a long period together appears to be that of Japan; between 1912 and 1937 she grew about 3 per cent per annim. The Soviet economy grew by about 5½ per cent per annum before the war and by about 7½ per cent since 1948. For mining and manufacturing alone—and this sector usually outstrips all others in any economy—the figures are: Japan 7 per cent, USSR 12 per cent."

Professor Wiles does not accept the view that this is being achieved at the cost of a very low standard of living. He says:

"Consumption is growing, as it happens, very fast. It is no mean achievement to have nearly halved the cost of living since 1947, while wages have gone up."

Professor Wiles is making no special claims for efficiency, productivity per capita, or for housing conditions comparable to those of our better-off workers in the West. Nor is he unaware of the inefficiencies at factory level now being grappled with by providing economic rewards for better-run concerns. He is concerned only with the fact that our economy does not allow us to achieve the rate of growth absolutely necessary for us to utilise our available capacity and achieve even a minimum programme of social betterment in housing, health, and education, nor can it do so unless our rate of growth rises to at least 6 per cent—which the economists declare to be at present impossible without still more disastrous inflation.

The Joint Committee of the U.S. Congress bears out Professor Wiles' conclusions. The best years of American economic growth were between 1867–1907 and 1922–27, when the annual increase was just over 5 per cent. From 1928 to 1955 it was only 3·6 per cent; and it has now fallen well below that. In the U.S.S.R. the rate of growth from 1950–55 was 10 per cent, that of U.S. 4·4 per cent. The U.S.S.R. was expanding at twice the rate of the U.S. Professor Wiles continues:

"We see that the overwhelming communist superiority in industry alone leads to a great overall superiority (in the whole national income). The effect of compound interest is very great over over a few decades. Thus, growing 3 per cent per annum faster than the United States, the U.S.S.R. could catch up from a starting point of half the United States' national income per head in twenty-three years."

Andrew Schonfeld takes up the tale. Today, industrialisation in Eastern Europe having overcome the problems of war devastation and the expansion needed to reach somewhere near the capitalisation of a modern industrial country, advance is proceeding at the leisurely pace of about 7 per cent, and more resources are being channelled into consumption. Even so

"Soviet industry is increasing its output at a speed which is wholly abnormal by capitalist standards. There can be little doubt that the Russians have found a way of multiplying their wealth faster than Western countries."

Nor is this because Russia is still at an early stage of development, but because of the high rate of investment, 25 per cent of the national income. Investment in capitalist countries falls off periodically, or as at present is deliberately restricted by raising interest rates and other forms of credit restriction, because more rapid expansion would create a runaway inflation ending in total collapse.

Schonfeld further points out that Russian industry never lacks a market to absorb its whole output, however high; because in a socialist economy production is carried out *only for consumption*. The government can always raise wages to the extent of purchasing the goods on the market. Moreover, the Russians can guarantee markets for long periods ahead to the industries making capital goods; while these are the very industries which are most uncertain under capitalism.[1]

Thus although both these economists are fully committed to capitalism and are critical of the shortcomings of the Soviet economy, they are compelled to admit that in spite of launching its venture under the worst possible initial conditions, following devastating

---

[1] *Observer*, June 14, 1959. See also Professor Alec Nove (Professor of Economics, University of Glasgow), *The Soviet Economy* (1965), and Professor J. P. Nettl, *The Soviet Achievement* (1967). None of these authorities are of course in any sense pro-Soviet.

F

wars and the succeeding difficulties, that country has broken through into a world still closed to our system.

In some ways a more interesting example of socialism in action can be found in East Germany, still regarded by most people who do not read the Business Supplements of *The Times* and the *Telegraph* as impoverished, hungry and backward—as it was ten years ago. The economic miracle that has raised it to the world's tenth wealthiest industrial nation has been noted in several economic journals and in a special economic report of the Federal German Republic (West Germany). We are unlikely to get a point of view biassed in a socialist direction in the *Sunday Times*, so let us refer to the Business Supplement for December 5, 1970 by Mr. Stephen Aris. He reminds us of the handicaps of the German Democratic Republic: it had little industry, almost all of which remained in West Germany, and no coal; "economically East Germany is infinitely weaker than its Western neighbour". It was largely agricultural, much more devastated by the war than the West, for the whole of it was fought over. Much industrial plant went to Russia in the form of reparations from both Germanies, though considerable help has since been forthcoming to East Germany. Many fled to the West, leaving a population of 17 millions.

Against this background let us see what progress has been made. Production has risen by 29 per cent and wages by 12 per cent, while prices have remained stable. The difference is accounted for by the fact that "they have carried through in the name of socialist planning one of the most thorough-going industrial re-organisation programmes ever attempted by a major industrial country". Not only have new industries been set up but the machine tool equipment has been totally re-vamped. There has been a tremendous housing scheme and in the new towns "the shops are bright and well stocked. And the goods are reasonably stylish and well designed. . . ." Luxuries are expensive, but consumer goods are plentiful and reasonably priced. Television ownership has gone up from 16 per cent to 66 per cent, refrigeration from 6 per cent to 48 per cent. Prices have remained stable for at least 10 years. I might add to Stephen Aris' report the fact that education and public health have been very thoroughly and efficiently developed.[1]

[1] *The Sunday Times* report has interesting things to say on central planning with the devolution of considerable autonomy to the factories and other concerns. There are, of course, considerable differentials in wages and salaries, very much as Marx himself insisted must be the case in the transitional years of building socialism. There was no utopian equalitarianism of that kind, or any idealistic attitude to incentives, in Karl Marx's proposals.

The development of these countries—and Hungary could equally well have been taken as another example—places a huge question mark over the structure of Western society. Socialism, as Isaac Deutscher says, is no longer an abstract question, an untested hypothesis, an optimistic speculation. Marxist theory has been carried from the sphere of theory to that of practice. We cannot close our eyes to what is happening.[1]

What has been achieved is full employment without inflation, steady increase of wages without increase in prices, continuous growth in production and investment without "over-heating" the economy, an uninterrupted and vigorous rhythm of economic activity which has not proved possible under private ownership.

For the West, armament booms have proved the only resource available to guarantee, but even that only in the short term, continuous and expanding productivity and have become the accepted stimulus to economic growth and employment. In Eastern Europe this has proved wholly unnecessary economically, a brake on real capital growth and a drain on prosperity. While the West fears a slackening of the arms race as likely to create poverty and unemployment, Socialist Europe "thinks confidently of the quickening tempo of their advance and of the prosperity that would come within their reach if only they could rid themselves of the burden of armaments".[2]

At the same time in the capitalist world the one factor that in a positive direction could, by rational standards, offer promise of an immense increase in prosperity for all sections, *automation*, becomes, like peace, a terrible threat. Those economists who concern themselves with the economic consequences of automation speak of the jobless men, like the surplus of unskilled labour in the United States which has now spread to include the craftsmen, technicians, and administrative sections of industry. Professor J. E. Meade of Cambridge, speaks of the "reduction in the total demand for labour", likely to follow automation, resulting in a large reduction in real wages even though there would be a steep rise in profits.[3]

This should be taken with what was said by Sir Leon Bagrit in his Reith Lectures of 1964:

"When the productive machinery becomes so efficient that the

---

[1] Deutscher, *The Great Contest.*
[2] *Ibid.*
[3] J. E. Meade, *Efficiency, Equality and the Ownership of Property.*

problems of distribution assume gigantic proportions, some much more intelligent and perhaps radical solutions will have to be found. We cannot possibly tolerate a situation in which people want more goods, with machines capable of producing them in abundance, and in which they are denied their share in these goods, simply because nobody has devised a method of distribution."[1]

What is so difficult for the Meades and Bagrits to understand is that "all the king's horses and all the king's men", all the economists and business organisations, "cannot put Humpty-Dumpty together again"; and they have tried every conceivable plan. It is not the Marxists who say this. They say so themselves, and say little else. Marx shows the reason for the basic disequilibrium which cannot switch demand over to correspond with output and at the same time maintain a steady rate of interest on capital and *on the reinvestment of profits*.

On the other hand, there can be no problem of this sort under social ownership. There is no dilemma and no conflict of interests where the community owns its own means of production *and the whole product*.

"As productivity grew, prices could be cut or money wages and stipends raised accordingly. (There need be no lack of demand short of the satiation of human want.) Such conditions would seem to be the prelude to utopia, not to catastrophe. It only *appears* as catastrophe in our present society because production is run by and for capital with the aim of swelling the tribute exacted by ownership rights, and because labour functions as a commodity with its price depending on the play of the market. The consequences of automation confront us as in a distorting mirror because the anarchic system under which we live is perversive of human values and human endeavour."[2]

We are concerned with one point only, an economic one, what the political implications are is another matter—and these could be quite different in countries in which constitutional procedures operated.[3] What matters is the emancipation of industry from limita-

---

[1] Bagrit, *The Age of Automation*.
[2] M. H. Dobb, *Argument on Socialism*.
[3] There need not be *one* pattern of socialist society any more than there is one pattern of capitalist society. We have been seriously misled by the appearance of socialism in a

tions imposed upon it by a theoretical system devised for the early stages of capitalism and now outmoded. This difficulty is the intellectual one of realising that economic like other conceptual systems are not *absolute*, eternal and unchangeable, but relative, historical, and subject to supersession when the time arrives for a shift of economic pattern— and that time is surely indicated by the intolerable piling up of contradictions and irrationalities in our own system—the situation today in the West.

Of course it is not only the revolutionary change of concepts that stands in the way of any full acceptance of the necessity of socialism; nor is it only the fear of having to sacrifice vested interests, which must almost inevitably create a powerful motive against change. There is also the question of carrying through such a transition by democratic means, a possibility now and for many years accepted by Western Communist Parties.

And for socialists there is also another problem. Is radical economic change of this fundamental character something bound to happen in the nature of things? Popper has repeated again and again his view that Marxism predicts socialism as astronomers predict eclipses; that for Marxists politics are impotent, and propaganda and education useless and unnecessary; that the social revolution will come of its own accord, and the workers have nothing to do apart from announcing its inevitable arrival.

Did Marx see the transition to a socialist society as inevitable and automatic, a process carried out by the dialectical development of capitalism according to the laws which Marx discovered? Nothing like this was ever imagined by Marx. He saw no dialectical process of change operating in nature and society by the process of internal contradictions passing automatically to a higher synthesis. For him dialectics was wholly an affair of man in history, of man learning on the one hand to control his world through knowledge of natural law; and on the other, man creating one after the other a series of

country with no developed industry, no literate proletariat, no democratic institutions, and behind it centuries of absolutism and backward religious traditions. Already, today, we have systems departing widely from the Russian model in China, Yugoslavia, Hungary and East Germany. Even more radical divergencies may be expected in countries like Italy and France. Nor among these experimental economies do we expect to find invariable success. Marx provided no blue-print because, on the new basis, progress had to be made by trial and error. There have been grave errors, but nowhere is there the slightest suggestion of going back to capitalism. Not even dissident elements in the worst-governed socialist countries want that. But are not the successes more important than the failures, in showing that the thing can be done, and done well?

technological advances and then consciously and intelligently adapting his economic systems, his institutions and ideas to the changing industrial basis; man changing himself in so far as he himself improves his tools and his economic methods and adapts himself to them. This is wholly a matter of intelligence and invention, of devising appropriate economic methods, in remodelling institutions. Nothing is determined, nothing automatic, *nothing certain*.

The very essence of Marxism is the rise of understanding, of comprehension. The movement of history is not imposed from without by the creative fiat of an Absolute Mind, nor is it the result of a dynamic urge or dialectical process within matter. It develops out of the redirective activity of human beings trying to meet their natural and social needs.

Is it possible for man to change the direction in which society moves? If it were supposed that this means imposing his own utopia then it would be quite impossible. It is rather the apprehension of what laws are actually operating now and with what consequences, and what new tendencies are implicit in the developed economy. Now for the first time plans for radical social reconstruction can be devised—to be tested in action, revised, discarded and if necessary others advanced, to be tried again. This is not only possible but urgently necessary, or the capitalist mechanism will get wholly beyond our control, or will by its stagnation involve us in unforeseen disasters and difficulties, and in dangerous unrest—the unrest of frustration, ignorance and anger.

Of all Marx's theories his interpretation of history has been most widely misunderstood. It has been supposed to represent a universal theory of human history proceeding in a predetermined course through the appearance and overcoming of the contradictions which arise within the successive phases of social development; this itself has been seen as determined by the economic factor, and that alone. Yet Marx never says more of history as a whole than that it follows the course of man's mastery of the external environment in order to satisfy his needs —at first the basic needs of food and shelter, but later broadening into all the cultural demands of civilisation.

On what he calls the "pre-capitalist economic formations" Marx makes only a few brief comments. His concern was with his own society, contemporary capitalism, its development and the transition to socialism. This is an empirical matter, not a question of any philosophical principle discerned to be at work in all successive forms of society before and beyond capitalism. Such a metaphysical notion would be flatly contrary to Marx's whole approach to philosophy and to existence.

Nor does Marx accept the notion of some inner principle moving history forward to its pre-ordained end, explaining the ordered sequence of events in terms of purpose—the unconscious drive towards the goal of human progress. Marx regarded all such metaphysical conceptions, which find their highest expression in Hegel's World Spirit manifesting itself in history, as indefensible. It is clear, then, that for Marx there is no force or principle of historical development; but only men doing what they can to build their lives in the world they inhabit.

What then is Marx's theory of history? It is that men make their own history, and cannot but begin to do so in the economic sphere, where they labour together to get their living and the wherewithal to create their civilisation. Marx does see this as a progressive process, but not because of any metaphysical or natural necessity, but because he sees that men never cease attempting to improve their techniques and enrich their culture, trying to overcome hunger, famine, deprivation and discomfort—and by and large they succeed. As far as nature is concerned, it is wholly neutral in relation to men's ends and desires except in so far as men are themselves operating as living, conscious parts of nature.

It will be for the archaeologist and the pre-historian to find what they can of the early stages of this process; and very much has already been discovered. Pre-history is a further department of highly specialised study, and raises many problems that do not come within the sphere of Marx's own work, beyond the obvious fact that the early civilisations represent an important stage in man's control of nature and development of settled and organised social life. But Marx rejected every suggestion that in asserting this fact he had attempted to interpret all history as the growth of a single civilisation. Any attempt to do so would raise grave difficulties over the transition from slave to serf economies, the collapse and disappearance of so many early civilisations, and the regression to the Dark Ages—surely not an advance on the *Pax Romana* of the Roman Empire.[1] Nor was Marx saying that human progress is inevitable. It has to be struggled for by men at every stage of development. It has frequently broken down entirely. Toynbee has described some twenty civilisations that have passed through the phase of positive growth, ultimately to decline and fall.

What then is Marx's conception of history? What it does assert is that the advance of civilisation consists above all else in the growth of man's knowledge of the ways to make things serve his ends, and to fashion out of them tools and instruments, and then, in what only instruments can in their turn create.

The method of organising human labour Marx calls the *Economic System*, and describes it in terms of the way in which men are related in their work. This may be, for instance, a community of small farmers, traders and craftsmen; or it may be a developed mercantile system; or it may be a feudal system of manorial lord and serfs; or it may be a system in which the owner of the means of production employs wage labour. Each of these distinct relationships involves customs, laws, institutions, property rights and duties, embodied in these very different patterns of social and economic life. Each one, involving different *classes:* lord and serf, merchant and craftsman, owner and wage earner, corresponds to a particular stage in the development of the social utilisation of the resources of production. The endeavour

---

[1] See Marx's *Pre-capitalist Economic Formations* (from the *Grundrisse*) and the Introduction by E. J. Hobsbawm.

must always be so to organise these relations, this pattern of getting the job done, as to make the best use of the available resources. This will of course change from stage to stage in economic development.

The system which is best for any particular period is that best adapted to improve the use of the available tools and machines and agricultural methods, both in efficiency, and by securing the largest possible distribution and utilisation of the food and other consumption goods produced.

But no system can hold good for all time, because tools and methods are constantly being improved; and this, in turn, requires new kinds of organisation to make effective use of them. Therefore economic systems need to be reconstructed from time to time if they are not to be calamitously out of adjustment to the developing resources of production. Thus it is inconceivable that modern industry, employing the resources of large scale machine production, should continue to be organised politically after the fashion of an absolute monarchy, or socially on the model of a feudal barony.

We begin to approach the clear distinctions between whole historic periods when we see how each complex pattern of social relationships (again let us remind ourselves of the vast difference between the feudal and the capitalist pattern of life) involves a system of rights and duties corresponding to the balance of classes. The *legal system*, of course, secures the appropriate conditions for the use of property and money. No economic system can develop smoothly without the aid of a legal system in harmony with its needs. This is why a radically new system of economic relationships always carries with it the necessity for a corresponding political and legal reorganisation.

For political systems too correspond to the basic social patterns: a society of hunters or fishermen is organised politically in a different way from a farming community or an industrial society.[1] Slavery in one phase, serfdom in another, and wage-labour in a third give rise to legal and political as well as economic concepts, and are expressed in different systems of law and different political constitutions.

What this amounts to in the last resort is a question of State power. The class whose economic interests are dominant in that particular pattern of society, be it the landowners, the industrialists, or a military caste, will control the State power and use it to preserve their order. Nor can radical changes in the class structure, such as the rise of the

[1] The French historians Thierry and Guizot showed how the changes in property relations were behind the revolutionary movements in France in the eighteenth century.

industrialists and the decline of landed proprietors, take place without a shift of State power to the rising class.

These economic, legal and political structures necessarily give rise to different ways of looking at the world: different values, ethical codes, different forms of caste and rank. There thus arises a typical "man" of the period: the knightly man, the gentleman farmer, the merchant adventurer, the industrialist, the banker—summarising the virtues and exalting the status of the leading group. These often claim to be universal and permanent types, but never are. They are closely linked with the human pattern of how man is associated with man in particular society; above all with the consolidation of that pattern through the power of ideas.

In a period of stability, like that in which the recently established industrial system got its new legal structure and instutions, its new code of ethics, its commercial rather than feudal values, everything tends to create a feeling of permanence, as if all this were the very nature of things, essential human nature. But should its own economic progress outstrip the economic pattern, which now begins to hamper it, a new class begins to make itself felt, a group that demands the modification of the economic pattern. When this new class takes over, it alters the social pattern and the economy, and proceeds to reconstruct the legal structure, and the values and ideals, to give it the complete control of the economy necessary to get the new system working properly.

Every such change is necessarily heralded by an ideological struggle, because ideas, philosophies, religion and ethical principles are the defensive and offensive weapons in every such change. Doctrines are patterns of social action.

Economic forces, therefore, play throughout history a creative and dynamic role. This has been, since Marx's time, investigated over a wide range of European history, but special attention has been given to the economic and industrial changes in the Reformation period and after; and to the relation of the fundamental economic revolution to constitutional reform and the new political theories of Locke and Bentham; and especially to the ideological struggles between Protestants and Catholics, which led to the establishing of a new individualistic ethic by the Protestants closely related to the requirements of business and commerce.

A religion which emphasised man's individual responsibility to his Maker gave the kind of spiritual attitude desired. This does not mean that these people were insincere, but that they had to conceive these issues in religious terms, for great areas of men's lives at that time were still integral parts of the sphere of the Christian tradition and the influence of the Church. Weber and Tawney have clearly shown how the Protestant ethic strongly reinforced the spirit of capitalism with its new emphasis on the individual, and how the Catholic ideology showed itself to be more consistent with feudal and pre-catholic social requirements.[1]

The rise of nationalism was another aspect of the development of commercialism. The growing capitalist class had to win the conditions necessary for their social advance, though this fell short of control of the state. But they saw and felt the struggle not in commercial or economic but in national terms. Given the economic situation in Europe at the close of the fifteenth century, it would be necessary, Marxists would say, that the loose unity of medieval Christendom should be broken up, and that the claims of the Universal Church should be repudiated, that strong Nation-States should be brought into existence, and that the rising business classes should escape from the restrictions placed on them by the Guild and the Church, and should make for themselves an ethic and a religious outlook in harmony with their changed economic needs. Merchants and manufacturers wanted to go their own way, untrammelled by codes of conduct which had been framed to suit the localised and regulated economy of the Middle Ages.

The English Civil War has been exhaustively treated by Christopher Hill, the Master of Balliol, and other historians whose approach is also fundamentally Marxist. Henry Pirenne's work on medieval Europe owes much to Marx. And one must not forget a whole series of brilliant studies on the decline and fall of the Roman Empire, especially those by Walbank, Rostovtzof, and Professor H. H. Jones. In fact no study of this absorbing period can today ignore the economic causes that played such an essential part in the three hundred years leading up to the final catastrophe.[2]

---

[1] Weber, The Protestant Ethic and the Spirit of Capitalism; Tawney, Religion and the Rise of Capitalism.

[2] A great deal of historical work today owes much to Marx without claiming to be Marxist. Butterfield declares that: "There is much evidence of a new spirit in historiography, which has with reason been attributed to the influence of Marx. Marxism has contributed more to the historical scholarship of all of us than the non-Marxists like to confess. It offers a corrective to that older view which evaded fundamental problems by seeing history as a field for the activity of disembodied ideas." Professor Finley, the

This immensely wide range of historical studies should clarify the meaning of the Marxist contention that political and ideological struggles which exert a dominant influence in shaping the general course of history are largely the outcome of the changing economic forces and conditions. The point is this: men make their own history; but they can make it, in a constructive sense, only by accepting the limitations and opportunities of the age in which they live. This implies not only that they must act in ways appropriate to their age but equally that they must think and feel in terms appropriate to it. It is in this sense that men's social ideas, as well as their political and social institutions, rest upon an economic basis. This by no means implies an economic or any other form of determinism. The fact that all thinking, in science, in legal questions, in everyday affairs is *about* the external world, its institutions, its values, its aims and ideas, does not mean that thought is a carbon copy of what it thinks about. Thought is always selective, creative, interpretative and value-directed. It can only be relative to what it thinks about; but if it were a mere *reflection* of its object, merely *produced* by these conditions, it would not be "thought" at all. As it *is* "thought", it exercises its own independent influence on what it thinks about, it interprets it, reaches conclusions, understands, and acts accordingly. It can, of course, so far misjudge the situation as to fail to understand the necessity of change, just as a doctor can make a bad diagnosis; in which case thinking obstructs and prevents effective control. But if it *does* correctly understand, then it becomes the real creative force of economic and social change and historical progress. Thus in the last resort it is *thought*, and not alone the object of thought, that determines human conduct and is the direct agent of historical change.

No one who appreciates this vital point will make the absurd mistake of trying to interpret all history in exclusively economic terms. What can be argued is that, however men decide to act, if they fail to realise the importance of levelling the economic system up to the requirements of developing technology, they are in for trouble.

Thinking and the action which follows will be ineffectual unless in harmony with the requirements of the economic situation. There is always an objective economic situation, but there is no correspond-

authority on the Ancient Greek and Minoan civilisations, declares that Marxism is built into his intellectual experience: "Marx put an end to any idea that the study of history is an autonomous activity and to the corollary that the various aspects of human behaviour —economic, political, intellectual, religious—can be seriously treated in isolation."

ing necessity in the development of ideas. They can go sadly astray, as well as rise to great heights of understanding and creative activity. There is no inevitability in history, because there is no inevitability in men's response to a given objective situation.

Another common mistake, sometimes shared by many who regard themselves as Marxists, is the identification of the social relations of production with the technical forces of production, and the consequent transformation of the creative role of social and historical thinking into the *technological interpretation of history*. This would mean that the tool itself, or the machine, would be the ultimate determinant of historical developments.

This ignores the basic fact that it was *thought* that devised the tool and the machine; that when man first began, there were no tools, no fire, no economy. His ingenuity, intelligence and thought constituted the primary creative activity. If great economic changes have decisive effects in history, it is man's thought that invents the new machines, or introduce dramatic improvements in them; and again it is man's intelligence that creates the new and appropriate forms of organisation and pattern of social relationships—the distinctive human community with its laws, ethical code, institutions, habits and attitudes of thought. It is *never* the mere fact of *nature* making its direct impression on the sense organs that effects anything. Animals for hundreds of millions of years received the same impressions and were *acted upon* by the environment, and nothing happened except their closer adaptation to the environment. That is indeed a form of determinism. Man, on the contrary, *acts upon* his environment and changes it to suit himself—creates a tool, lights a fire, builds machines. This activity is not the *product* of the environment it is the creation of a *new* environment by human intelligence and direction.

When Marx says that the impulse in social development comes from the enlargement of the productive forces, which demand a new form of human association, this is not mere adaptation to the machine. There are two reasons for this: firstly, because that enlargement was itself entirely due to the stimulus of the existing system of social relations; secondly, because the reorganisation is itself a creation of the intelligence and one requiring creative thought.

The social relations of production (which are always property relations and the foundation, also, of culture) cannot therefore be regarded as the automatic reflection of technology, for the development of technology is directly dependent upon the system of social relationships. As Marx himself says,

"The materialist doctrine that men are the products of circumstances . . . forgets that circumstances are changed precisely by men. . . . The coincidence of the changing of circumstances and of human activity can only be conceived and rationally understood as revolutionary practice".[1]

The mistake is always for the baffled student of Marxism to separate two inseparable aspects of a real unity (as is also done when "mind" and "matter" are conceived as independent entities). This leads to insoluble problems, whether we are discussing technology and organisation or basis and superstructure.

"What these gentlemen all lack is dialectic. They never see anything but here cause and there effect. That this is a hollow abstraction, that such metaphysical polar opposites only exist in the real world during crises, while the whole vast process proceeds in the form of interaction, and that here everything is relative and nothing is absolute, this they never begin to see. Hegel has never existed for them."[2]

There is always, and continuously, reciprocal interaction. In every society improvements in technology, invention and discovery are going on all the time under the prevailing way of life and encouraged by it; at the same time every advance requires a modification of methods and ideas, of the way of life; and these new methods and ideas not only *suit* the new techniques, but, because they do so, foster them, so that once more they forge ahead and demand *further* social and ideo-

---

[1] Marx. *Thesis on Feuerbach*, III. That technological change is not the final cause of social development is clearly shown by the disappearance of chattel slavery in Western Europe in the 12th century. Feudalism was a full grown system of production long before that date and certainly does not emerge from the appearance of advanced techniques *within* the slave system, associated with a new class which overthrows the slave owners. "The breakdown of the ancient mode is therefore implicit in the socio-economic character. There seems to be no logical reason why it must lead inevitably to feudalism." (*Precapitalist Economic Formations*, Introduction by E. J. Hobsbawm.) For further evidence that technique itself does not determine the mode of economic production, one need but point to the use of large-scale machinery in such different economies as those prevailing in the U.S.A. and in the U.S.S.R.
[2] Engels to Conrad Schmidt, October 27, 1890.

logical changes. This is what is meant by dialectics. There is nothing metaphysical, nothing mystical about it.

It was the economic determinism of some of his own followers to which Engels was referring when he wrote to Schmidt in August, 1890:

"The materialist conception of history has a lot of friends nowadays, to whom it serves as an excuse for *not* studying history. It was this sort of nonsense that wrung from Marx the indignant—'Well, in that case, all I know is that I am not a Marxist.'"[1]

The same theory lends itself to the pure metaphysics of "an inevitable pre-determined process, an economic law of motion, as ascertainable as the laws of physics",[2] or the immanent law of a continuous irreversible movement from phase to phase, driven by the appearance and resolution of an endless series of contradictions, that Karl Popper brings forward as the Marxist historicism which he refutes in *The Poverty of Historicism*. Popper argues that Marxism is a deterministic system of this sort. Since it is possible to predict eclipses, Marxists think it should be possible for sociology to predict revolutions.

But Marxism has never made any such claims. Marx himself contemptuously repudiated the suggestion that *Capital* contained an historico-philosophical theory embracing all history. It formulated no "universal laws" of history. As Maurice Cornforth says:

"You can read right through the historical works of Marx, and of all other competent Marxist historians, and not meet with any formulations of any such laws. . . . The historical works of Marx himself do not proceed by trying to show how the later events necessarily followed from the earlier ones in accordance with inexorable laws, but by showing how people, in the development of social production, became involved in certain contradictions and problems, and how they acted to resolve these contradictions and problems. And the basis is always the adaptation of relations of production to forces of production".[3]

Another very common interpretation of Marxist historical theory is that *self-interest*, the "economic motive", is held to be the sole

---

[1] Engels to Schmidt, August 5, 1890.
[2] John Bowle, *Politics and Opinion in the 19th Century*.
[3] M. Cornforth, *The Open Philosophy and the Open Society*, p. 138.

cause of historical progress and the effective force in overthrowing capitalism and establishing socialism.[1] But Marx very plainly stated that the *motives* operating in hisotry have always been ideological and often religious. His problem was to explain why certain ideals prevailed at one time rather than at another and to discover what factors bring into being the ideals for which men live and die. He came to root all ideals and ideas in the class nature of society, because the class representing the dominant mode of production will have strong views as to the value of these institutions for the whole society, as representing all the noblest ideals and values of human society. They will inevitably identify the particular social order which they have created, and which they control, with the principle of order itself, and will regard the threat of a competing order as synonymous with chaos and the disintegration of morals and civilised values.

Marx attacked Bentham and Stirner precisely because they conceived man on the pattern of an egoistic and self-centred petty-bourgeois shopkeeper, whose every act is determined by calculation of the possibilities of personal gain. What he wished to do was to go beyond the idea which *insists* on the motive of economic interest as superior to that of working for the common good, thus establishing a system that will only work under the drive of the economic motive. What Marx wanted to do was to establish a society in which man can at the same time work for society and for his own good, in which therefore for the first time he lives under the conditions in which man can be truly human. Thus in the same society the class situation gives rise to two opposed ideas, one representing the *status quo*, the other a rival group struggling for power.

Marx's theories point towards the future; but they are not utopian, for he points out that the existing methods that have developed so dramatically and successfully under capitalism, have led to a situation in which technology has outrun the existing economic pattern. Therefore if we are to get our industrial potential operating, and not running below capacity, that will only be after the removal of the limitations on economic growth enforced by our present economic and financial system.

This is not a "prediction" in an astronomical sense. It is a reasonable

---

[1] It is of course equally likely that the critic will condemn Marx for the directly opposite reason, as Dr. George Steiner does in his "Eliot Memorial Lecture". He sees Marx as advocating Christian idealism, calling upon man to renounce selfishness and "leap out of the shadow of his petty needs".

analysis of a situation that has become menacing and obstructive, and a suggestion as to how we may have to modify our methods to get beyond it. It is no different in principle from analyses and proposals relating to many other problems. Soil erosion develops and calls for irrigation methods on a colossal scale, beyond the scope of individual efforts by small farmers. Thus the Tennessee Valley Authority comes into being to effect a social control rendered necessary by the gravity of the situation.

Marx's hypotheses are not "explanations" designed to show how things are and must be; they are developments of the "logic of situation", suggesting certain ways of dealing with frustrating problems. They are not predictions but proposals to be tested. And like other scientific theories these proposals are always capable of being refuted. If capitalism were to break out of its limitations, secure rapid economic growth in all developed countries (not just in the lucky ones), and swiftly industrialise the under-developed ones; if it were to develop all its resources and overcome world poverty, if it were to guarantee employment and rising wages, then Marxism would stand refuted. Conversely a socialist organisation of society should be able to show that it is on the way to achieving these very things.

The transition which is effected when the socialist reorganisation of society is attempted, requires more than the situation and the contradiction, more than the ripeness of the system and obstructed potentialities, more than a rational solution. Negatively it requires the overcoming of the class interests that block advance. Positively it requires a great rise in the level of popular understanding and political consciousness, and that is not predictable in an astronomical sense, and not automatic, and not the direct consequence of technological pressures and necessities.

Marx does not see the transition immediately confronting us as one which the whole community, envisaged as a classless democracy, can consider dispassionately from the standpoint of the good of the whole community, and in entirely rational, organisational and economic terms. It involves a conflict of interests and the resolution of that conflict. Above all it requires enlightenment. That enlightenment, Marx supposed, would arise primarily among those most hampered and oppressed by the irrationalities of the old system, those most obviously denied the blessing of increased prosperity and economic security. This will include not only trade unions but also blue-collared workers, technicians, scientists, teachers, doctors—all those who find unnecessary limits placed upon what they can do and want to do for themselves and for society, limits imposed solely by the financial mumbo-jumbo and the economic maladjustments of an economy in crisis. Any such understanding is unlikely to arise in the minds of those whose interests are bound up with the financial mechanism of this very system, whether on the side of investment or on the side of financial manipulation.

When large masses of people begin to see how the existing economic forms, and the interests associated with them, are hampering economic growth and how absurd, frustrating and paralysing the concepts and laws, the operative principles of the system are, they will be ready for the positive statement of a new system of thought, new institutions, and new ethical and legal principles, all of which are involved in the necessary organisational changes. But this cannot but challenge the position and interests of the dominant class, both ideologically and economically.

Thus when the bourgeoisie rose to power, the gathering strength of the rising class then had to be directed towards a *political* victory, as Marx always insisted. In a democratic society the battle will, as he said himself, "be fought to a finish in this ultimate political form of bourgeois society".[1]

Marx neither invented the class struggle nor did he bring it into existence in order to exacerbate political feeling and whip up the revolutionary passions of the workers. Class interests are already there, and class privileges, and class exploitation. Even so it is not of the wickedness of the capitalists that Marx wants to convince the workers (in fact he says again and again that he lays no such charge against them): it is that the class structure of society prevents, by the operation of economic law, enough being done on behalf of the working class and impoverishes the whole of society. Of course advances can be made, and Marx fought hard against those who said that this was impossible; but economic obstacles necessarily appear: inflation, cuts in the social services, unemployment, war—and it is clear that the limit has been reached. Meanwhile, outside the areas of exceptional advantage, the unprivileged remain on or below the poverty line, and the system offers little hope of their relief. Nor can the deadlock be broken unless the strong hold of owning-class power and privilege over the economy is broken; that is why class struggle cannot be avoided.

On what condition does the radical change necessary to release

[1] Marx, *Critique of The Gotha Programme*.

the forces of production depend? Lenin, in his article *Frederick Engels* (1895) wrote:

"People could not conceive of the workers acting as an independent force. On the other hand, there were many dreamers, at times geniuses, who taught that governments and ruling classes had only to be convinced of the injustice of the existing order, for them to bring about peace on earth and universal happiness . . . In a word almost all the socialists of the day and in general all the friends of the working class looked upon the proletariat as a sore and nothing else, and watched with horror the spread of this sore with the growth of industry. . . . In contrast to this universal terror, Marx and Engels based all their hopes upon the continuous growth of the proletariat. The more proletarians, the greater their strength as a revolutionary class, the nearer, the more possible would be socialism. In brief, the service rendered by Marx and Engels to the working class was that they taught the working class to know itself, to be conscious of itself and to put science in the place of dreams."

The French socialist Blanqui had little faith in the working class and a great deal in the few dedicated spirits he gathered round him. Their policy, said Marx was "to make revolutions extempore without the conditions for revolution". They considered that the essential requisite was a small, but disciplined, illegal revolutionary organisation. This was the policy of the *minority* revolution, which *after* the seizure of power would win over the majority of the workers to their side. They would therefore work and fight for a *minority* dictatorship.[1]

Marx rejected this policy. He believed that no "vanguard" will succeed "unless it can arouse in itself and in the masses a moment of enthusiasm in which it associates and mingles with society at large, identifies with it, and is felt and recognised as the *general representative* of society". Thus it becomes "in reality the social head and heart". The revolutionary energy and consciousness of its own power is not enough. It is the proletariat *itself*, and not a revolutionary élite, that must be enlightened. Marx spoke of the proletariat becoming philosophical, of the "lightning of thought penetrating deeply into the virgin soil of the people".

Theory becomes a force if it *grips the masses*, Marx declared. A

---

[1] The policy of certain Maoist and other ultra-left revolutionaries, calling themselves, for some reason, Marxists.

revolution cannot be a matter merely of a minority securing the consent of an unenlightened majority. Lenin too, in his *What is to be Done?* called for "mass consciousness in theoretical as well as in political and organisational work", he wanted to raise consciousness and understanding to a much higher level. He warmly approved of Kautsky's conviction that this socialist consciousness does not arise spontaneously; we must not wait patiently for the labour movement to come to a comprehension of socialism. Such a policy simply leaves the workers subordinated to bourgeois ideology.

Marx himself did not envisage Communists forming "a separate party opposed to other working-class parties" (*Communist Manifesto*)[1], because it was their task continuously to push forward the others, and because *they* clearly understood the significance of the "historical movement going on under our very eyes", and could communicate this understanding to the proletariat as a whole. Lenin, later, saw the importance of a "vanguard"—the Party, but such a body has failed if it cannot enlighten the rank and file.

Fundamental change is not possible until the overwhelming majority of the proletariat are brought to an awareness of the situation, of what is happening to them, of what exactly stands in the way of advance, of their role in history. Nothing happens until men come to the consciousness of their condition and their united power, and find within themselves the understanding and strength to create out of the old a new form of society. "Communism is for us not a state of affairs to be established, an ideal to which reality will have to adjust itself. We call communism the real movement which abolishes the present state of things."

In our time this has been clearly seen by Antonio Gramsci. Socialists, he asserted, must win the support of the majority. If they do not, they are either inept or totally unrepresentative. He had no use for the mass totalitarian party whose members display only loyalty of a military type to their political centre.

He was convinced that economic conditions do not themselves create a socialist mentality. It is our task to repair the gap by raising the level of consciousness of the workers. The influence and understanding which thus comes to pervade the majority is what Gramsci means by the "hegemony of the party". He does not mean that the Party rules an unenlightened mass movement. What it must *not* attempt, at any price, is the brute one-way indoctrination of the

---

[1] *Marx subsequently treated the whole organised working class as his party.*

workers by a "vanguard". Workers have to train themselves to become not merely wage earners but producers aware of their place in the process of production "in all its levels from the factory, to the nation, to the world". This is the first phase of the revolution, through it the whole working class will develop that hegemony which depends on its new level of consciousness and thus makes it, in Gramsci's terms, a "class".

If the party is not doing this, it is useless and in danger of establishing its own dictatorship over the workers in conditions of crisis, upheaval and social collapse. It may hope in the long run to exercise authority as a benefactor on behalf of the blind and passive masses, but socialism requires more than acquiescence, it demands the whole-hearted participation and cooperation of the masses in establishing the new order.

Of course at any one time the actual consciousness of a class may fall far short of the consciousness of the position, role and significance which it could rise to in that period. But there is a *potential* consciousness which can and must be realised if social progress is to be effected. The *real* consciousness is no measure of this potential and we cannot therefore acquiesce in it as limiting and determining the political possibilities of any particular time.[1]

It is necessary to say that the "potential political consciousness" of the working class is by no means static. It rapidly rises in conditions of struggle. It enters a higher, more significant stage still with the conquest of political power. Thereafter it becomes a matter of vital importance to realise that the *potential* political consciousness requires every effort both to raise it and to realise it, since the whole achievement of socialism depends upon this factor.

Gramsci develops the position established by Lenin in *What is to be Done?* that the economic and political drive is powerless without its ideological accompaniment, lacking which the working class inevitably absorbs the ideology of capitalism, which hamstrings all its political and economic efforts.

If the ruling class controls society it is not only through its institutions, and its control of the coercive power, but because it has achieved intellectual and moral authority, spontaneous and willing consent, from all classes. "It evokes spontaneous loyalty by its own prestige."

This has to be attained in turn by the new economic-political bloc, the working class and its allies. The achievement of this hegemony

[1] This conception is that of Lucien Goldmann. See his *The Human Sciences and Philosophy*.

goes far beyond the political objectives of the parties and the economic aims of the unions. The bloc must fight for its intellectual and moral values, and establish its claims to be a ruling class by creating an acceptable philosophy or world-view.

Gramsci points out that unfortunately, the "determinism, economism, and materialism" of the post-Lenin Communist Parties has left no room for such a world view, and therefore the correct leadership is lacking.

It is only through such a sweeping victory on the cultural front that adherence of other groups, as representing a higher and more comprehensive culture, can be obtained.[1]

Political struggle today is waged on the cultural front. It is not at the moment only a political struggle of manoeuvre but a cultural battle of position. In the West, the civil society with its institutions, educational, cultural, legal, ecclesiastical, is far more important within the State complex than it was in Russia in 1917. That is why the main victory must be won here. This is the major task of Marxists in the advanced coutries of the West. As Marx said, *"before the proletariat fights out its battles on the barricades, it announces the coming of its rule in a series of intellectual victories."* It is on *this* front that the next battle must be won.

Only a democratic struggle informed and energised by understanding, and by realising its truths by struggle in action, can build a cooperative society. It cannot be created by the wise for the foolish, by the energetic benefactors for grateful and passive recipients. But active democracy must be continued *after* victory in the whole process of building socialism. To attain political power and thus be in the position to start a new line of development, *to change direction*, does not mean that socialism is now here, "at a stroke"! A new and extremely difficult period of transition is beginning and the democratic participation in the struggle for reaping the fruits of victory. It is not enthusiastic obedience to direction from the vanguard that is required, nor just discussion of ready made directives handed down from above, but participation in working out schemes and applying them, consultation and sharing in decision making.

There is always the danger of concentrating power in the hands of a particular group. This invariably imposes limits on development, as it manifestly does under capitalism, and certainly must under socialism. Marx would never call an essentially bureaucratic

[1] Antonio Gramsci, *Intellettuali.*

society "socialism". If the revolutionary *avant garde* becomes a new bureaucracy we again experience the alienation of power, and the division of people into subjects and objects; a perpetuation of ideological ways of thinking; control of the mass media; and limitation of political and spiritual freedom.

In revolutionary periods we experience what fully shared political thought and action can mean. This must at all costs be continued and maintained in the period of construction. By participating in activity of this sort the individual develops an important dimension of his social being and realises new potentialities.

Thought and bold experiment, determination and real devotion to democratic procedures, must be given to devising ways and means of popular involvement in discussion prior to decision and in actual decision making.

Society itself must have responsibility in the determination of general policies and objectives. Political leaders must be controlled by assemblies, opinion-finding conferences, and popular vigilance. Socialism must mean not only economic liberation from class interest but liberation for participation, for active engagement in all social, political, economic, and cultural spheres. No real revolution can be achieved without such general participation, without full opportunity for ordinary people to share in decision making. As Marx said, "the freedom of the individual will be the condition of the freedom of the whole society".[1]

Marx of course envisages the eventual disappearance of a class society of any sort, because its continued existence is incompatible with the full utilisation of contemporary economic resources. There lies ahead, for the first time in history, the possibility of satisfying the needs of all men, not only of some, because the creation of an industrial society for the first time in history gives us the possibility of overcoming poverty. This is a change which not only overcomes poverty but overcomes the alienation due to some men using others for their personal economic ends, the alienation of men feeling their class inferiority, their commodity status, their deprivation.

This way out is not the discovery of another *law* system to which we bow, using it for our purposes. To use law for a chosen purpose makes no difference to the necessity of the law itself. Man's development is not law-controlled in this sense, as are the operations of nature,

[1] *Communist Manifesto.*

but from start to finish men introduce the new factor of intelligence in tool-making, problem-solving, organisation and planning.

If Marxism endeavours to make social development itself as law-determined as nature, it is missing the significance of man and his reason. So long as man is law-governed on the level of nature, even dialectical nature, he remains a product and cannot change society. If the social system goes wrong he can only be destroyed with it. That is why even capitalism, left to itself, does not destroy itself and automatically pass over into socialism. Left to itself, crisis does not end capitalism, it is the automatic, cybernetic mechanism, to restore equilibrium at the expense of the workers. It is *man* that ends capitalism, that overcomes it and replaces it—not law, not history.

The evolutionary process leading up to man produces him, but the man that appears proceeds thereafter to make himself. Man is not only a product. A product results necessarily and automatically from the immediate physical antecedents, including of course the external conditions. This is not so as far as man is concerned because he introduces his intelligent understanding of the situation which does not, as *simply mirrored*, decide his action. If man is simply *acted upon* by his environment, and if man's thinking is simply a reflection of external facts, man will remain for ever the victim of environmental pressures —whether physical, economic, or ideological. He is of course both limited *and enabled* by the physical laws of the situation, but what happens depends upon his *penetration* of the situation and his intention of altering it. In the historical situation we are considering, it depends on his challenge and rejection, not his passive acceptance, of existing ideological, economic, and social pressures.

This, of course, is where the socially-minded materialists who recognised the fact that man is moulded by his social environment found themselves in a dilemma. They also knew that it is *ideas* that change the world and hence engaged in critical reformist propaganda. But if men are conditioned by their environment, how can they possibly reach the ideas which are fundamentally critical of it and thus change it?[1]

There is no answer to this question if we accept the materialist

[1] This was the problem that Plekhanov wrestled with throughout two of his most important books, *The Monist Conception of History* (in the English translation *In Defence of Materialism*), and *Essays in the History of Materialism*. He came to the correct conclusion, i.e. that man himself created the environment which influences him and can and does re-make it.

view of perception which Marx rejected—that ideas merely *reflect* things as they are. Consciousness appeared to Marx in a role altogether different from that allotted to it by the positivism of the later 19th century. So far from merely "reflecting" an ongoing process, it *transformed* the total situation in which it was embedded. Thought is able to do this because at certain moments in social development a revolution in the mind, a new theory, acquires the character of a material force. The relation between theory and practice here becomes a dialectical one when *some* men, and then *more* men, have their consciousness raised to the level of awareness of themselves, their situation, its contradictions, and of what can and must be done to overcome them. This immediately demands a frontal attack on the apparently eternal and unalterable law systems of capitalism, its values, its ideals, its legal institutions, and of course its economics.

We must therefore be careful when we say that "being determines consciousness", because for the older materialism it leaves things as they are and imposes a rigid determinism. When Marx says that "with me, the ideal is nothing else than the material world reflected by the human mind and translated into forms of thought", we are compelled to see that "translated" means "critically understood", and it is this notion that Marx continuously explains and urges from his first statement of the dialectic in 1844 and its elaboration in the *German Ideology*, to its final and complete exposition in the *Grundrisse* of 1857-8.

Nothing less than this delivers us from that materialism which was the ideology of developing bourgeois society and from a paralysing determinism. There is, of course, *also* the recognition of *physical* necessity in utilising *physical* law; but there is no such necessity in seeing how and for what purposes to use those laws; that requires a different kind of "reflection", i.e. *critical* consideration. Professor Ryle admirably illustrates the union of the two modes of thought when he points out that a golfer is subject to the law of ballistics *and* obeys the rules of golf, and *plays with skill*!

The coming of socialism is not something that happens like storms, and droughts, and earthquakes—which represent, as do the evils of capitalism, external determination. It comes only when men have the intelligence and the will to make the best of the ripened conditions —but the ripened conditions themselves will not bear fruit.[1]

[1] Nor, as we remarked earlier, is man's recognition of a necessity independent of himself, in which he must acquiesce, the freedom we are talking about. The cork on the wave is

With man's comprehension of his task we leave the realm of external determination and enter the realm of freedom. Marx has an excellent phrase to express the transition. "We shall make", he said, "the fossilised conditions dance to their own tune." And we do this by lifting reality to the level of thought.

not free. On the contrary what is going to happen depends wholly on man understanding what he has to do. We may hope and anticipate that he will; but his enlightenment and decision is not a phenomenon of the same character as the falling of a stone, or the boiling of water at 100° C.

12

THE ROLE OF IDEAS IN HISTORY

The transition from capitalism to socialism is by no means automatic. Essential to it is the theoretical awareness which arises only when the historical situation has matured to the point of resolution. The theoretical concept, the idea, arises when the situation can be clearly evaluated in realistic terms and not before. This is not a utopian illusion. It is not a voluntarist decision independent of conditions, but neither is it an automatic historical change independent of the reason and the will—nothing is more emphatically and continuously contradicted by everything that Marx consistently taught. And nothing is more emphatically and continuously alleged by critics of Marxism in the face of this plain disavowal by Marx himself.

For Marx the first step must be a *theoretical* one, an intellectual conviction, a deeper understanding of a paradoxical and menacing situation. It is in fact that familiar experience in history, and especially the history of science, that leads to what Professor Kuhn calls "the paradigm shift"—"a transposition in the mind", "the policy of picking up the opposite end of the stick". Herbert Butterfield, dealing with the same question, finds in such periods of change "spectacular proofs in history of the fact that able men who had the truth under their very noses, and possessed all the ingredients for the solution of the problem, were somehow incapacitated from realising the implications of the situation".

What brings about the sudden revolution in the mind is the accumulation of irrationalities and contradictions. Of course, the original theory always advances explanations of these, endlessly coping with more and more paradoxies and absurdities, but doing so with less and less conviction. The credibility gap widens, until one day total disbelief supervenes—and the new theory takes possession of the mind; one which at once provides the key not only to clarity of thought but to practical advance (as, for example, in natural science, the advances in medicine that followed the discoveries of the circulation of the blood—and of the function of oxygen in metabolism).

Looking back on any outmoded science it is difficult for us to imagine the condition of affairs before the change, or to comprehend the mystification involved in the older explanations on the one hand and the resulting anarchical condition on the other. In his important study of radical changes in scientific thought such as the Copernican theory of planetary movement round the sun, the circulation of the blood, and the theory of evolution, Professor Kuhn points to "a profound awareness of anomaly as necessary for a change of theory—failure in normal problem-solving activity—breakdown of ad hoc theories to explain this or that contradiction, paradox, or crisis."[1] Basically it is the stubborn anomalies, and then the fact that the new theory makes sense of the muddle and sets things working again.

What results is more than a modified theory, says Kuhn, *it is change of world view*—as if we were transported to another planet. We see new and different things. We experience a re-education of perception. Thus what is required is first and foremost *to see the point*—an intellectual revolution. Such periods in history, whether we are considering the transformation of feudalism to mercantilism, or the Reformation, or the break-up of the medieval philosophical synthesis, or the Copernican theory of the solar system, are times of theoretical discussion and new intellectual convictions. Marx speaks of the necessity for "logic, insight, courage and clarity" when the change he envisages arrives.[2]

Marx devoted his whole life to intellectual enlightenment: hence his lectures, his pamphlets, his activities in connection with the First International, his books, his letters, his stream of advice and explanation directed to the Social Democratic Party in Germany. His whole career was one of education. It is a strange misunderstanding to imagine that the whole process of social change would go on "automatically", with "mind merely a by-product", and adsolutely powerless; or to imagine that, independently of ideas, changes of a fundamental nature take place in the economic structure "and some decades or centuries later a change takes place in the ideas."[3] Clearly ideas must appear somehow which indicate the necessity for radical economic and political change. Moreover they must appear *before* that change, since they are indispensable if it is to be brought about. Do they arise spontaneously in the working-class movement?

Lenin in his *What is to be Done?* says that the merely spontaneous

[1] Kuhn, *The Structure of Scientific Revolutions.*
[2] Marx, *Introduction to the Critique of Hegel's Philosophy of Right.*
[3] Carew Hunt, *The Theory and Practice of Communism.* Issued by the Foreign Office for the briefing of members of the Diplomatic Service.

movement of the working class is quite unable to effect the transition to socialism. "The level of consciousness required can only be brought to them from without . . . Modern socialist consciousness can arise only on the basis of profound scientific knowledge. . . . The endeavour to do without theory has the result of limiting those who attempt it to the narrowest and most parochial forms of empirical opportunism."[1] Kautsky comments on this: "The endeavour of practical persons to have no truck with theory runs counter to the whole spirit of Marxism."[2]

Perhaps the clearest statement of all on the indespensibility of ideas in social change is to be found in the *Short History of the Communist Party of the Soviet Union*, in the section on Dialectical and Historical Materialism, generally regarded as written by Stalin:

"There are different kinds of social ideas and theories. There are old ideas and theories which have outlived their day and which serve the interests of the moribund forces of society. Their significance lies in the fact that they hamper the development, the progress of society. Then there are new and advanced ideas and theories which serve the interests of the advanced forces of society. Their significance lies in the fact that they facilitate the development, the progress of society; and their significance is the greater the more accurately they reflect the needs of development of the material life of society.

New social ideas and theories arise only after the development of the material life of society has set new tasks before society. But once they have arisen they become a most potent force which facilitates the carrying out of the new tasks set by the development of the material life of society, a force which facilitates the progress of society. It is precisely here that the tremendous organizing, mobilizing and transforming value of new ideas, new theories, new political views and new political institutions manifests itself. New social ideas and theories arise precisely because they are necessary to society, because it is *impossible* to carry out the urgent tasks of development of the material life of society without their organizing, mobilizing and transforming action. Arising out of the new tasks set by the development of the material life of society, the new social

---

[1] Lenin, *What is to be Done?* (Quoting Kautsky with approval, p. 30.)
[2] Kautsky, *Neue Zeit*, 1901–02, XX, No. 3. *On the new draft programme of the Austrian Social-Democratic Party*.

ideas and theories force their way through, become the possession of the masses, mobilize and organize them against the moribund forces of society, and thus facilitate the overthrow of these forces which hamper the development of the material life of society."

In the face of this it is surprising to find in Professor Acton's recent book *What Marx Really Said* the statement that Marx's views

"contradict the beliefs of most of those taking part in social movement and political revolution and who believe that they are altering society by putting forward new ideas, new outlooks and new concepts."

Marx is saying (according to Acton) "that it is not ideas that change history". Of course ideas that have dropped from the sky do not change history; but ideas derived from an *understanding* of the structural incoherence of society, resulting in proposals for the reconstruction of society based on an appreciation of all the factors involved. Precisely the same kind of mental activity is involved in all scientific discoveries.

Ideas in social thinking, as in all other subjects, must follow the facts and understand them. But understanding them is more than passively reflecting them. Marx insisted that knowledge is never passive reflection but is derived from active grappling with reality.[1] Ideas are always the result of activity and *for* activity, for grappling with, altering and manipulating what is understood *in terms of that understanding*. If one has discovered the cause of a disease one can proceed to cure it, or better still prevent it. Ideas *react back upon the situation which gave rise to them to effect its transformation*. What begins as an effect, becomes itself a cause.

This of course is the dialectical process of action, interaction, and then further action, which marks the development of science, and of all social change. So far from being determined, it is wholly dependent upon the depth and accuracy of comprehension. Nor does effective action complete the process, it continues it, for the changed situation must again be examined to see what further changes it requires. This also is the case in social change.

Marx sees social change as beginning with the process of examining

[1] Hence his emphatic rejection of Feuerbach's mechanistic materialism and naive "reflection" theory of knowledge. See Marx's *Thesis on Feuerbach*, I.

the defects of the economic structure, indicating the causes of the anomalies and irregularities, and then suggesting the reconstruction that might overcome them. What is needed is not an overall theory of all history, but a scientific analysis of an empirical situation. Nor is the suggested solution the end of the matter. He was perfectly aware of the imperfections of the period of reconstruction that must follow, and of the inevitable shortcomings of the transitional stages to socialism which society would begin to traverse. That he anticipated the arrival of "the millenium" is a gratuitous misrepresentation of Marx's position.[1]

All new theories when applied reveal their defects and demand amendments, sometimes rejection. They are never final. Popper declares that Marx's theories are astronomical predictions of the approaching millenium. All that the Marxist is expected to do is to wait for its arrival. On the contrary, it is a working hypothesis to deal with an economic breakdown, a working hypothesis which has to be tested. In the testing it will certainly reveal its defects; it will demand revision and modification. Used in its new form it will again be tested, and again reconstructed. This is the procedure which Popper himself describes as "the logic of scientific discovery". It is exactly what the procedure of Marx's ideas in practice has proved to be. Yet Popper constantly affirms that Marx's theory is so constructed as to be incapable of being tested, that it is one of these pseudo-theories that is compatible with any facts whatsoever.

Marx's theories have been repeatedly modified in the light of their application and in the light of historical changes. Never do they appear as an abstract explanatory scheme to be imposed on all the facts, equally applicable at any period. On the contrary, they are always empirical, and frequently found to be inadequate in one respect or another—as when Marx realised the impossibility of revolution following the collapse of the German Revolution of 1848. His writings on social struggles in France, on the First International, on Napoleon III, on the Commune of 1871, show a progressive modification of his views and theories. He was often wrong, as Darwin was, as Galileo, Priestly, Harvey and Newton were, as every great scientific pioneer was—but that does not detract from the "paradigm shift" these men effected, the mental revolution which opened new vistas for mankind.

That is why even those who have profound disagreements on many matters with Marx nevertheless recognise the immense importance of

[1] See his *Critique of the Gotha Programme* and Chapter 15 in this book.

this radical transformation of the understanding of the process of historical change. Schumpeter calls it "one of the greatest individual achievements of sociology to this day", and Patrick Gardiner of Oxford in his book on *The Nature of Historical Explanation*, speaks of the success of the Marxian theory "in emphasising factors previously ignored by historians, and in bringing to light previously unsuspected correlations between different aspects of social development. Theories of this kind may indeed be regarded in some respect as pointers to types of historical material which may prove relevant to the understanding of a particular historical situation . . . their significance lies in their suggestive power, their direction importance."

One of the reasons for the view that Marx saw men's thoughts and ideas as "a kind of vapour which mysteriously arises from the material foundations",[1] and thus no more than a powerless epiphenomenon, is the belief that Marx was a materialist in the sense of reducing all things human to matter in motion, a crude reductionism of the "nothing but" kind, once popular in certain circles in the 19th century and represented in the works of Karl Vogt (Marx's bitter opponent), Büchner and others. Marx never came near any of these theories, and emphatically repudiated them. His whole life bore tribute to his passionate belief in the importance of ideas, of the defects in the economic structure, the irrationalities and the potentialities of the existing situation, being comprehended intellectually; in history "coming to consciousness", reaching the level of understanding itself in enlightened men. To think of this as a mere "vapour" arising from a "material foundation" could hardly get farther from Marx's thoughts.

Marx has also been much misunderstood as regards his theory of the superstructure. This too can very easily be turned into something nonsensical. In fact it is a theory familiar to anthropologists and sociologists who find in each particular civilisation a pattern of "structural functionalism" in which all the different aspects of a culture belong to the single pattern; the religion, the kinship rules, the ethical code, the political institutions are not independent (as if the religion of the Aztecs could just as well have been the religion of Classical Greece), but intimately related to the whole historical complex of institutions.[2] When sociologists go on to speak of "historical speci-

[1] Gardiner, *op. cit.* It is surprising that Gardiner who finds himself compelled to acknowledge the importance of Marx's theories of history, should then be guilty of a solecism of this kind.
[2] See Hodges, *Wilhelm Diltley, an Introduction.*

ficity" they mean that one such total of thought and life pattern belongs to each form of civilisation—a conception also sketched by Oswald Spengler in his *Decline of the West*, and elaborated in Toynbee's *Study of History*. This approach has only to be carried one stage farther to see the culture as closely related to the pattern of human relationships, as connected at one period with the agricultural economy, at another with the institutions of slavery, later with the feudal economy of medieval Europe, and then with the rising mercantile system, and finally with capitalism. The close relation of ideological to economic structure in the rise of capitalism has been discussed by Weber and Toynbee among others.[1]

It is in this sense that the institutions are suited to the way men are associated together in production, and exchange, and trade, and personal service, and the ideological systems with them. Feudal institutions, of course, reflect feudal relationships of overlord and those owing him fealty. Weber shows how the religious pattern and the moral code change from that of Catholicism to that of Protestantism when industrialism and *laissez faire* replace the corporate ideas and simpler mercantile pattern of pre-capitalist society.

Marx goes beyond this quite acceptable view of the unity and mutual dependence of structure and function when he points out that the superstructure *reacts back* on the infrastructure to play an essential part in serving it, inspiring it, justifying it, providing it with ideas, ideals, a moral code, and the works of imagination which play such an essential part in the entire life of any society, and also acting as a powerful stimulus to the forces of production. Ideas and institutions are in constant process of mutual modification, sometimes gradually, sometimes more rapidly and drastically.

It has sometimes been asked how, if the institutions and ideas which arise on the basis of an economic system lend it support, opposing ideas, contradicting these and proposing radical change, can possibly come into existence.[2]

But one must surely ask where these ideas and institutions that are now under criticism themselves came from. They must have replaced other forms of social life. According to this objection that could never

[1] Both Marx and Engels were well aware of the relative autonomy of ideologies, that, by definition, they are not manifestly related to the sub-structure, that they have an independent life and development of their own, and are carried over from the period in which they are highly relevant to later periods in which they become obsolescent.
[2] For instance by Wetter in his *Soviet Ideology Today*, and Raymond Aron in *The Impact of Marxism in the Twentieth Century*, a contribution to *Marxism in the Modern World*.

G

have happened either. But clearly the whole process of social development is a continuous process of economic and social improvement and adaptation, or primitive man could never have taken the first step beyond the life-style imposed upon him by his environment. It is clear that the objection rests upon the erroneous view that knowledge is merely the impress, the reflection, the effect of the material world, and of external forces of an institutional and ideological nature. It was the position in Marx's time of "all materialism up to now". Marx rejected it out of hand on philosophical grounds—man knows not passively but actively, as Kant had shown. Marx never taught that man's relation to his environment, whether material or social, or to the economy, or to institutions, was a passive one—that he was merely acted upon by these forces. Marx's whole position, from its earliest formulation, was exactly the opposite.

Man's reaction to his environment is one of investigation, criticism, endeavours to alter and reorganise it, to control and use it for human ends. Above all this means a critical attitude to existing conditions to find out how to remove defects and improve techniques and methods. Man is continuously effecting material and technological changes, superseding existing tools, machines and methods. Clearly if he is capable of the intelligence to invent and introduce a new machine, he will have the intelligence to devise the methods necessary for its use and the new organisation under which it will work efficiently. That this is precisely what he has been doing for tens of thousands of years makes the objection a rather foolish one. As Marx says, the superstructure devised to provide the best conditions for the technological basis was constructed by men for that purpose, that was how it came into existence. If it ceases to serve that purpose will they not improve it and reconstruct it? While they were engaged in their earlier task of making the one that is now obsolete, they were of course working under the influence of the previous system, but that did not prevent them remaking it, institutions, ideas, legal system and all. It is also necessary, in order to effect such drastic changes as this, to replace the political authority, that part of the superstructure which maintains existing institutions. This had to be done in spite of the fact that the conditions under which the wresting of power took place included the existence and exercise of opposing power.

Every growth in the productive forces creates faults in the superstructure, and reveals the inadequacies in the ideas which belong to it and support it. The result is that social change always involves a battle of ideas, a conflict of ideologies. A further consequence is that the ideas of the existing system and the superstructure they represent are bound up with the interests associated with the old order, and become transformed into a class-fortress and base of reaction, and even for counter-revolution. Because theory and practice have got into the hands of opposing groups, the major steps in the development of the productive forces cannot always transform the superstructure in an evolutionary manner. Change is resisted by violent means, and counter-revolution may have to be suppressed to secure the implementation of the democratically expressed will of the majority.

By the time such a revolutionary situation has matured, there is a whole new superstructure latent in the rising group. It develops from all they have learned from the growth of the productive forces, and becomes the starting point for the superstructure of the new society, which therefore is one which starts on a higher plane than that of the overthrown society.

Marxism sees the process of change in capitalism during the transition to socialism as originating firstly in the advance of the technology —but this very advance is an achievement of the intelligence and is fostered, encouraged and urged forward by the organisation of capitalism, which "cannot exist without constantly revolutionising the instruments of production" (*Communist Manifesto*); secondly, by the criticism and improvement of the methods of working; and thirdly, by the economic and institutional changes rendered necessary to create favourable conditions for getting the best out of the improved productive apparatus. This involves changes in institutions, ideas, habits, even moral ideas, as Weber and Tawney have shown, and changes also in political power. Faced with objective facts that obstruct the economy a tension is generated which will ultimately bring about the appropriate modifications of the superstructure.

The first thing that Marx had to do when he laid down his first principles was to deal with precisely the objection we have been considering to radical social change—the *materialist* objection. It is strange that the difficulty should again be raised in our day to Marxism itself, which got off the ground by demolishing it as a materialist fallacy, i.e. that ideas are just a product of the infra-structure.

Ideas and institutions have to serve the social structure. They do not just *reflect* society, they serve it and constitute it, they create the mind of the age. During any particular period of social change a matter of some consequence concerns the "new men" now moving into positions of power in government and industry, the political leaders, lawyers, philosophers and scholars. In the 19th century the law was vigorously overhauled by Jeremy Bentham; liberty was discussed by John Stuart Mill; John Locke had already equipped the merchant class with constitutional theories and a new philosophy to justify it. Thus the law, the State system and the ethical code of the nation came to correspond to the pattern of social relations. The new business class replaced the landed gentry, a new pattern of political government was gradually fashioned. There followed the less directly affected spheres of art, literature and other cultural activities, nonetheless influential.[1]

Every sensible theory can be turned into nonsense. If we say that automatically and instantly, the moment a fundamental social and economic change occurs, all the institutional and cultural aspects change from the old to the new, we are not describing what Marx had in mind. Many old institutions go on under their own momentum for years after they are obsolete. But if they are out of tune with society, they lose their old significance even if they survive, and eventually decline and die away, while new ones gradually take their place.[2]

What is changing *most* profoundly is the climate of opinion, the ethos of the period. This is much more closely related to the fundamental pattern of human relationships than is usually realised. Consider a medieval troubadour of the 14th century, the courtly love game, the illiterate but powerful and gallant manorial lord, the closed corporation of the Church with its great variety of orders and ecclesiastical ranks, the small guildsmen and the merchants. The mental life of this period is *not* that of 19th-century England, or that of 1769 or of 1569. The slow but irrevocable change of spiritual climate in such periods of transition is well described by Plekhanov:[3]

"So long as the social relations do not change, the psychology of society does not change either. People get accustomed to the prevailing beliefs, concepts, modes of thought and means of satisfying given aesthetic requirements. But should the development of production forces lead to any substantial change in the economic

---

[1] Two interesting discussions of this period of transition are MacPherson's *Political Theory of Possessive Individualism* for the early stages, and Polanyi's *Origins of Our Time, The Great Transformation*, for the later.
[2] Plekhanov, *Essays in the History of Materialism.*
[3] Plekhanov, *The Materialist Conception of History.*

structure (that is to say the human relationships in industry, business, trade and above all the relation of the leisured class to those 'gainfully employed'), and as a consequence, in the relations of the social classes, the psychology of these classes will also change and with it the 'spirit of the times', and the 'national character'. This change is manifested in the appearance of new religious beliefs or new philosophical concepts, of new trends in art or new aesthetic requirements."

The relation of the ideas and values and philosophical beliefs of a period to its social pattern, gives us what the sociologist calls the "historical specificity" of its culture, and the Marxist its "ideology". To this question we must now turn.

13

REASON AND REVOLUTION

"It is the energy of thought which moves the world", writes David Kugiltinov in a recent issue of *Soviet Literature*. This was Marx's view. The fundamental revolution, without which no radical political and social change ever comes about, begins in the mind, as the recognition of an anomalous situation and a critical examination of its cause.

It can never be a mere *reflection* of an irrational situation, the result of which would only be some despairing cry about 'the human predicament' or the 'absurdity' of existence. There is no automatic and mechanical production of radically critical ideas. They require us to challenge and overthrow the ideas, the economic and political theories, which reflect the existing structure and constitute its superstructure— the ideas and institutions which maintain and defend it.

It is a fundamental shift in the point of view, the loosening of former modes of thought, the categories, as the philosopher calls them, a break through to a new insight. And for Marx this change has to take place not in a minority, though no doubt that there is where it will start, it has to permeate a whole society, becoming the effective theoretical understanding of a whole class, and proceeding to the recognition not only of the basic economic mode of production to be replaced by a socialist system, but of the political victory necessary to bring this about.

Nevertheless the view is still sometimes expressed that understanding can only *follow* and cannot *precede* a political victory. But Marx, in his second period, after abandoning the strategy of a minority revolution, appears to have envisaged a very thorough permeation of the working class by socialist ideas. This is what Marx meant when he spoke of "raising reality to the level of thought". Before the political battle is fought and won, he said", a series of intellectual victories must be achieved".

Opinions differ as to the extent to which such a revolutionary consciousness must extend beyond the minority. Marx saw the immediate aim of the German Revolution of 1848 as a very limited one, involving and depending upon the bourgeoisie who only wanted a constitution. He envisgaged a development of the revolution by stages, the working class eventually taking command and proceeding to establish socialism. But later Marx came to accept the necessity of a *majority* revolution which would require the understanding and acceptance by large numbers—a considerable majority, not a bare majority—of what is involved in the first stages of a really socialist order, and the transfer of political power to the working class and its allies. This is the situation anticipated in a literate, advanced industrial society.

Such a situation is not possible, however, if it is only the "vanguard" who understand the situation, and have the socialist aim as their ultimate objective. To secure power on such a basis would by no means guarantee support for a subsequent socialist programme.

What this means is a fundamental shift in the point of view from which we see our society, and in particular its economy; a loosening of fixed modes of thought *that are not realised as modes of thought,* but taken for granted. To see what is meant let us again consider what has happened in the history of science, as when for instance the idea of the earth as the fixed centre of the universe around which the sun, the moon, the planets and the stars revolved attached to their crystal spheres, gave way to a totally different conception, that of the sun as the centre and the earth moving round it. This is known as the Copernican revolution. It is only one of a series of radical shifts in our basic categories which have from time to time shattered our universe of discourse.

But is is not only in science that this happens. Every distinct civilisation has not only its own form of political organisation, for example a feudal society, or an absolute monarchy, or a republic; but we can ask what religious rites and sanctions, mythologies and sacraments, permeate it and sanctify that political order? What is its technological basis? Is it the hand loom or the steam engine? And after all that, we may still ask what is its total world view, its value system, its conception of the nature of man.

The changes in scientific thought were themselves not merely new *ideas* about a specialised set of theoretical concepts, mainly of interest to experts. The old astronomy was part of an entire religious, social and philosophical world picture. To change it was to disintegrate a world order and the minds that conceived it:

And new philosophy calls all in doubt
The element of fire so quite put out
The sun is lost, and th' earth, and no man's wit
Can well direct him where to look for it.
When in the planets and the firmament
They seek so many new; they see that this
Is crumbled out again to his atomies.
'Tis all in pieces, all coherence gone,
All just supply, and all relation.

(John Donne, 1631)

The same mind- and world-shattering change took place when the
great medieval synthesis, inspired by the Scholastic philosophy and
the Catholic Church, gave way to the new world of the Renaissance;
and after the still more drastic change of the Enlightenment under the
influence of Descartes, Newton and the French *philosophes*, when men
were called upon to break with traditions and authorities which had
so long fettered mankind and to create through reason a new order of
things.

Of course in our day we are generally no more aware of the framework of our thought, through which nevertheless we perceive and
understand our world, than a fish is aware of the water in which it
swims. Everything is taken for granted and not thought about at all.
The conventions of our time, its unquestioned assumptions, are as
much part of us as our breathing. R. G. Collingwood, the Oxford
philosopher, believed that the task of philosophy was to disclose the
unquestioned assumptions of each age—those of its science, but also
those of its political thinking, its religion, and its morals. He showed
that the complex of such presuppositions for each period of history was
different—one for the Graeco-Roman world, quite another for the
Middle Ages, and so on. These presuppositions are not, he argued,
mere airy speculations but determine the entire structure of the
science, the law, the economy and the politics of each period.

Every age considers its world view eternal; but it is not; it gives way
to another, because each while it lives is unconsciously working to
turn itself into the next. The task of tracing these transitions is an
absorbing one and helps us to become self-critical about our own
presuppositions and their dissolution. We come to realise that if the
transition is delayed or obstructed then a whole civilisation can become

fossilised, otiose, paralysed and impotent. It may take a long time to die, but die it will. History is littered with defunct civilisations.

How then does one world order become obsolete, disintegrate or fall into decay, and give place to another? Some of the features of this process can be seen if we return to the less complex problem of radical changes in scientific thought. If we consider the Copernican revolution, we realise that long before the new theory emerged came a period of uncertainty and doubt, when inconsistencies and contradictions multiplied. These begin to loosen rigid modes of thought and helped men to break through to deeper insight. What happens in this period is the steady undermining of categories over the whole field of thought. A volley of perplexing questions is directed against the orthodox position. Its weaknesses, disadvantages, shortcomings and sheer irrationalities are demonstrated. Circumstances must play their part. This is not an intellectual game. The difficulties belong to the developing situation, they are not logically inherent in the system. They develop as the maturity of the old system pushes its principles to consequences which are intolerable.

Kuhn in his book on *The Structure of Scientific Revolutions* calls the change forced upon us by these difficulties the *paradigm shift*. The paradigm is the model, the whole structural system within which the laws appear—even though it is the laws that are seen, and not the hidden pre-supposition.

"A more profound awareness of anomaly is necessary for a change of theory. The state of Ptolemaic astronomy was a scandal before Copernicus, Galileo and Newton arose in a welter of anomalies".[1]

Only after the failure in the normal ability of a system to solve its problems; after the break-down of supplementary explanations to explain these failures; after problems thought to be soluble are suddenly seen not to be (under the existing rules)—only after every possible attempt has been made to reduce the facts to rational propositions, and in social matters, only after grave hardships, the danger of collapse, grave unrest and disturbance, only after the authorities supporting the old theories virtually abdicate, does the new hypothesis suddenly appear not absurd, but obvious. This is the beginning of the paradigm shift.

This is the kind of thing that takes places on the much wider field

[1] Kuhn, *loc. cit.*

when any system of categories, or even an entire world order, breaks up. These are the symptons that we recognise in our own period of transition. On every side the feeling is growing that we are coming to the end of things. Discussing the confused economic situation in the United States the Business Supplement of the *Guardian*, commenting on the panic at the "ominous phenomenon of that grip of stagnation and rising unemployment combined with apparently uncontrollable wage and price inflation", goes on to say "what haunts the financiers and politicians more than they care to say is the vague fear that the cause of the recession is not really understood at all. It is a suspicion that the American people are for the first time doubtful about the survival of their society, and their system of government." The same sudden feeling of unreality, of the insanity of things, comes over us when we hear of Canadian farmers being instructed and subsidised to put so many hundred acres of good wheat land out of cultivation to keep up the price of wheat, and of French farmers being subsidised to root up apple trees to keep up the price of apples and cider, while tons of good apples are destroyed for the same purpose. And all this in a world in which millions are short of the bare necessities of life. What disturbs one more than all this, is the complete failure of those most directly concerned to see anything odd in what they are doing.

It was when Marx saw the irrationalities and contradictions of developed capitalism and was convinced by his economic analysis that this disequilibrium was built into the mechanism of the system that he saw the beginning of world change, the crumbling of concepts, a final insanity in the nature of things. He saw the paradoxes, the insoluble dilemmas, the bankruptcy of the theoreticians long before the full picture had developed. Today the thing itself stares us in the face.

But the business of overhauling our concepts, of reconstructing our system of thought is not an easy matter. It requires a certain intellectual courage and considerable effort. Yet, if man has learned to master nature, to give himself and his environment the character of a world civilisation which he has made for himself to live in, if man has done this, it is because he is capable of real scientific thinking. Man is the only animal who thinks so hard that he transforms the whole structure of his life by its means. Everything human is due to man's power of thinking hard.

What is it that has to be turned upside down, taken to pieces and put together again in a different pattern? It is what we call the *structural pattern of society*, which too many people regard as absolutely permanent through the ages. Some even hold that it is constituted in that particular pattern because its plan is built into the human mind as part of its constitution. Let us look at that pattern. It is basically one of human relationships making up an organic whole in which each individual plays his own part, a part determined by the pattern and functioning of the whole, like the organs of a living body. But with man this role is consciously played, and should be played only if the good of the whole is the way in which the good of each is realised. History shows many of these structual patterns: one is that of master and slaves, another that of feudal lord and his men, ours is the private owner of the means of subsistence and his purchase of labour power as a commodity. Each pattern has its special type of man, of class, of class relationship, each has its own values, principles, moral code, and economic laws, its own political institutions, religious apparatus, and cultural activities and forces, for they are forces. Consider Plato's "Just City" with its fixed principles, reached only by the rational intuition of the trained philosopher, who alone therefore is fit to rule. Consider Plato's rigid stratification of men into those of gold, of silver, and of brass and iron. The men of iron to work, and not to think. The men of gold to think and not to work. And note also how the conception is inculcated by telling the people "the noble lie". The ideological myth of men being inherently of different metals and ordained from birth persuades them of the rightness of the status they are to occupy. Here is an *order*, an institutional system and also a mental pattern—one-dimensional, and incapable of allowing the rational process to transcend the limits of its structure.

At this point we have to learn that the very essence of life is found not in the perpetuation of established order but in its frustration. Failure to recognise that the present system is dying will allow us to construe the events of the day in terms of its inadequate forms. When this happens, as is the case today, we become aware of disorientation and bewilderment, a sense of chaos and unreason—the frame of mind of much contemporary literature and drama.

But an irrational state of affairs need not be a signal of defeat. In the evolution of scientific thought it frequently marks the first step in a spectacular advance. The multiplication of anomalies is exactly what compels us to reconstitute our theories on new principles, on a higher level.

Then begins the process of reconstruction leading to a different structural system, a tradition-shattering process in contrast to tradition-bound thinking. The assimilation, rational comprehension, and above all control of new facts cannot be accomplished without a reconstruction and re-evaluation of *all* existing facts as we know them. For example the sun has to be seen not as a small satellite of the fixed earth, but as a star, millions of miles away, around which a tiny object, the earth revolves. Impossible! Absurd! But true.

And so faced with our social, political and economic irrationalities, which we are shortly to examine, Marx suggest that they cannot permanently be comprehended and controlled within the world view and assumptions of a system which after all only appeared two hundred years previously, as something contradicting all rational views then, as new, revolutionary, rather absurd. But historically, it had to come. It was an advance. It liberated our efforts, it afforded new scope. But why should it be regarded as eternal, as *absolute*, as unalterable in basic structure? Historically, says Marx, its world view must give way, but only when it can no longer cope with the facts it exists to make sense of, only when, instead of fostering expansion and development, fuller control, human freedom, the system interposes obstacles, forbids advance, even moves backwards, only when it involves intolerable absurdities. It is then that we begin to move to a radically new form of order beyond the contradictions, where we can achieve that measure of control the lack of which involves us in despair and a growing sense that the universe is essentially absurd, just as in its own sphere, in the development of science, the intellectual miracle opens up a new world.

Normally in our scientific work we assume that progress takes place by surmounting our difficulties one by one, always allowing for a margin of error; by adding fact to fact; by extending our system by a process of 'piecemeal modification'. We go on using the same laws and principles, trying this way and that, modifying here and extending there to get beyond the anomalites. This is also the way we work in the social science, in economics and politics. But real scientific advance does not take place by adding fact to fact, and by small modifications of existing theories, but through the collapse of accepted principles, through an historical series of crises followed by an intellectual revolution.

This is also the way in which progress has taken place in social and historical development, and the lesson we have to learn is that this is how it is taking place today.

"The modern age", said Lord Acton, "did not proceed from the medieval by normal succession, with outward tones of legitimate descent. Unheralded it founded a new order of things, under a law of innovation, sapping the ancient order of continuity."[1]

What alarms us is the fear that in society this must mean a violent upheaval—the catastrophic overthrow of the existing order. That has been the case when for many years a bankrupt order has been maintained, usually by force, against a rising tide of discontent and suffering. It has not always happened that way, nor need it under constitutional government as Marx himself insisted. Nor is it the case that a radical change of this sort means the total destruction of "the system" which anarchism loudly calls for. The pattern goes but not the content. Marx, who spent his life fighting the anarchists, from Proudhon to Bakunin, pointed out that every step in the development of capitalism, except those which take place when it goes into reverse gear, points in the direction of socialism.

Capitalism in its last stages is pregnant with socialism, as Lenin used to say. This is the truth of Kautsky's position, but he thought that the last step would be one of continuity, whereas it is one of discontinuity. Nevertheless it is a discontinuity which preserves everything positive that has appeared under the system that is replaced. The transition does not present itself in the form of a general catastrophic collapse of capitalism but an interlocking series of political and economic struggles. It is also supposed that Marxism anticipates not only a catastrophic transition to socialism but an almost instantaneous ending of the whole system of capitalism and within a few months or years the appearance of an entirely new order with new ideals, standards of conduct, "new men". This, again, was never Marx's view, who said,

"Only through years of struggle can the class which overthrows cleanse itself of the mire of the old society and become fit to create a new society. You must pass through fifteen, twenty, perhaps fifty years of war not merely to change the system but to change yourselves and render yourselves fit for political rule."[2]

---

[1] Acton, *Lectures on Modern History.*
[2] Marx, summary of the meeting of the Central Committee of the Communist League September 15, 1850 (quoted from Mehring, *Karl Marx*).

And Lenin said much the same thing, "The human material with which we seek to build socialism has been corrupted by thousands of years of slavery, serfdom, capitalism and the war of every man against his neighbour."

The change of paradigm is only the precondition of socialism, and reconstruction of the concepts is only completed during a long and difficult road towards establishing the new order. Past changes in man's history were never instantaneous, the kind of changes we are considering occupied centuries. But there are nodal points of transition, just as in biological evolution the air-breathing amphibian is not a new kind of fish, even though the lung fish is an interesting intermediate form. Nor is the mammal only a curious, haired, warmblooded reptile. The new stage is a qualitative leap. Applied to society, this is Marx's concept of revolution. The battle of ideas precedes radical change, and continues long after it. It impels, dialectically, the series of organisational changes which precede and then follow the crisis of transformation.

The years leading up to the period of transition to socialism have an ideological character of their own. As difficulties multiply and the dilemma becomes more hopeless we hear less and less, not more and more, of socialism. Fifty years ago it was debated, written about and discussed in the House of Commons. Today it is hardly mentioned except in Pickwickian fashion as a "boo" word for any kind of government intervention that runs counter to business interests, or for welfare measures to aid the victims of capitalism.

Nor in recent debates, in which the deadlock is frankly admitted, is it possible to mention the fact that highly industrialised countries operating successfully a fully socialist economy, notably the Soviet Union, are insulated from both inflation and unemployment and are maintaining a high rate of growth. There is a complete mental block which does not allow the economies of East Germany, Hungary or Romania to be mentioned. To do so would be felt to be unpleasant, improper.

But contradictions are multiplying and are apparent in the prevailing climate of financial and economic crises: one day in Western Europe, the next in the United States; in the decline of economic growth in the older capitalist countries; in the existence of a vast amount of apparently ineradicable poverty inside as well as outside the areas of advanced capitalist development.

This had been brought about by the immense pace of technological achievement in the last 250 years compared with the extremely slow changes in previous ages, which meant slow economic development and the relative stability of social systems and civilisation. This pace in our time has been the result of an unprecedentedly large investment of human ability in constructional engineering and the means of obtaining and using mechanical power, and in successful improvements not only in technology but in agricultural and animal breeding.

It is questioned today whether the economic and social organisation for distributing the potential product, and determining its nature in terms of the social welfare of people, has kept pace with and is appropriate to the resources now available to overcome want.

Nor is the ideological climate which came into existence in an age of nascent capitalism and economic scarcity the most appropriate world of discourse and ethical feeling for the age of monopolies and mass production. A society cannot maintain its social cohesion unless a decisive majority of its members hold in common a viable and relevant system of guiding ideas and ideals. That is another reason why it would seem that there must be impending an intellectual revolution, to reorientate our world in relation to these enormous technological changes and urgent social demands.

In our time the world is distracted by violent conflicts of interest, disequilibrium, hopeless dilemmas in which each way out leads to disaster of one kind or another, recurring breaks in the continuity of development, and inexplicable arrest of economic growth. In one respect the problem is different from that in the natural sciences, because the social reality under consideration itself undergoes change; and also because paradigm change has not merely to overcome innate conservatism but involves the interests of individuals, groups, classes and nations. Resistance to change is therefore likely to be tougher and more bitter than in science. That is why the social revolution is a more difficult affair, for the new and more effective control of the economy is hampered by resistance to the modifications of the structual forms of the old society, which are artificially preserved beyond the point where they are economically useful, by the interests they represent. Gradual evolution is thus prevented, and when the discrepancy becomes sufficiently great, society must experience a period of social conflict or perish.

Another grave difference from scientific change is the fact that the contradictions are not so deeply felt by those in the position of maintaining the status quo. Wars in distant lands, poverty thousands of miles away, or out of sight in the slums, cannot often be expected to distress those in comfortable circumstances, beyond at best generous donations to charities such as Oxfam. People who are individually merciful and considerate are seldom intelligent enough to see the needs of others as vividly as they recognize their own; and where privilege is threatened reason has no difficulty in finding proof that such privilege serves universal ends. But a culture which tries to hide its cruelties by moral pretensions that do not change the facts can only exacerbate the feelings of those who know the facts and continue to suffer.

None of these obstacles to readjustment of basic theory, to the paradigm shift required by society, can in the last resort prevent social change, for it is neither intellectual satisfaction nor an important advance in science that is at stake but society itself. There comes a time when reconstruction is the only alternative to rapid decline and internal anarchy and disintegration. It is no longer merely the short-comings inevitable in any economic system which demand improve-ments without requiring the basic pre-construction of the system; it is something far more serious. Kuhn points out that all scientific theories are troubled by anomalies, and that these have to be lived with until in numbers and importance the irrationalities and contradictions become intolerable. It is at that point that we are ready to welcome a radically new approach to the whole problem. This is also so in society. It can always be argued that any system will have its defects. Those anxious to conserve existing institutions will be prepared to put up with a good deal of illogicality and downright misery among the un-privileged, and with genuine difficulties for themselves. They will always hope for a turn of the tide, for a restoration of confidence, for some new monetary policy, or for a change of government that will put things right. The question is: when do we reach the point at which the alternative to radical change is worse that the change we dread? A huge question mark hangs over the structure of Western society, which is now subject to the most searching scrutiny. The basic principle of capitalism is that if the private interest of investors and manufacturers are allowed full scope, ultimately the goods needed will be produced, prices will be kept down by competition, capital will flow where profitability indicates public demand. The introduction of a great deal of government control and assistance, pressure of trade unions, nationalisation of certain industries, has not changed the fundamental aim of industry, which is still subject to the pressures and requirements of economic law. The basic allocation of resources is still made in pursuit of an adequate return on invested capital. Production decisions are still regulated in terms of financial requirements without reference to social consequences, as far as that is possible. The great corporations, partly assisted and partly controlled by government, are as much subject as the small businesses of Adam Smith's day to monetary control. Production stops or is restricted where it is not profitable. So far from the public interest being served, the basic demands of the masses being supplied, the world's resources being directed and utilised to satisfy human need, enormous areas of that need cannot be met, within the terms of capitalist economic law, even though the resources are there.

The capitalist economic system, even when government has contributed control and assistance, has failed to secure the satisfaction of human needs rendered possible by the immense resources now available and the potentialities of industry to utilise them. Here is the source of the great contradictions of modern capitalism which constitute the basis of the Marxist analysis of the modern world.

It was Marx's *Capital* which revealed this basic irrationality of capitalism, its fatal movement towards increasing irrationality and frustration, its inability to overcome the fetters of its own system upon the forces of production it has so successfully and triumphantly developed. *Capital* is not a treatise on economics, demonstrating the labour theory of value, the theory of increasing misery, and the ultimate collapse of capitalism. Marx starts from the presupposition of the system as it was expounded in his day by the leading economists[1] who themselves maintained the labour theory of value. Marx has indeed been described as the last of the great classical economists.

He was concerned with the operation of this system to accumulate capital from surplus value and by investing it in new industries continuously to expand the forces of production. Marx draws attention to the heavy cost this process of exploitation involves, but lays stress on the tremendous achievement of capitalism in this respect. But he then shows how a system which is entirely concerned with enlarging the volume of investments is not concerned basically with what industry should be about—satisfying human needs and the ultimate distribution and consumption of the product. Beyond the point at which industrialism is completely established, it runs into insoluble contradictions. It fails to utilise its potential capacity. It even begins to

[1] Ricardo, McCulloch, James Mill, William Petty.

slow down the rate of economic growth although human welfare urgently demands it.

Marx is not basing his criticism on the rapacity and hardness of the heart of capitalists, nor on a denunciation of the injustice of exploitaion. His argument is an historical one! That there is not *one* unalterable and eternal system of economic laws, but a succession of such systems, each fulfilling its task in turn and then giving way to the next, just as political and legal and philosophical systems have done, just as successive forms of civilisation have done. Marx derives the structure of these forms of society from the pattern of human relations in production. He regards each pattern of economic activity as carrying out its task, preparing the way for the next and then giving way to its successor. The existing system is the latest and is constructed to create and expand *capital*. This it has done. But it cannot fully utilise this capital. This can only be done if economic law is seen not as a final and complete science, as absolute truth, but historically, as serving its purpose and then suffering radical transformation to a new system primarily concerned with the *utilisation* of capital, of developing industry for human welfare—this will be a *socialist* economy, and in it the pattern of human relations will be that of common ownership and cooperative production for use, not class ownership and production for profit, that is to say for the maximum return on invested capital.

Marx does not advocate this on utopian or moralistic grounds, as an ideal system. He sees it as rendered necessary by the contradictions appearing and intensifying in modern capitalism, and also in *the many important changes in capitalism itself*, particularly its huge aggregations of capital in corporations and the ever growing role of governments in industry and finance, which prepare the way for socialism, which carry industry right up to the point at which social ownership and control is all but inevitable, and is the obvious next step. This is the point in history at which Lenin said, "Socialism looks out at us through all the windows of capitalism".

I said, "all but" inevitable, because Marx never for a moment thought the transition could take place automatically. It requires the immense development of political and economic consciousness in wide sections of the community which we have been discussing. It requires ideas, an intellectual revolution, or the result will be not progress but decline and disintegration.

Such a period of transition can be one of alarm and despondency.

Such advances in civilisation are processes that all but wreck the societies in which they occur. For some almost any tragedy would be a better alternative than socialism. But "better dead than red" is a value judgment that a twentieth-century human being is entitled to make only for himself, and not for any other human being, either alive or unborn. If "better dead than red" is his considered judgment, he can act on it without much inconvenience to his neighbours, but he is not entitled to take with him the rest of his present and future fellow human beings.

As long as the human race remains alive we can be confident that it will outlive any of the habits and institutions that it has introduced into its social and cultural heritage. Man's cultural heritage is less durable than man himself. It is not a built-in part of human nature, but merely a man-made product which its maker is free to modify if he chooses. While there is life there is hope.

14

THE ILLUSIONS OF THE EPOCH

The paralysis of the modern mind, its hopeless entanglement in the contradictions of our economic system, is due to more than an intellectual error that hard thinking could dispel. It is more like those post-hypnotic compulsions which force a man to do something absurd, or the hypnotic condition that persuades a man that he is freezing cold or cannot move his arms. Marx describes the hypnotic coma which has a whole civilisation in its grip as "the illusion of the epoch". We are the victims of an ideological crisis, not simply an economic one.

Jung has persuasively invoked the collective unconscious to explain certain myths, religions and fairy tales. Far from being a childish fancy, the fairy tale expresses some widespread experience of mankind, some haunting fear or buried problem. In *The Sleeping Beauty* the whole court and countryside falls into a deep sleep around the princess, until a kiss from the youth who cuts his way through the forest of thorn bushes awakes her. That, says Jung, has been mankind's fate many times. We could add that in the course of history there come periods of decline into stagnation, blindness, paralysis, until some newcomer hacking his way through painful obstructions awakens the sleeping world.

The experience of a civilisation entering such a period of decline and stagnation is one we are familiar with. It seems impossible to make headway, the obstacles appear insurmountable and for the difficulties of our industrial system the economists appear to have no remedy.

Marx suggests that this paralysis reflects the end of an historic period when the reorganisation of society is due. The theoretical and philosophical basis is inadequate for the tasks before it and there can be no advance before there appears a new understanding of man and of his economy.

The system of ideas underlying the social order at any period in its history Marx calls an ideology. It is a closely knit system of beliefs, determined largely by economic forces, and reflecting the position of the dominant class in that period. Every form of social life is motivated and limited by its conceptual framework. For long periods, for centuries, such a *Weltanshauung* or framework of thinking, feeling and acting, dominates men's lives and finds expression in their work, in political institutions, in their religion, their art, and in the values, customs and morals of the age.

But there comes a time when its work is done and the world this philosophy has created moves towards a change of pattern. But the dissolution of such a system of ideas is unimaginable to almost everyone. It is not that some established theory *within* the system is threatened, it is that the conception of the entire framework of existence, the whole system of beliefs and categories, the basic pre-suppositions of the age, is in process of disintegration.

A society cannot maintain its social cohesion unless a decisive majority of its members hold in common the guiding ideas and ideals which are furnished by such a philosophy, if we may call it such—a cosmogony, a theory of the nature of man, some conception of the purpose of life and the direction of history. This not only provides an explanation of the meaning of life, but a basis for the code of duties and obligations which hold society together and in which it finds its rationale.

From the appearance of a class society the ideology serves the further purpose of securing the privileged in their rights and reconciling the subordinate classes to their subservience, thus providing a pattern of social relationships that is accepted as natural and right by all.

An ideology has an important persuasive role to guide the individual and give him a sense of purpose. It is by no means basically a vehicle for the coercive pressure of society, the authority of the State being secondary to the forces that work from within by faith and conviction, making the individual believe that he is fulfilling himself by obedience, even if in fact he is becoming alienated. Every society, every authority has to be *accepted*. It must obtain the consensus of the majority; and it is the ideology which secures this. It is thus thoroughly functional, and is related to social practice especially in establishing the distinct and necessary role of different classes and callings.

An important form which ideology takes is that of religion, which provides consolation for those born to servitude and suffering, while it sanctifies the authority of those born to rule. No human society, before the rise of science, is conceivable without a religious system to sustain and inspire it. As Engels said of the Christian Church

"A religion that brought the Roman world empire into subjection and dominated by far the greater part of civilised humanity for 1,800 years cannot be disposed of merely by declaring it to be nonsense created by fraud."[1]

At the time of its full development all the achievements of civilisation depend upon its structural pattern and its ideology, and these have been considerable. History is not a long series of errors, follies, frauds and injustices from which we are emerging in our age of enlightenment with nothing but pity for the dark ages now left behind. But from the standpoint of a new phase in historical development, the ideology of the old order cannot but be regarded as based on illusion, mystification and false conceptions which men have made for themselves. What has to be overcome in such times is the conviction that these beliefs have a permanent and absolute validity.

It is however only when the historical conditions are ripe that this criticism can be effective, and then it will be accompanied by the emergence of new social and economic forms which have been growing and maturing in the womb of the old order, and by the appearance of new men, new groupings, with new ideas.

When such a period of radical change arrives,

"Morality, religion, metaphysics, all the rest of the ideology, and their corresponding forms of consciousness, thus no longer retain the semblance of independence. They have no history, no development; but men, developing their material production and their material intercourse, alter, along with this their real existence, their thinking and the product of their thinking."[2]

This can be misunderstood. Such forms of thought are not unmediated, they do not appear as pure creations of the mind, as mere intellectual errors. They are related to historical conditions; which give rise to them and cannot do without them. But, as Engels later explained, the ideas of any age also have a connection with those of the preceding period, and are by no means solely determined by the contemporary situation. However, the more radical the social changes the more drastic the modification, and the more inevitable is it that a new ideology or new theories will appear.

[1] Engels, *Bruno Bauer and Early Christianity*.
[2] *The German Ideology*, Part I.

Thus, when social change is on the agenda the ideologies which were once taken for granted and which represent the pre-suppositions of the decaying world-order appear, in Marx's phrase, as a "false consciousness", their real causes in the needs of the old pattern of society not being recognised. No epoch of history can be understood in terms of how it views itself, to do so would be to share the "illusion of the epoch". This notion is familiar to us from the works of Freud, who showed how often what a man thinks of himself and imagines to be his motives are quite different from what he really is and why he behaves as he does, as Marx had said as long ago as 1859 in the Preface to his *Critique of Political Economy*.

Marx examines the ideologies of the declining capitalist era from this point of view and finds them closely related to the condition of alienation for which the class system is responsible, alienation affecting all classes in society; but this "false consciousness" is also a characteristic of *religion*, of the *State*, and of the system of *economic law;* in other forms it is also reflected in the philosophies of the time, and the utopian ideals of the rising movements of protest.

Religion was for Marx the most significant ideological form of alienation; and the premise of all criticism of society and of philosophy must, he says, be the *critique*[1] of religion.

Following Feuerbach, Marx sees religion as reflecting all that man has been deprived of by the exploitation of a class society. It is what gives him consolation and hope in a world which strips him of his manhood and which merely uses him as a means for other people's ends.

Although this is one important aspect of religion at certain periods, neither the anthropologist nor the historian would find it an adequate account of religion which has undoubtedly played an indispensable and creative role in the development of civilisation; and Marx himself never meant it to be. In the course of history, so far from only inculcating submission, religion, as Lenin says, has frequently been a revolutionary force when "the democratic and proletarian struggle took the form of a struggle of one religious idea against another",[2] as was the case when it inspired Cromwell's Ironsides in the Great Rebellion of 1640.

A second aspect of the ideological expression of alienation is found

---

[1] By a *critique* Marx means not a destructive criticism, but a critical evaluation. All his important works are critiques, including *Capital*.

[2] *Lenin*, letter to A. M. Gorky, November 1913. *Collected Works*, Vol. 35, p. 128.

in the conception of the *State*. In his *Introduction to the Critique of Hegel's Philosophy of Right* Marx argues that the State does not really represent the control of society in the interests of all, as it claims to do. In fact, in a capitalist society, it reflects the conflict of interests between the classes and is in effect the instrument of class power, imposing laws and using coercion in the interest of the rulers. When the class society is ended and alienation has been overcome by a society based on social ownership, the State, as an external coercive authority, eventually disappears. This however demands the overcoming of the last remnant of resistance to the people's interests, and the drastic reconstruction of the state apparatus.[1] During this period of transition the State operates through genuine democratic forms to complete the reorganisation of society in the interests of the whole community. So long as an authoritarian state apparatus continues in the period of transition to socialism there is still a long way to go before we can claim that a real socialist society has been built.

There has been a good deal of misunderstanding as to the position of the individual in socialist society. Marx never conceived him as subordinated to the state power. Aldous Huxley once wrote, "The aim of communism is to deprive the individual of every right, every vestige of personal liberty and to transform him into a component of the great Collective Man." This has never been part of Marxist theory. Marx himself emphatically declares that "Above all one must avoid setting up society again as an abstraction opposed to the individual. The individual *is* the social entity. His life therefore an expression and verification of social life."[2]

The conception of the system of *economic laws* under capitalism constitutes a third major feature of the ideological expression of alienation under capitalism.

Marx devoted the whole of *Capital* to the discussion of this form of ideology, especially as it is expressed in such concepts as "commodity" and "money", and in the operations of the all-powerful "market". These entities stand over against man, who finds himself dominated by his own products and subject to the illusory sway of his own organisation and artifacts. The "commodity", that which is bought and sold, including "labour power" itself, Marx shows to be the key

---

[1] After the creation of the first socialist state, one cannot expect the disappearance of state power while there is the possibility of military intervention from capitalist forces.
[2] Marx, *Economic and Philosophic Manuscripts* (Milligan translation), p. 104.

concept. It involves and envelops social relations between living men, operating with its own laws and imposing its own consequences. Men within the system can enter into relations with one another only through *commodities* and the *market*, through money. These come to mask the real relationships, and Marx uses a special term to show the irrational character of the power it exercises. "I call this *fetishism*", says Marx, "which is attached to the products of labour as soon as they are produced as commodities and which is consequently inseparable from the production of commodities."[1] Among primitive people fetishism and magic express nature's dominance over man and the illusory sway of man over natural forces. In our economic world these reifications also exercise something like a supernatural power, though they are really, once again, only creations of the mind.

Robinson Crusoe,[2] says Marx, knows economically exactly what he is doing. He knows why he has to work and for what. His object is the direct production of the necessities of life and their consumption. Remarkably, he can do this entirely without money! The economists must be shocked. The relation between him and his means of subsistence is "simple and transparent". This is not at all the case under capitalism. Here the production of commodities is enveloped in fog. The operations of the market are not transparent, the are *opaque*. The commodity thus has a "mystical character". Its mystery is the power of money and capital, and the supremacy of the "market" over common sense and human needs. This gives rise in turn to an *opaque* society, in which money holds sway over human beings. It is this that gives the inverted reflection to society in which men see commodities ruling them and forget that it is they who have themselves made the money-commodity-market system, and could unmake it tomorrow if they wanted to. But until this happens they continue to live in the fog of mystification and

"The life-process of society which is based on the process of material production does not strip off its mystical veil until it is treated as production by freely associated men and is consciously regulated by them in accordance with a settled plan."[3]

Capitalist ideology is responsible for this "reification", that is to say the creation of an entity out of an abstraction which exists only in the minds of those who live in the self-created world of this transient

[1] Marx, *Capital*, Vol. I, Chapter 1, Section 4.   [2] *Ibid.*   [3] *Ibid.*, Section 3.

ideology and which is responsible for the whole tragic absurdity of the capitalist economic impasse and all its irrationalities.

But there is nothing absolute or eternal about the economic system of capitalism.

"By knowledge and by action men can disperse the heavy clouds of fetishism and transcend the conditions that gave birth to it. An economic destiny is relative and provisional, and is destined to be transcended once men have become aware of their possibilities and realise that this transcending will be the essential, infinitely creative act of out own age."[1]

Marx makes the ideology of "money" the theme of one of his *Economic and Philosophic Manuscripts*, taking Shakespeare's *Timon of Athens* as his text to drive home the corrupting nature of the money fetish. He shows how in this play Shakespeare attributes to money the quality of a visible deity "transforming all human and natural qualities into their opposite, the universal confusion and inversion of things."

The following passages are worth quoting verbatim:

"Money, since it has the *property* of purchasing everything, of appropriating objects to itself, is therefore the object *par excellence*. The universal character of this *property* corresponds to the omnipotence of money, which is regarded as omnipotent essence . . . money is the *pander* between need and object, between human life and the means of subsistence. But *that which* mediates my life, mediates also the existence of other men for me. It is for me the *other* person . . ."[2]

Gold? yellow, glittering, precious gold? No, gods
I am no idle votarist. . . . Thus much of this will
    make black white; foul fair;
Wrong, right; base, noble; old, young, coward valiant. . . .
    Why, this
Will lug your priests and servants from your sides;
Pluck stout men's pillows from below their heads:
This yellow slave
Will knit and break religions; bless th' accurst;

[1] Marx, *Capital*, Vol. I, Chapter 1, Section 4.
[2] The emphases are Marx's own.

Make the hoar leprosy ador'd; place thieves,
And give them title, knee, and approbation,
With senators on the bench: this is it
That makes the wappen'd widow wed again;
She, whom the spital-house and ulcerous sores
Would cast the gorge at, this embalms and spices
To th' April day again. Come, damned earth,
Thou common whore of mankind, that putt'st odds
Among the rout of nations, I will make thee
Do thy right nature.

Shakespeare attributes to money two qualities:

1. It is the visible deity, the transformation of all human and natural qualities into their opposite, the universal confusion and inversion of things; it beings incompatibles into fraternity.
2. It is the universal whore, the universal pander between men and nations.

The power to confuse and invert all human and natural qualities, to bring about fraternisation of incompatibles, the *divine power* of money, resides in its *essence* as the alienated and exteriorized species-life of men. It is the alienated *power* of *humanity*.

What I as a *man* am unable to do, what therefore all my individual faculties are unable to do, is made possible for me by means of *money*. Money therefore turns each of these faculties into something which in itself it is not, into its *opposite*."

It would seem that Marx regarded capitalist society as corrupt and damaging to human nature, a social order based on exploitation and, at this stage in its development, rent with contradictions. But this does not mean that its "false consciousness" condemns it as without positive feature, or that the illusions of its ideology are destitute of any degree of truth.

In every ideology there is always an element of truth, and since truth is strictly relative to conditions, when a system of society is advancing or has reached stability, its values and institution must be regarded as relatively acceptable, and its culture as containing much of permanent significance. That was true of the Graeco-Roman world of Medievalism, and supremely of the Renaissance.

It is also true of capitalism, which Marx saw as a necessary phase in social development, and indispensable to the coming era of productivity which would at last overcome the problem of poverty and human degradation. Marx pays a high tribute to the bourgeois economy in *The Communist Manifesto*, and he fully recognised and appreciated its cultural achievements. His point was that the disequilibrium of its economy and the slowing down of its growth indicated the necessity of "going beyond" it, of *negating* it so as not simply to destroy it but in doing so to develop its own potentialities, fulfil its promises, and carry forward in developed and completed form all that was good in it—which was much.

It is when we reach this stage that the ideas and institutions which served capitalism and the whole of society well became outworn, less and less useful, and finally obstructive and dangerous. However important an ideology, it cannot claim validity beyond the conditions and needs of society. When these demand radical change, and the controlling and supporting ideas and principles of the older order stand in the way of that change, the time has come for their radical criticism and rejection. They have no claim to dogmatic finality.

The matter may become more serious. The ideas and principles of capitalism as an ideology constitute the whole world outlook of our society, of our view of man and his nature, and of the social relationships of society. We should be aware of the appalling evils which mark the development of industrialism and are still with us. These evils have been mitigated by the pressure of public opinion and organised labour. In spite of the crude selfishness and money values of capitalist society, men have always been better than their creed. There has been generosity and pity, fellowship and self-sacrifice, dedicated work for the community—not only for personal gain. But as a social order moves towards its end, privilege is threatened and the whole structure appears threatened and unstable. Now the principles of capitalism are more vigorously asserted, its ideology is buttressed by every kind of theoretical support and the modern mind falls more completely under its domination than before.

At the same time there grows up a counter-ideology of protest, in the earlier years expressed in moral and utopian terms. The French socialists St. Simon and Fourier, Robert Owen in England, the vehement sermons of John Ruskin, Thomas Carlyle, and the romantic protest of William Morris are all examples of this ideology.

In the later stages of capitalism these protests are in turn answered by a new development of the ideology of capitalism with its theories of man as a predator by nature, his aggression congenital and ineradicable. There is also renewed emphasis on the importance of genetically superior groups and races, coupled with *élitist* theories of government and the rejection of democratic principles. Behaviourist theories become current which regard men as constituted by conditioned reflexes and only controllable by pains and rewards, like laboratory animals—"the ratomorphic view of man".[1]

For, especially in an age of transition, there is not *one* ideology but two or three. There is, of course, the ideological expression of the existing class forms of society, whether feudal or capitalist; and, since the new order is already growing up within it, we have a rival, antagonistic ideology, representing the class aspiring to power, yesterday the rising bourgeoisie, and, today, as capitalism declines, those groups in the old economy who are fighting for an altogether new form of society.

As we shall see, the ideology of capitalism itself goes through three stages: its initial, combative, progressive form when it is establishing itself; the organised form which justifies and stabilises the system when it has arrived; and the ideology of capitalism in decline—partly aggressive and desperate, sometimes ruthlessly abandoning democratic forms, sometimes negative and despairing—the ideology of anarchism and defeat.

Only when the process of social development gives rise to scientific understanding of the rise and fall of economic systems does a theory capable of being experimentally verified and tested in action take the place of ideology conceived as a "false consciousness".

Man's historical progress is bound up with man's mastery over nature, including his own nature. For as each stage in economic development is basically a pattern of human relationships—today one of buying and selling human labour—men become in their habits and ideas, in their ideologies, the creatures first of the succession patterns of pre-capitalist formations, and finally of a competitive free-for-all. They then attribute their behaviour to the predatory character of human nature—an ideological explanation if ever there was one. When man changes this system to a cooperative pattern, he brings an environmental situation into being which encourages and fosters a

---

[1] We are not criticising the findings of science, but the superficial and highly speculative theories of non-professional writers, or in some cases like Lorenz the illegitimate extrapolation of work on fighting fish and geese to man. Behaviourism is a scientific theory but a questionable one.

new type of man, the cooperative type, which in time, guided and inspired by the new ethical, legal and artistic forms of culture, and the new theories of society, will help to create new men.

Turning from that modern world in which man is by definition all animal and unrestrained self-seeking in a congeries of possessors and pursuers, to Marx's "categorical imperative to overthrow all conditions in which man is a humiliated, enslaved, despised and rejected being", one asks—which is the ideology and which the truth? Or, perhaps, which ideology has the most truth in it and the less illusion?

The dominant ideology becomes the unquestionable assumption of the time, uncritically accepted by writers, broadcasters, reviewers and leading journalists, so that the public mind cannot but see things in this pattern. It is the pattern, of course, that fully supports the economic principles of individual enterprise, economic competition, and the survival of the fittest. It supports the view that these sectional economic intersts are final and absolute and ultimately secure the interests of all.

We have systematically taught and insisted on the principle of each man getting all he can, as the rule of our society; but we are now alarmed at the determination with which the trade unions are doing exactly that. Are we still so sure that the ultimate motive in industrial and personal life should be financial gain?

In the early days of capitalism this was vigorously contested, first by Carlyle and Ruskin, and William Morris. It became the creed of the early socialists and found its prophetic voices in Bernard Shaw and R. H. Tawney. Today this is regarded as little more than ineffectual idealism. It is no longer a conflict between two rival faiths as it was in the Ruskin-Morris period, but the acceptance by our intellectuals, and those concerned with propaganda and communication, of the ideology of private and sectional gain. The protest is now relegated to the preachers and saints, to the ineffectual believers in the brotherhood of man and utopia. Our ideologists assure us that there is no rational foundation for the idealism of the reformers.

This makes clear first what is meant by an ideology being accepted not as a theory which can be questioned, but as the manifest truth of our world. But there is another and parallel tendency in modern thought, which reflects the growing irrationalisms of capitalist society. It arises from these current views of man, but also from the consequence of this reduction of man and society to purposeless mechanism. This is the ideology of a world that has lost its meaning. It is immensely reinforced and verified by the social unrest, wars and uprisings, and economic dilemmas of our time.

Today nihilism, the philosophy of the absurd, the growing conviction that progress is an illusion, takes us beyond the ideology of capitalism to the ideology of decadence.

Albert Cornu, the French Marxist, has drawn attention to the shifting character of ideologies as a class society passes through its inevitable phases of development. This is a useful reminder that since society is not as stable and permanent as it would wish to be, so ideologies must not be supposed to be absolute and enduring. Cornu therefore distinguishes three phases of ideological development:

1. The *conservative* and justifying ideology of the dominant classes in a period of relative stability. It halts development in the present, to which it gives an absolute value.

2. The *reactionary* ideology of a class in process of decline and disintegration. At this stage philosophy denies essential value to present reality, and either points beyond to the spiritual world and the life beyond, or lapses into nihilism and pessimism.

3. The *revolutionary*, Utopian ideology of the yet insufficiently developed classes who desire to change the social order, turning away from both past and present. This tends to determine dogmatically the general shape of future reality.

A few words may be necessary to make Cornu's view clearer.

(1) There are three exceptionally interesting examples of *conservative* ideologies in stable societies. The first is Plato's theory of the fixed castes—the men of gold, the élite, who alone have the right to govern; the men of silver—the soldiers and administrators; the men of iron and brass, who are the workers. Plato derives this political plan from ultimate and eternal principles revealed to the rational intuition of the philosophically minded, chiefly the principle of Justice, which Plato interprets as "keeping every man in his place". What is to be noted here is that the ideology which determines the political system is the system of absolute *ideas*.

The second example is furnished by the feudal system, with its rigid stratification of King, noble, knight and serf, each with his duties and his responsibilites. Now this system also has its ideology in the theology of the medieval Church with the Pope, the bishops, the clergy, and the laity, inculcating the hierarchical principle of absolute authority emanating from God, from which derived the divine right of Kings.

The third example is the Indian caste system and the theology of Karma, which teaches that if you are born in a lowly station it is because of your sins in a previous existence. Hindu philosophy and religion is a revealed system of absolute truths and doctrines which justifies and perpetuates the status quo.

(2) Beyond the stabilising philosophies comes the *reactionary* ideology. In its positive form we have found this in various theories of man and society which reduce the human to the animal and all existence to the mechanical interaction of physical entities.

In its negative form we find its expression in such statements as "I feel profoundly in the depths of my being that in the last resort nothing matters",[1] or from a distinguished dramatist:[2] "At the end of my work there is nothing but dust: this complete disintegration." He is important, says a well known dramatist critic,[3] "because he gets so close to seeing Nothing". These are not isolated cases, they reflect a very widespread malaise expressed in a whole culture of despair. Yet without some vision of the world, including those elements and order without which society lapses into anarchy, how can civilisation endure? Perhaps in the lower stages of life man can maintain his life with mere glimpses of reason; but one philosopher at least has come to the conclusion that "when civilisation culminates, the absence of a coordinating philosophy of life spells decadence, boredom, and the slackening of effort".[4]

(3) The *revolutionary utopian* ideology arises as the first phase of the revolution, before enlightenment has reached the masses, and before the ripening of the social and economic conditions. This according to Marx is a useful, prophetic and inspiring kind of ideology, but only as the fore-runner of *praxis*, of effecting a working understanding of the development of society now in its final stages. Praising it in the period before practical measures were possible Marx regards it after that, and in our time, as in effect negative and reactionary.

(4) Following the *utopian* period we reach the pragmatic level of scientific socialism. Scientific not in the sense of reducing men to molecules in motion, and society to the resultant of economic forces

---

[1] Leonard Woolf, in *Downhill All the Way*, Vol. IV, in his autobiography.
[2] Samuel Beckett, 1956. It might equally have been Pinter.
[3] Mr. Ronald Hayman in the *Observer*.
[4] Whitehead, *Adventures of Ideas*.

in unconscious interaction, but in the sense of a theory continuously in process of being tested and revised in action.

At this level, says Marx, we leave ideology behind, just as we leave behind the philosophies that only *explain* the world. We have begun, with conscious if imperfect understanding, to change it.

But, it may be asked, if all ideas are relative to historical conditions, is not Marxism too? There is, however, a difference: for Marxism is not simply a theory about society but a *method* of investigating society and its historical sequence of forms of order. As such a *method* it vindicates itself only by its success; unlike dogmatic theories, it is constantly improving its own methods, and like other scientific theories is under constant criticism and revision.

Marx's theories of social development are the fruit of such a methodology. Clearly if the methodology is sound the working hypotheses derived from it have a reasonable measure of truth, as tested, of course, in action; and unlike "ideologies" proper, which are affirmed dogmatically, Marxist theories are under constant revision[1] on the basis of the corrections made as they are applied in practice.

Marxism, offering itself as a theory not merely to be argued about but to be tested, a theory which appears only as the interpretation of a concrete situation for immediate, and limited, action, is on every occasion having its theories refuted or corrected; and, one believes, in part verified. Do we say then that Marxist theories are conditioned, relative to actual situations, never final, never certainly true? This is the case. They are true so far as they work and have that measure of validity and nothing more. They remain imperfect but useful, carrying us farther and by doing so creating new situations from which new hypotheses will be derived, theories which like all scientific hypotheses are self-corrective, capable of and demanding endless transformation and improvement through the course of history.

[1] If anywhere Marxist theories are advanced as dogmas which cannot be criticised or revised, that in itself excludes them from being considered as either Marxist or scientific.

H

15

THE COMING OF SOCIALISM

Man makes his own history, said Marx. And he makes it only when his political understanding rises to the point of knowing what is really going on around him. Society moves forward in this phase of development only in so far as the overwhelming majority knows and wills the next step. Nor is it for a moment the mere *willing* of a utopian alternative to capitalism. Marx rejects utopian socialism as in our day a reactionary diversion from commonsense. The *next step* is but the beginning.

It depends on the ripening of the conditions, which means that the transition to socialism becomes possible only

(1) When the economic system is beset with contradictions and absurdities.
(2) When instead of fostering the development of the productive forces, it begins to restrain and impede them.
(3) When there has developed the education, organisation and political consciousness of a considerable majority of those responsible in one way or another for the world's work, until the point is reached that these groups see the necessity for change and are aware of their power through the democratic process to bring it about.

Marx rejects the seizure of power by a minority; and where constitutional government exists, sees the possibility of a peaceful and democratic transition to socialism; though he never overlooked the possibility of an attempt at counter-revolution *by* the capitalist class after power had passed into the hands of the people by constitutional means.

How then are we to suppose that the revolution is going to happen?

Marx was not given to prophecy and made no blue-prints or tactical plans for the revolution. There are, in fact, a great variety of ways towards a socialist society. The way forward today cannot be restricted to the methods by which socialism has been established up to now, which were occasioned by the exceptional conditions following two world wars. There are certainly other ways. And we cannot ignore the fact that socialism has now been established, in its initial forms, in a large part of the world; and is already developing successfully along various paths.

As long ago as 1920 Lenin wrote to the leaders of the movement in Trans-Caucasia calling upon them "to avoid any mechanical copying of the Russian pattern. They must skilfully work out their own flexible tactics."[1]

Today the policy of the Communist parties in Britain, Italy, France, Spain and of most other, if not all, Western countries, is to proceed *in alliance* with other progressive forces to find some better way out of the economic confusion of our times rather than to blunder on at the expense of the interests of all but the financiers, and from these beginnings develop a widely based movement in the direction of socialism.

As to what form that socialism might ultimately take, the more one considers the special conditions and possibilities in the West, the clearer becomes the need to be ready to accept greater *diversity*, both as to aim and method. There is already considerable diversity in existing socialist societies: Russia, China and Cuba are following radically different paths; and in Europe, Yugoslavia, with its industries in direct control of the factory workers, presents a different kind of socialism from the central control we find in some other socialist countries. The variety is great and will be greater when well established democracies take the socialist road, with multiple parties, free elections and a free press. Thus the diversity in the socio-historical origins necessarily leads to diversity both in the paths to socialism and the forms the new society takes. It is quite impossible today to fit this diversity into any sort of straightjacket, to make it uniform. The period of independent and multiform socialism is not merely hoped for today. It has arrived.

There is no Marxist blue-print for socialism. Marx is at the farthest possible remove from those utopian sketches of the ideal society that we find in Thomas More, Morris, Bellamy and others. Marx has been criticised, often by the same person, at one moment for formulating a comprehensive programme and predicting its inevitable arrival in the future "with the certainty of an eclipse" (Popper), and at the next moment of leaving us completely in the dark as to where we are going and what we are going to do after the revolution. Thus Sir Isaiah Berlin in his Romanes Lecture for 1971 on Turgeniev and Russian

[1] *Collected Works*, Vol. 32, p. 160.

Anarchism, after describing the Anarchist position—no doubt he had Bakunin in mind—as the call to pull the whole system down, destroy it, and then after "shattering it to bits", leaving us to build it up again "nearer to the heart's desire", immediately attributed this proposal to Marx, who had spent his life in refuting it and one of whose bitterest enemies was Bakunin. Not deterred by this fact, of which he was well aware, Berlin[1] with a flourish quoted Marx as declaring, "He who calls for a programme for the coming socialist order, is nothing less than a fool and a reactionary"—evoking a storm of applause from his audience in the Sheldonian Theatre.

What Marx actually said was very different. He rebuked the *Utopian socialists* for "playing with fancy pictures of the future structure of society, which at this stage of affairs can only be basically reactionary."[2] He went on to say that "the doctrinaire and necessarily fantastic anticipation of the programme of action for a revolution of the future only diverts us from the struggle of the present."[3]

All social thinkers are aware that the fictional Utopia, and there have been many from Campanella's *City of the Sun* and Sir Thomas More's *Utopia*, to the *New View* and *Report* of Robert Owen and Edward Bellamy's *Looking Backward*, can never be more than an imaginative exercise and, as Marx declared, when a realistic programme is required by the maturing of conditions which make immediate action possible, utopias are worse than useless. But, as Berlin very well knows, the rejection of utopian dreams is not the same thing as having no principles of social progress and no projects for the steps anticipated for carrying forward the transition to socialism. Marx, and Lenin after him, had a good deal to say about that, and Marx, in particular in his last published work (1875), prepared a constructive critique of the Gotha Programme of the German Social Democrats.

What has to be done when the time comes for action depends on men's ability to understand the possibilities of a highly complex situation. For this the Marxist analysis of social crisis may offer guidance. Then everything depends on judgment, and on the determination and energy to carry a reasonable project to a successful conclusion. The succession of actual situations, each following and arising out

---

[1] Sir Isaiah Berlin knows better. He has written an excellent brief life of Marx and is fully conversant with Marx's repudiation of Bakunin. He also knows quite well as a former professor of political theory that a social philosopher does not have to provide finished blue-prints for the future in order to be taken seriously as a social and political thinker.

[2] *Marx to Sorge*, October 1877.   [3] Marx to Nieuwenhuis, February 1881.

of the other, cannot be anticipated or predicted, and Marx made no attempt to do so—very wisely. Looking back on a period of rapid change and development we can see the causal sequence: but that does not mean that it could have been predicted, or, that it was pre-determined.

Marx, therefore, makes no attempt to lay down the precise sequence of steps in the transition to socialism. Nor does he predict the course they follow. He is not a fortune teller or a weather prophet. Nevertheless, he has a great deal of understanding of the causes and conditions of social maladjustment, and of the trend of economic reorganisation necessary to overcome them; and he has a great deal of light to throw on the social forces and new groupings which arise in such crises, and the trend of political struggles in which they engage.[1] He thus provides the kind of understanding of the situation which in our time is emerging, which is of invaluable help when we come to probe in realistic terms the "logic of situation" confronting us.

So far from confidently predicting success, Marx fully realises the chances and perils of the revolutionary struggle. In 1848 in *The Communist Manifesto*, at one of his most optimistic moments, he says that the struggle may not end in victory, but in "the common ruin of the contending classes". In 1850, repudiating the demand of his associates for "revolution now", he declared that the workers "must go through fifteen, twenty, perhaps even fifty years of war and civil war, not only in order to alter existing conditions but even to make themselves fit to take over political power." In 1852 he was despairing of the British workers at that time: "This most bourgeois of nations is apparently aiming at the possession of a bourgeois aristocracy and a bourgeois proletariat as well as a bourgeoisie."

Writing to Liebknecht on February 11, 1878, he complained that "the English working class has been gradually more and more deeply demoralised by the period of corruption since 1848 and has at last got to the point when they are nothing more than the tail of the Liberal Party. Their direction has gone completely over into the hands of the corrupt trade union leaders". He was far from anticipating an immediate revolution in England.

What working-class movement, then, did Marx at that time consider as on the point of winning the world for socialism, or as having any chance of doing so in the immediate future? The answer must be

[1] See, for example, *The Eighteenth Brumaire of Louis Bonaparte* for the manœuvres and critiques and inter-play of forces in France in 1851.

—none. So much for the frequent assertions that Marx anticipated an immediate revolutionary uprising of the proletariat of Western Europe.

Socialism is for Marx not even the *inevitable* outcome of human history.

"It cannot be produced by economic fatalism, nor by some mysterious finality of history, nor by a decree of 'society'. The living individuals acting on its behalf may be defeated. Humanity may enter into confusion and chaos. The solution is indicated within the total movement; it gives a direction to our view of the future, to our activities and our consciousness, it does not abolish them. How could economics and social automatism be brought to an end automatically?"[1]

Has Marx then no prevision of the future? Indeed he has, but it is limited, provisional and lacks any kind of predictive finality. It is often said that his predictions have been falsified. He made none of the character suggested, few of any kind. What is remarkable is not how few of his anticipations were verified, but how many.

He did not predict the coming of revolution in the industrial West in the near future. Indeed, he said that the first break through might well be in a backward country being developed by Western capitalism. Discussing the contradictions making capitalism decline, he says:

"This contradiction need not necessarily come to a head in this particular country. The competition with industrially more advanced countries, brought about by the expansion of international intercourse, is sufficient to produce a similar contradiction in countries with a backward industry."[2]

As was the case in Russia in 1917. Indeed, many years later Marx anticipated the outbreak of revolution in Russia, not in the advanced industrial West. He thought that as a consequence, Russia could effect the transition from feudalism to socialism without having to go through the painful years of bourgeois capitalist development. He did, however, expect the revolution in Russia to spread rapidly to the West, where it would find the conditions ripe for the transition

[1] Henri Lefebvre, *Dialectical Materialism.*   [2] *German Ideology*, Part I.

to socialism; and he saw the revolution not as occurring in one isolated country, but as a world phenomenon.

On the insuperable difficulties of capitalism Marx was right, in spite of the optimism of the late fifties, and "the end of ideology" talk, which saw the triumph of "democratic socialism". It is not possible to think or write in that vein any longer. It is certainly not the view of our economists today, or of authorities like Professor Galbraith who says, referring to the world economic crisis of 1929–31: "The only thing certain on the fortieth anniversary of the 1929 debacle is that some day, without fail, there will be another disaster." Professor Leontiev of Harvard would agree with him, and go farther. Speaking of Marx's "brilliant analysis of the tendencies of the capitalist system" he also bears witness to "the truth of his theory of the inescapable obstacles to economic expansion."

"The record is indeed impressive: increasing concentration of wealth, rapid elimination of small and medium sized enterprises, progressive limitation of competition, incessant technological progress accompanied by an ever-growing importance of fixed capital and last but not least, the undiminished amplitude of recurrent business cycles—an unsurpassed series of prognostications."[1]

Marx believed that the growing contradictions of our society clearly point to the necessity of radical structural change; but he does not imagine that the course of the transition "can be predicted with the certainty of an eclipse", or will take place automatically and with inevitability. On the contrary, what happens will depend upon human understanding, decision and responsibility. He sees this comprehension arising in the class most closely identified with the developing forces of production, and which experiences the pressure of its oppressive working on their own lives. He sees in their organised strength the most likely instrument of economic and political re-organisation. He is also aware of the inevitable resistance of those whose economic interests are bound up with the existing system and who will be unwilling to acknowledge that the time has come to supersede it. Necessary change necessarily involves struggle and this will become in the end a political struggle for the control of state power.

Economic and political forces alone, however, are not sufficient

[1] Proceedings of the 56th Annual Meeting of the American Economic Association.

for this task. Ideological conflict, preceding political victory, is of primary importance. The ideas and institutions comprising the supporting ideology of the existing order must be subject to radical criticism, and other ideas must replace them, and other institutions be fought for. Marx regards the development of a new consciousness as the necessary prerequisite of social change. Ideas are not merely secondary, the reflection of established institutions, of the social structure as it is. If so, change would be impossible. The difficulties and anomalies of the system in its last stages of development give rise to *critical* ideas, especially in those who bear the brunt of these contradictions. These are the effective agencies of further change. Thus, when an economic system develops contradictions obstructing its further growth, the effect on men's minds is not a mere reflection of the fact so that they have to accept the situation. On the contrary it results in criticism and the alteration of structure of the economy.

The essence of Marxism is here. Social change does not happen of itself, so that we become conscious of it and acquiesce in it or find ourselves taking part in it, swept along on the tide of history. Without man's understanding of his economic situation, and that means his discovery that economic law and its consequence—the hitherto uncontrolled forces of the market—is a temporary, imperfect historical phenomenon, overdue for demolition, an obstruction to social progress without this understanding, the impersonal laws of capitalist society move irresistibly, not towards socialism, but to economic paralysis, the permanent subordination of the working class, further decline and decadence, to the end of our civilisation.

Marx sees the role of consciousness as *understanding*, and the development of that understanding to *criticism* of received ideas and existing realities. Before the majority revolution there must arise a movement of men that doubts the built-in virtue and final truth of existing institutions. Whoever excuses them or justifies them, whatever his hopes and actions in pursuit of a better society, is himself a paralysing and not a liberating force.

Marx sees this development of consciousness appearing in an advanced, a matured economic situation, and not before. Its indispensable function is to free the world from all existing formulations of the present state, its social and political structure, and the economic laws of capitalism. Therefore Marxist thought is not imagined as a *doctrine* which has to be taught to men before they can be effective in changing the world.

There is no "theory" standing over against the world, only a changing society. That is why what Marx saw and understood in 1860 is not what we see and try to understand today. We have to develop our own understanding of our world. Truth is not the doctrine but in the situation, as Marx well knew:

"We must not say to the world, listen to us for we possess the real truth. Instead we must show the world why it struggles, and that consciousness is something which it *must* acquire even if it does not desire to do so. The reform of consciousness consists only in this and thus one makes the world master of its consciousness, that one awakens it from its dream about itself, that one explains to it its own actions."[1]

Marx sees this stage of the development of man as the end of a long historical process which the anthropologists and the historians have described. At each stage man improves his control of the environment by some form of economic, that is to say social, organisation, related to the level of his technology. In building his social order he makes himself—his mentality, his institutions and his culture matches the social pattern. His pattern for thousand of years has been a class pattern in the sense that the privileged have used the unprivileged as slaves, as serfs, and now as labourers; it has created its own modes of thinking, its ethics, its ideology, its values, and above all its human types.

The capitalist system is seen by Marx as the highest and most productive plane of economic development so far; but its economic methods lose their progressive character in the last phase of its progress. It is at this stage that man finds himself under the sway of forces and principles which the economist treats as the absolute and inescapable objective laws of his system. Men are deluded into thinking that these laws and institutions which they themselves have made exist independent of their will and must for ever exercise power over them. Today they do not facilitate economic growth and secure human freedom—they restrict and obstruct, and they frustrate. The awareness which is now for the first time possible, because the whole structure cries aloud for basic reorganisation, reveals the social cause of this frustration and obstruction, and gives rise to man's determination to change the system. It is at this time that consciousness withdraws from the old

[1] Marx-Engels *Gesamtausgabe*, Vol. I, pp. 345–6.

theoretical systems, economic theories, institutions and ideologies to re-create society with new thinking, a new economy and new institutions. The last phase demands this extent and depth of understanding before man can enter the period of transition to a socialist society.

Marx devoted much thought, over the whole of his life, to the problems of man's conscious participation in social development. It was the core of his philosophy of man. But he does not formulate one consistent and final theory. This was characteristic of all his work. He never felt that he had said the final word on any subject. It always lay open for further criticism and re-statement. This was the case with the sequence of theories he advanced between 1848 and 1875 on the transition from capitalism to socialism. We have here not one pattern, but three contrasting patterns or models, advanced at different stages and reflecting changing conditions over a long period. They can briefly be described as the pattern of *minority revolution*, the pattern of *majority rule*, and the pattern of *competing systems and peaceful transition*. The tactical disputes between these methods still divide Marxian socialists.

1. The Minority Revolution

Although Marx only considered this possibility for a very few years at the outset of his political career, this tactic has frequently been revived and followed. It took its origin theoretically from Blanqui[1] who believed in the revolutionary leadership of an élitiest type, and particularly from the circumstances of the German Revolution of 1848. Although Marx always differs from Blanqui (later to a greater degree than in 1848), in 1850, in the formation of the "Universal Association"[2] the signatories included three members of the Communist League, including Marx and Engels, and two Blanquists. Its aim was "to overthrow the privileged classes, to subject them to

---

[1] Blanqui was a revolutionary socialist who proposed to overthrow existing society by the *coup de main* of a small revolutionary élite, who would after their victory impose their will upon the whole of society, including the working class. Though sympathising with the masses, Blanqui had neither a socialist theory nor definite proposals for improvement; nor had he any need for the participation of the workers in the struggle for socialism, or their education and enlightenment. Marx had little use for this "phantasy of overturning an entire society through the action of a small conspiracy".

[2] It has to be remembered that these societies, with imposing titles were not mass organisations: indeed they had no general membership at all but consisted of small groups of devoted revolutionaries, often in exile. Blanqui conceived every revolution as a coup pulled off by a small revolutionary minority.

the dictatorship of the proletariat, and to continue the permanent revolution until the attainment of socialism". What did this mean?

The German Revolution was a struggle for constitutional government and nothing more. Marx and Engels returned to Germany to take part in it, and deliberately put the whole question of socialism aside for the purpose. But they had in mind after a victory of all the Liberal sections of the movement, from the big bourgeoisie to the small men, the farmers, and the workers, a *further* struggle, first against the big bourgeoisie, and finally to secure political power for the proletariat. This was what was meant by "the permanent revolution". There was no suggestion of the victorious proletariat representing a majority, even of the working class and peasantry; but it was anticipated that the measures of reform they would introduce would *eventually* win the support of the majority.

The Revolution was in fact defeated. Marx found that in any case the proletariat was not nearly sufficiently advanced for the task it was given to perform. He therefore broke with those of his associates who were still committed to the policy of "socialism now", whom he accused of replacing "critical observation with dogmatism; a materialist attitude with an idealist one".[1] From now on Marx believed that only the worsening of economic conditions would give the revolutionists the possibility of rousing the workers. For a short while he hoped that the economic crisis of 1857 might provide the opportunity, but his thoughts had already moved from the tactic of the Minority Revolution to an entirely different conception.

The *locus classicus* for the rejection of the Minority Revolution is Engels' Introduction to *The Class Struggles in France*. Here Engels explains why he and Marx abandoned the tactic of minority dictatorship: "History has proved us wrong."

But the rejection of the possibility of "revolution now" was based on further reasons; the economic pre-conditions had been ignored. *Had* "all the productive forces capitalism has room for" been developed? Blanqui had entirely overlooked, or rejected, the theory of productive forces and relations, the theory of primary economic change in social developments, and the fact that social consciousness can only arise if social facts have reached the point of giving rise to revolutionary ideas.

[1] Marx's supporter Schram went so far as to fight a duel with Willich, in which Schram was slightly wounded.

As Marx began to understand this,[1] his tactical thinking began to move towards the patterns of working for a drastic change in working-class consciousness as conditions worsened, and of agitating for the formation of a separate working-class party, opposing all other parties previously formed by the possessing classes (Statute of the First International, 1864).

Engels in his Introduction to Marx's *The Class Struggle in France*, sums up the reasons for the change of tactics:

"The time of surprise attacks, of revolutions carried through by small conscious minorities at the head of unconscious masses is past. . . . With the successful utilisation of universal suffrage, however, an entirely new method of proletarian struggle came into operation, and this method quickly developed further. . . . And so it happened that the bourgeoisie and the government came to be much more afraid of the legal than of the illegal action of the worker's party."

2. The Majority Revolution

Marx anticipates a growing unification of the workers in their unions and the spread of political consciousness because of the inevitable pressure of economic conditions. It was generally believed at that time that universal suffrage would inevitably mean the victory of the proletariat on the political field. The idea of the workers voting for the political parties of the capitalists was unthinkable.

When Marx helped Guesde in 1880 to frame the programme of the French Socialist Party, he wrote into it the clause which declared that such political aims "must be sought for by all means available to the proletariat, including universal suffrage, which can be transformed from an instrument of deception—as up to now it has been—into an instrument of emancipation." Marx saw the electoral struggle not only as a means to majority rule, but as an important means for organising and educating the workers.

When that majority had been won, Marx saw the results as "the democratic rule of the immense majority in the interests of the immense majority". Marx is now speaking, not of "dictatorship" in the sense of minority rule by force, but "proletarian rule" on the basis of a

[1] Marx nowhere explicitly rejects his former tactic and embraces the tactic of the Majority Revolution. But the new policy is very clearly stated in all his activities in connection with the First International.

political victory for the majority. The revolutionary dictatorship of a representative body is not contrary to democracy, but is an energetic way of action by the new democratic institutions to abolish the old undemocratic ones and to safeguard the new democracy's own existence and extension. This involves a thorough-going reconstruction of the institutions of the bourgeois state. Marx recognised that this would be most likely to provoke resistance.

This policy did not suggest that the winning of elections was a substitute for the revolutionary conquest of power. It was a preparation for it. The political revolution, therefore, precedes the social revolution, leading to a majority revolution which now exercises dictatorship over the recalcitrant minority. When the working class wins political power, it will use "political coercion to continue its class struggle against the capitalists until the economic conditions which give rise to classes have been abolished or transformed. The dictatorship will last as long as this process of social transformation."[1]

It is important that we should see that Marx, *at this stage*, sees no possibility of taking any real steps to socialism *before* obtaining power, even though the working-class struggle can stave off attacks on wages and improve conditions.

It might be thought that this is the last form of Marx's tactics, but in his *Inaugural Address* of 1864 he opens a new perspective where he cites instances of socialist institutions developing inside capitalist society. Is it, after all, possible to develop capitalist industry and bourgeois institutions *in the direction of socialism* to a much greater degree than had been supposed possible even though revolutionary change is still necessary to complete this development and establish a socialist order? This brings us to

3. *The Pattern of Competing Systems and Peaceful Transition*

The possibility of improving conditions under capitalism and of carrying forward important modifications of capitalism itself led to several competing patterns of transition. The first, which was developed by Bernstein, saw this process as carrying with it the necessary political changes anticipated by socialists. You cannot change society industrially *without* changing it politically, he argued. Therefore capitalism *becomes* socialism by an evolutionary process.

Kautsky, on the other hand, while he agreed with Bernstein up to the point of *starting* within capitalism the process of transformation

[1] Stanley Moore, *Three Tactics*, quoting Marx's reply in Bakunin's *Statehood and Anarchy*.

(just as capitalism has started within feudalism), held that the process could not be completed without winning power. For Kautsky you were a "reformist" if you held that the transition to socialism could be started *and finished* without political victory—the political elements being products and phenomena of the industrial.

How far did Marx himself travel in this direction, which departs radically from the tactics both of the Permanent Revolution and of the Majority Revolution? This raises three questions:

(a) How far can real improvements in working-class conditions proceed under capitalism?

(b) Did Marx recognise any structural changes within capitalist industry in the direction of socialism?

(c) What views did Marx hold as to the possibility of a peaceful transition to socialism by democratic means?

(a) On the first issue, Marx always insisted that through trade union pressure hours of labour would be shortened and wages held or increased. He opposed the French and German socialists who asserted that the "iron law of wages" made this impossible. Nor did Marx see the whole working class falling into a condition of impoverishment. He saw the hopeless position of the more or less permanently unemployed, but as Lichtheim says, "There is no warrant for the assertion that Marx expected real wages to fall until the entire working class was at, or below, subsistence level."[1] The tendency was to keep costs (i.e. wages) as low as possible in view of market pressure, but Marx again and again insisted on the countervailing factor of working-class organisation, including not only trade union pressure but the established standard in any particular country in any particular trade, which might be well above the average. So that the job of the working class is to take advantage of every means available, industrial and political, to improve its position where possible, to win victories on the wages front, to secure all possible reforms. Marx never ceased to urge this and himself to take an active part in these day-to-day struggles.[2]

As to "increasing misery", attempts have been made to justify the phrase as referring to the reserve army of the unemployed, or to a relative increase in the gap between rich and poor in spite of a very

[1] Lichtheim, *Marxism, An Historical and Critical Study*, p. 189.
[2] See the *Minutes of the First International*.

real improvement in conditions or to the increasing insecurity of the working class in a period of permanent crises and the threat of war.

But it can hardly be denied that since the Second World War, although the working class does suffer many disadvantages, much poverty still remains, and the gains won by hard struggle are in real danger of erosion by inflation, unemployment and the curtailment of social welfare, the standard of the majority of workers has risen.

This position is already being attacked and, if capitalism continues to govern economic development, the present economic situation seems more likely to lead to "gradualism in reverse gear", and real decline, than further improvements and greater security.

(b) On the second question, attention must be drawn to the long and important sections in Capital, Volume III, on the rise of the Co-operative Societies and on the development of capitalist amalgamations and the disappearance of the owner entrepreneur, who is replaced by a salaried managing director. In these chapters, describing the coexistence of the new and old, Marxism appears to affirm the thesis that the economic transition to socialism can start before the working class attain power.

But progress can only go so far. The contradictions which Marx had demonstrated to exist in capitalism will inevitably obstruct further development. Therefore the time must come when the developments within capitalism in the direction of socialism must give place to a struggle for political power, in order that these potentialities can be realised.

(c) Did Marx himself believe that this power could be obtained by constitutional means and the transition to socialism be effected by peaceful means? In fact Marx on several occasions expressed the view that the peaceful transition to socialism was possible for countries with democratic constitutions. The very general belief that Marx worked for a violent uprising, the overthrow of constitutional government and the establishment by force of a revolutionary dictatorship is entirely false, though critics of Marx frequently believe that "Marx expected that the revolution would be violent and perhaps bloody, and its success would depend upon smashing the state."[1] The Observer, reporting on student unrest, is of the same opinion: "Karl Marx, in putting the use of violence onto a pseudo-scientific basis and endorsing his theories with the attitudes of a neo theology, bears some historical

[1] Acton, What Marx Really Said.

responsibility for both Stalin and Hitler."[1] There could hardly be a more total misrepresentation of Marx's view than what is attributed to Marx in these two statements. In an interview with *The World* on July 3, 1871, Marx formulated his position in these words:

"In England the way is open to the working class to develop their political power how they will. There an uprising would be foolishness, when the goal can be reached more quickly and certainly through peaceful agitation."

At Amsterdam in 1872 Marx said that "we do not deny that there are certain countries, such as the United States and England, in which the workers may hope to secure their ends by peaceful means." He went on to say that in those continental countries where democratic constitutions do not exist, the State machine must be overthrown; but that it is not necessary in Britain. But as he said elsewhere on many occasions, it can and must be reconstructed after electoral victory. Engels takes the same position;

"Where popular representation concentrates all power in itself, where one can do constitutionally what one will as soon as one has the majority of the people behind one, in democratic republics like France and America, and in monarchies like England where the dynasty is powerless against the will of the people, there the old society can grow peacefully into the new."[2]

On the Erfurt Programme of the German Social Democrats, Engels declared that

"If one thing is certain it is that our Party and the working class can only come to power under the form of the democratic republic. This is ever the specific form for the dictatorship of the proletariat."

Marx, in his *Critique of the Gotha Programme* had also said that

"the class struggle has definitely to be fought to a finish in the ultimate political form of bourgeois society."

---

[1] *The Observer*, October 27, 1960.
[2] Engels, *Zur Kritik des Sozialdemokratischae Programmestwherfes, 1891*.

Although Marx held this view, "he certainly never forgot to add" says Engels, "that he hardly expected the English ruling classes to submit, without a 'pro-slavery' rebellion, to this 'peaceful and legal' revolution." Could this be averted, perhaps, by compensating the capitalists? Engels reports that "Marx told me (and how often!) that in his opinion we would get off most cheaply if we could buy out the whole lot of them."[1] Lenin subsequently concurred. In *Left Wing Communism* he declares that

"it was perfectly admissible to think of paying the capitalists well, of giving them ransom, if the circumstances were such as to impel the capitalists, providing they were bought off, to submit peacefully and to pass over to socialism in a cultured, organised manner."

As we have already pointed out, Marx did not see the necessity for "smashing the state apparatus" where political power could be secured democratically, but the first task after that would be an "energetic dictatorship" (meaning "the rule of the immense majority not the minority") "to eliminate the remnants of old institutions, to proclaim the sovereignty of the people . . . work out the new constitution . . . and take the necessary measures to safeguard its own existence and the conquests of the revolution from all attacks."[2]

Social democracy, Engels asserted, would not let itself be provoked in assuming power. But if the reaction should revoke its own rules of legality, it would only fare the worse, for in that case socialists would be free to take the sternest measures to resist counter-revolution. They would not therefore "deny themselves the right to counter any attempt to overthrow the constitution by force". And he rejected the pacifist pleas of those who "demand from us that *we, we alone of them all*, should declare that in no circumstances will we resort to force and that we will submit to every aggression, to every act of violence not only as soon as it is merely formally legal—legal, that is, according to the judgment of our adversaries—but also when it is directly illegal. Indeed no party has renounced the right to armed resistance in certain circumstances. None has ever been able to relinquish this ultimate right."[3]

[1] Engels, *The Peasant War in Germany.*
[2] Marx, articles in *Neues Rheinische Zeitung.*
[3] Engels, *Letter to Bebel*, November 1884.

We have some important contributions from Marx on the problems of transition which electoral victory, or any other forms of obtaining political power, will involve. In 1875, the German Social Democrats drew up a programme for the Gotha Congress of the Party. Marx and Engels prepared an extended criticism of their proposals, which were sent in the form of long letters to Bebel and Brache. The main document is known as *The Critique of the Gotha Programme*.[1]

The *Critique* is as near as Marx ever came to the formulation of a policy for the transition to socialism. And it is almost entirely negative! But guiding concepts for future advance are suggested by these very criticisms.

(1) The German "Marxists" in their Party Programme demanded an equitable distribution of the proceeds of labour. Marx pointed out that the whole product of labour could not be apportioned by wages, since a considerable proportion was required for fresh capital and for social services.

(2) Rejecting the notion of equality of wages for the period of socialism which must precede communism, Marx laid down the principle of remuneration according to value of the work—differential wages. The well-known slogan "to every man according to his needs" was declared to be utopian and postponed to the future as the ultimate goal.

(3) Marx rejected equalitarian principles, pointing out that the rights demanded could never be higher than the economic structure allowed. But rights would be left behind altogether when plenty is available for all. "Then and only then will it be possible to get out from under the narrow perspective of bourgeois rights and society at last will be able to inscribe on its banner: 'From each according to his capacity, to each according to his needs'."

(4) Marx severely criticised the programme for regarding all those outside the organised working class as "one reactionary mass". What about the craftsmen, small industrialists, farmers, and many other groups? Are they to be lumped with the big capitalists as "reactionary" and treated as such? If so, socialism will never be realised.

Marx and Engels always called attention to the importance of the allies of the proletariat. Engels, writing to Bernstein in 1882, says: "The idea that the coming revolution will begin on the basis that the whole world will be divided into two armies—on one side ourselves, and on the other the whole 'reactionary mass', is clearly

---

[1] Not published until 1891, it was closely studied and annotated by Lenin.

a childish one. It is to say that the revolution must begin at Act V and not at Act I, in which the mass of all opposition parties is united against the government and its stupidities, and thereby wins victory." Lenin, too, speaks in the same terms of the importance of the non-class conscious proletarian and semi-proletarian masses, and goes on to say that to imagine that the workers need no allies is tantamount to denying the social revolution altogether. "Whoever expects a 'pure' social revolution will *never* live to see it. Such a person pays lip-service to revolution without understanding what revolution is."[1]

(5) Finally, we come to the State. Marx neither rejected the proposal that within the existing state structure the socialist programme could be carried out nor did he demand that the state should be dissolved. On the contrary, the workers should make full use of state power, but having "won the battle for democracy" the constitutional power in their hands would be used to *establish* democracy at all levels, and this would mean the gradual but complete reconstruction of the state apparatus. "The workers", Marx says in *The Civil War in France*, "cannot simply lay hold of the ready-made machinery of the state and use it for their own purposes." It was created to serve the purposes of another class and of an exploiting and ruling class. It must therefore be democratised from top to bottom, and made responsible to the control and supervision of the people. By "the dictatorship of the proletariat", Marx did not mean the dictatorship of the Party over the proletariat, or the rejection of democratic procedures and the subjugation of the "reactionary mass" by dictatorial rule, but the carrying out of the will of the majority in spite of whatever opposition it met from the defeated minority.

Marx unquestionably believed that a worker's government would be more democratic, more respectful of freedom, and more humane than any of the older governments. He conceived of proletarian government as being, from the very beginning, more truly democratic and liberal than anything known in bourgeois Europe; and by democracy and freedom he meant government truly responsible to the governed, and as scrupulous a regard for the rights of the individual as is compatible with the existence of government. The "dictatorship of the proletariat", as Marx and Engels conceived it, is proletarian democracy. Whatever falling short of Marx's own principles the exigencies of history or the shortcomings of his followers may be responsible for, there can be no doubt what Marx's Marxism stands for.

[1] Lenin, *Collected Works*, Vol. 22, p. 356.

Beyond the establishing of a socialist government, Marx saw not the immediate appearance of a socialist society, but a long period of revolutionary transition from what he called the first stage of socialism to the higher form, which he called communism. It is the guiding principles of this transition which he discusses in the *Critique of the Gotha Programme*.

Clearly he was entirely right to make no attempt to provide the generation whose task it is to enter this period, with blue-prints and instructions. He never lays down doctrines and theories; he always insists on an evaluation of the concrete situation. Clearly the complex of possibilities, difficulties, external pressures of an international character, the immense differences in the societies entering upon this phase—some advanced and already experienced in democratic methods, others backward and with no experience, throw the whole responsibility onto the new democracies themselves.

It is now that man takes the first halting steps to make his own history, to achieve his own destiny, and there are no guarantees against failure. From now on man learns by trial and error.

What remains problematic is whether in the generation for which opportunity opens in the ripeness of time the occasion will be seized. One contemporary Marxist who saw the whole course of revolutionary struggle during the past fifty years has this to say on the possibilities and perils of our times:

"If the chance to make a revolution is missed, then development of the economic forms of capitalism might well proceed along a different course, and the opportunity for revolution would never come again."[1]

[1] George Lukacs, *History and Class Consciousness.*

16

THE INEVITABILITY OF SOCIALISM

It has been supposed that if Marx established a philosophy of history and a theory of social development, this necessarily involves determinism. We are corks swept along on the tides of history; and whether we like it or dislike it, support it or reject it, it makes no matter. Socialism is inevitable. This conclusion might indeed follow if the entire development of reality followed strict dialectical laws in the sense of an irresistible process of contradiction and resolution carrying first nature and then society from lower to higher levels; in which case the laws governing human history would be only special instances of universal principles. In that case, just as stars and planets have been precipitated from nebular vapour, just as vertebrate animals have developed from unicellular life, so, inevitably, will communist society develop out of the contradiction of capitalist society.

However widely this may be accepted; even if some forms of Marxism[1] have been as deterministic as this, there is no support for this position in the writings of Marx. Marx had no dialectical theory of nature and never inserted into nature the Hegelian principle of a logically unfolding contradiction. Marx was concerned only with the dialectic of man's relations with nature, not with nature itself. He discusses man's economic development, therefore, and especially the two historical phases in the development of capitalism: a deterministic phase, followed by the phase of conscious, rational control. It is in the deterministic phase of capitalism that we find "tendencies which work out with an iron necessity towards an inevitable goal". This was not a Marxist discovery. It follows from the capitalist economic theories which explain the operation of the laws of supply and demand, of the monetary mechanism, of prices, of the flow of capital and so forth. Marx develops the understanding of this system to show the difficulties and obstructions it leads to, and the possibility of *intelligence* surmounting them by replacing the capitalist system with the social ownership of resources and their rational control and organisation for human ends. The necessity is confined to the automatic operations of

[1] Notably German Marxism before 1914.

the capitalist system, which are so by definition—its advantages are declared to be that the search for maximum profit, for the employment of capital which secures the best return, works inevitably to produce the highest efficiencey, that is to say the greatest total economic benefit to society. Marx argues that while in its earlier stages capitalism greatly expands production, the welfare of the whole community is ultimately secured only if it is sought deliberately and rationally by society itself.

It is a distortion of the Marxist theory to argue from the inevitable consequences of the operation of *capitalist* economic laws to a similar necessity in the transformation to socialism.

"When capitalism is negated, social processes no longer stand under the rule of blind natural laws. . . . There can be no blind necessity that terminates in a free and self-conscious society. Not the slightest natural necessity or automatic inevitability guarantees the transition from capitalism to socialism."[1]

Wherever we find in expositions of Marxism any form of determinism, we may be sure that we are very far from any theory which can be attributed to Marx, yet it is frequently argued that Marx held a deterministic theory of social development. Thus we find in John Bowle's *Politics and Opinion in the Nineteenth Century*, that he speaks of, "An inevitable pre-determined process, an economic law of motion as ascertainable as the laws of physics." Karl Popper equates what he calls Marxist "historicism" with the predictive methods of Newtonian physics. Marx is supposed to show that if it is possible for astronomy to predict eclipses, then sociology can predict revolutions.[2] He is supposed to have pictured society moving inevitably through pre-determined stages as a consequence of a mystic force, called the historical imperative; this rendering politics impotent and unnecessary.

This conception is supported by the claim that Marxism is a scientific theory. But not all sciences are of the pattern of physics and astronomy. A scientific theory is any theory that is not accepted until it is verified by experiment and observation, and put to the test in practice. And there is a further difference between the theories of natural science and sociological theories in which men and their ideas and actions are concerned.

[1] Marcuse, *Reason and Revolution*, p. 318.
[2] Popper, *The Poverty of Historicism*.

Engels correctly points out that when we come to understand natural law we become its masters. We are no longer merely acted upon by it, we utilize it for our own purposes. This is the first level of human freedom. But if we go on to describe Marxism as a cast-iron system of sociological laws from which the inevitability of socialism can be deduced with mathematical certainty, we have entirely failed to understand what Marx was getting at. Firstly, it is, even on the physical level, a mistake to consider natural laws as having a legislative and coercive authority. They are highly conditional generalisations, and by no means absolute. But, secondly, are there any laws of history like those of physics or chemistry? Marx does not attempt to show that this is the case. On this level we do not take advantage of laws operating independently of ourselves as we do in science. We solve the concrete social problem before us in terms of our intelligence. If we reorganise on the basis of common ownership, we do so not because there is any law compelling us to do so, but because reason shows us that this is the way out of our difficulties.[1]

In these circumstances we may, taking a great variety of factors into consideration, *anticipate* a result that is desirable; and if the situation *demands* action, we can act on the basis of our estimation of the possibilities. We shall, of course, modify our plans as we go forward on the basis of success or failure, and there is plenty of scope for error. This at once shows a fundamental difference from the utilisation of physical laws.

Sir Karl Popper and Professor Ayer have no grounds whatever for saying that Marxism is a theory which is compatible with *any* set of circumstances, being so constructed as to be satisfied whatever the consequences of putting it into effect. Marxist proposals are manifestly liable to failure, or to defects which must be corrected when experience reveals them. Popper and Ayer[2] must have in mind theories which are merely *explanatory*. Such theories can be devised to explain any kind of historical event and they are open to this objection. If, for instance, one says that there is a "providence" that brings ultimate good out of present evil, clearly the existence of present evil does not negate the theory. But there is no Marxist theory which says that, whatever happens, some natural law working independently of human wills is manifested in the event. On the contrary, the Marxist says that if you

[1] A *law* would mean an invariable sequence of cause and effect, but how can this be the case for *one* event in world history?
[2] Popper in *Conjecture and Refutations*, Ayer in *Metaphysics and Commonsense*.

don't understand you will meet with disaster, but if you try to find out what is wrong and by sheer intelligence devise a means of overcoming your difficulty, the result will verify your hypothesis. If it does not, then your hypothesis is mistaken. This is the course pursued, for example, in medicine, in agriculture, in engineering. It proceeds by trial and error, and so far from its hypotheses being compatible with any result, they are subjected to the kind of test which can refute them, or show their defects.

But in the social sciences no *laws* working independently of human wills are involved, since what happens depends wholly on our participation in the situation. It is not, as Popper supposes, that events *will go forward anyway*, and we, seeing that it will be so, get on the band wagon, or "give history a shove"; on the contrary, the desirable result follows *only* if we play our intelligent, co-operative and active role, only if we pursue a *sequence* of controlling decisions, each derived from our renewed estimation of the developing situation which *we* are continuously changing; and if each of our decisions is not too far off the beam. This is not determinism!

It has sometimes been argued that the same forces which create the situation also create the people who will intervene, and determine their thoughts and efforts. This is the oldest form of materialistic determinism. It is a self-defeating theory because it explains and justifies whatever is done or not done. In the long run it can only lead to passivity, to prophecy, to a self-satisfied course of always saying "We told you so", or "It had to happen thus".

There is no suggestion of any such attitude in Marx. What happens is our responsibility. We can fail to respond to the situation; or we can respond erroneously and fail; or not enough of us can respond, and we can fail. For Marx there is no inevitability but on the contrary the alternative: "either socialism or a descent into barbarism". Marxist theories of history do not guarantee against the extermination of society.

There is, however, another kind of predictability, based on an estimation of what men who possess intelligence may be expected to do. We may expect the inventor of the tool (primitive man) to be followed by others who improve the tool. We may expect men, who possess intelligence, to devise the forms of economic organisation which enable them to make the best use of their tools. This, in fact, is what they have done throughout the course of history. Our anticipation is that they will do it again, when the capitalist form of organisation is found to be inappropriate.

Life is full of occasions on which we anticipate the course likely to be followed if people use their wits. There is no determinism here. The determinism would be seen if they did *not* use their intelligence and became the victims of forces they could neither understand nor control. When medical science first discovered cases of bacterial disease, it could be anticipated that the organisms responsible for other diseases would also be discovered, and that preventive measures against infection and other methods of coping with bacteria would eventually follow. It could then be anticipated that many diseases would die out or become rare; that the population would increase and so on. There is no determinism in this. It depends on the continued and progressive exercise of intelligence, on the *use* of new methods, of learning from their use, of experiencing failures as well as sucesses, on qualitative advances (inoculation, vaccination, anti-biotics) and on continued and increasing understanding of the rules of health by the general population. None of these things come about by the operation of natural law by itself, which we merely observe, and then predict the consequence. Everything follows from our intelligent discovery, by the utilisation, improvement and enlargement of our knowledge and our methods.

All this is obvious, not recondite and difficult. We are not plunging into metaphysics or intricate exercises in logic. Why then should difficulties and misunderstandings arise when precisely the same kind of process is going on in the diagnosis of social disease, in new methods of treatment, in considerable "break throughs", comparable to the great discoveries in medicine? Partly it is intellectual conservatism, but it is also, surely, the resistance of vested interests.[1]

This raises the question of the resistance to, and the ideological distortion of, unwelcome ideas in the interests of the *status quo*. The tenacity with which capitalist principles are maintained in the face of criticism and new ways of thinking is surely related to the class interests threatened by a radical change. Marx spoke of "so many bourgeois prejudices behind which lurk in ambush just as many bourgeois interests".

We should be very foolish if we believed that the Walls of Jericho will fall down if we march round and round blowing our trumpets and announcing irrefutable truths. For it is not only that the basic economic principles of capitalism are regarded as well established and inescapable, but we have to contend with other ideological conceptions

[1] Just as witchdoctors resist the coming of modern medical treatment.

and institutions associated with it: the legal system, contemporary ethical standards safeguarding property rights, money values, and a large number of institutions reflecting class privilege and authority, among them religion in certain of its aspects.

This is why Marx insists on an ideological battle which must accompany the direct political struggle. In fact he goes so far as to assert that intellectual victories must precede political victory. This does not mean that we shall have to convince all the interests that stand in the way, but we can do a great deal to shatter their self-assurance and conviction. When power is robbed of the shining armour of scientific, ethical and philosophical theories by which it defends itself, it will fight on without that armour; but it will be more vulnerable and the strength of its enemies will be increased.

It is just as important, if not more important, to undermine the unquestioned acceptance of the prevailing class ideology by the great mass of ordinary people of every condition. If socialism comes, not automatically, but only when the great majority understand and are ready to act, social change depends first and foremost upon the recognition that the whole philosophy, world view, system of legal, moral and economic thinking of our society is open to question.

So far from socialism arriving by the inevitable processes of history and social development, the maturing conditions require a conscious, hard-won battle of ideas, a revolution in the mind, and the active, responsible and energetic entry of millions of people into the difficult business of changing existing institutions. This is very far from an inevitable automatic process of evolutionary development.

Here we must meet a very reasonable objection: is it not intellectually indefensible to declare about any system of beliefs that its only justification is that it serves class interests? If that were really what we are doing, it would indeed be reprehensible; but that is not our position. The psychological, economic or social course of peoples' beliefs have no bearing on the evidence which makes them true or false. No one has any right to look for unconscious motives and determinants in the thinker instead of first examining the validity of the arguments themselves. Whether we are concerned with the question of capitalism, or of Marxism, the case must be debated on its own merits. It is only when the case for capitalism, as its own defenders state it, has broken down, that we have the right to ask *why* such a shaky case should be maintained, *why* its exponents will not for a moment even consider the Marxist case, or, if they do, only after they have themselves restated it in a way which exposes it to easy refutation. The unmasking of ideologies, in the sense of showing the class interests that prompt them, is only in place when the belief that is unmasked has been shown to be without adequate foundation.

Determinism is characteristic not of socialism but of capitalism itself, as manifested in the irresistible operations of economic law in slumps, crises, unemployment, inflation. The only way to freedom is by escape from the determinism of the capitalist economic system; but the only way of escape is by overcoming first of all the illusions of the epoch, the ideologies, which hold the mind in thrall. The goal of history, said Hegel, is freedom; and so said Marx. The only inescapable system of law that Marx finds is in the laws which the economists themselves insist we *must* obey. Marx begins his writings by reflecting on the slavery of the capitalist system, and the alienation in which it involves its victims. He is concerned with one theme from these beginnings in 1843 to his death forty years later, and that is freedom. *Capital* is concerned to show, as capitalist economists then and since have also been at pains to demonstrate, that capitalism requires of us submission to its rules. But Marx's intention is to show that these laws belong to the historically conditioned *structure* of a given society, the pattern of its social relations—in this case the relations between investing employers needing an adequate return, and propertyless workers selling their labour at the market price. It is this structure and its operations that give rise to the law system, which is therefore not part of the eternal and absolute nature of economic life as such, but temporary and passing. It is the aim of Marx to show how one law system gives way to another, and how ultimately that *kind* of imposition from without belongs to a particular form of human association but gives way to the freedom of *rational* control of resources in a different one. Thus he is revealing the periodic phases of social re-organisation, directed by human intelligence under changing conditions—not determined by the conditions, but by the mind and will of men. This, as Cornforth says, "is not, and could not be, a law governed process in the strict determinist sense that there are pre-ordained laws which allow nothing to happen except what does happen."[1]

The question for man, in relation to nature, is how to make use of its laws; the question for man, in relation to *society*, is how to transcend

[1] M. Cornforth, *The Open Philosophy and the Open Society.*

the law system of a class society and its determinism, and find freedom in a class-less society.

But does not Marx insist that all men are controlled by economic motives? If it is not the sytem that determines us for ever, is it not the built in disposition of "economic man"? In that case, would not Marx be revealing an inner psychological drive as irresistible as any economic law? This, again, is to interpret Marx in terms of the views he is rejecting. Marx attacks Bentham and the economists precisely because they conceived man on the pattern of an egoistic and bourgeois shopkeeper whose every act is determined by calculation of personal gain. His own view was that the essential nature of man was social, and, in Aristotle's sense, *political*—meaning coming to its fulness in the corporate life of the city, the community. Economic man is distorted, limited, undeveloped and unhappy. Man finds his real self only in fellowship and in work for that common good in which each shares and which alone maximises the personal good of all. It is a mistake, according to Marx, to confuse individualism with personal fulfillment. The man who seeks his own welfare and nothing else becomes retrograde and drags the world back to the level of the beast of prey. He diminishes himself and loses himself. The true personality grows in inverse proportion to its egoism. It is here that Marx is in the fellowship of the Carlyle of *Past and Present*, of Ruskin and Morris, and in our own day of Tawney and the humanist tradition.

There remains the belief that Marx at any rate makes the economic basis the "ultimate" factor in history. If we mean the recognition that we have to secure our subsistence before we can do anything else, then that is indeed so; and the only people who fail to acknowledge it are those whose subsistence is being looked after by other people, who have never endured real poverty, never faced unemployment and always had a roof over their heads. It is the moral superiority of the complacent and the comfortable over the less fortunate; and, rather than an indication of a finer and more spiritual attitude to life, it is a particularly unpleasant and contemptible one. But we secure the basis for ourselves not because we have no desires other than material ones but in order that we can enlarge our needs (and Marx was always talking about that) to include the fulfilment of competence in the crafts and professions, and the re-creation of the spirit in the life of the arts. What Marx is pointing out is that this cannot be achieved by some at the expense of others without spiritual poverty and social insecurity for rich and poor alike.

What has to be made clear is that Marx never separates "the economic factor" as if it could exercise an independent and ultimately final
determination. He never uses such expressions as "in the last analysis
it is the economic factor that prevails", as Engels sometimes does.
There is no *single* determinant. The "economic" pattern which is
thought to be ultimate, is after all an *effect* before it becomes a cause,
and it is always being modified by being made more appropriate to
its job of fulfilling human lives, even if that is to increase the food
supply to overcome world poverty—which our spiritually minded
critics may regard as a low and materialistic aim.

The "economic" never exists outside the always concrete, historically
changing complex of society, including man's spiritual life and its
expression in many varied forms. How does man *begin?* There is no
economic determinant. His own urgent need is not created by a tool.
It urges him to create a tool. At every stage we find the inter-penetra-
tion of needs, means, ideas, political pressures—some stimulating, some
obstructing. Economics is not the *factor* that creates the future; what
comes nearest to it is "association" in the world's necessary work,
which can be of various kinds; and Marx is seeking the association of
co-operative labour and common ownership as the means of personal
fulfillment and the attainment of a *common* good. This, he believes, is
the only way to create "the conditions in which it is possible to be
fully human".

Man as we find him is already, in his society such as it is, doing its
essential work in one way or another, every way being some form of
co-operation, *even under capitalism.* In this society we find customs,
laws, religions, institutions, ideas, moral codes. It is not created by
fate, or by history, or by technology, or by economics, but by man.
He is born into such a form of society and has to adapt himself to it;
but he at once sets to work to develop it and change it, the better to
satisfy his needs and demands. No force, or factor, technological or
evolutionary, does this. *He* does it.

We must not separate the infra-structure (the economic or technological) from the super-structure of institutions and ideas. They are
inseparable, and constitute a developing whole—developing only
through the rational activity of man. Faced with this task or that
problem, this possibility or that challenge, men bring their intelligence
to bear on a variety of issues. They are inventing and improving their
machines, reorganising the factory, legislating, organising trade unions,
educating, engaging in political conflict, philosophising, moralising,

all at once. Change may be proceeding more obviously in the technological field at one time, and in the organisational field at another, or the main issue may be political, or it may be ideological. What we must avoid doing, or we break the unity of a dialectical process, is to separate the technological from the economic and then argue: Which comes first, the hen or the egg? or make the equally grave mistake of separating the ideological from the economic. They are inseparable, but nevertheless distinguishable. But it is impossible to rebuild the integrated concept of the organic whole by juxtaposing the separated aspects of a dialectical unity.

The historical picture is of man bringing nature under control. As he does so he makes and remakes his society through the development at one and the same time of his techniques and his methods of operating them. Always he is creating new needs, not simply satisfying the basic animal needs with which he starts; and this is an essential part of the development of his own personality. "History is the natural history of man," says Marx. His economy and his whole society is a process of continuous change. The dialectical process is that of solving in action the problem posed by one period of change in order to bring about the next.

Well, if it is not the "economic" form of society that is the ultimate determinant, is it the tool, the technology? Is this, when all is said and done, the very heart of Marxism? We have already answered this question, in the negative. Granted that at particular times, social advance demands technological improvement, the *technological base cannot advance by itself*. It is controlled, stimulated and driven forward by mental, social and ideological considerations. Machinery functions and expands under the economic and cultural conditions of rising capitalism, and let us remember that by "economic" we mean a form of human association of a co-operative nature even under capitalism: production *under capitalism* is essentially social, said Marx. When these conditions become inadequate, and no longer allow the rapidity and degree of growth we require, what happens? We begin to *think* about the situation, to search for its inadequacies and flaws. It is changes in our ideas, followed by changes in organisation, that get things moving again—the whole thing very much the activity of minds.

It is this development that creates a new economic structure which again improves and develops the technology. History, said Marx, is "the activity of man in pursuit of his ends". Men will everything on the human level. Whether we are asking how exactly the technology advances, or how it is the economic form is modified, always the answer must be· leading ideas in the minds of engineers, scientists, organisers, stimulated by needs, by ideology, by ethical ideas, by theories; or, if it is the economy we are considering, once again there is no change apart from a dissatisfaction, and a rational investigation of the structure to see how it can be modified and followed by an intelligent and willed process of re-organisation.

The mistake of imagining that the technological level is the final determinant should also be apparent when it is realised that the same technological base underlies both the socialist economy and the capitalist economy in the world today—clearly technique in itself does not determine the mode of economic production.

Underlying much of this fear of determinism is the notion that man is most free if he can get away from the obligations and restraints of communal life. He thinks he can do so if he creates a system in which every man is *free* to follow his own economic interests and there is a minimum of interference. When he does so, he finds he has set in motion destructive economic forces which he cannot control. Where is his freedom? By his individual economic freedom he has created un-freedom. What he then cries for is release from the pressures of the very society he has thus created. If he secured it, he would only find himself where he was at the beginning.

How economic individualism under the banner of freedom creates its opposite, while socialism rooted in social obligations and respon-sibilities secures and realises it, is perhaps the most important of all the discoveries of Karl Marx.

17

MARXISM AND HUMAN FREEDOM

Man has to learn that there are different kinds of restraint and obligation. There are those which are imposed on him by the mechanism of a capitalist society, where the good of *that* society is not the good of all but of some, and the rest suffer coercion, either of class law, class privilege, the state of that privileged class, or of economic law. *That* is determinism. There are also the restraints and obligations he could willingly accept because they alone secure the maximum common good, which is not the good of the state, but by democratic control and purpose the good of all. That service and bondage alone is freedom.

There is one other road to freedom that gets nowhere. The *existentialist* is perfectly right when he says that choice must not be coerced. But he is wrong when he says that to choose with a *reason*, to choose what rational enquiry shows to be the effective way to secure the desired end, is to abandon free choice. There is a distinction between a compelled choice, and a reasoned choice. If one does not make this distinction, then the free choice is wholly arbitrary and without reason. That is either impossible or a form of madness. Real freedom is the freedom we find if we *know* what to do. *Knowledge* is the key to freedom, not the absence of compulsion.

But if socialism requires us to submit to the irresistible laws of social change, and if those laws are formulated by the theoretical authority which can insist on obedience to them as the only sure way to socialism, then there emerges not only an orthodoxy involving the disappearance of free enquiry, but an autocracy replacing democracy—turning into rigidity even things which ought to be the exemplification of elasticity.

A Marxist system of social science might become an orthodoxy carrying with it the authority to declare what its laws are exactly and how they are to be applied; as such it could represent the ideology of a bureaucracy.

"The most dogmatic philosophies are all bound up with one or another bureaucracy, for every bureaucracy possesses a system of knowledge in self-justification, which sets standards for filling its ranks and promoting its members, for legitimising the hierarchical order."[1]

Sartre is right when he says that any system of laws, which are laws in the same sense as the laws of physical science, though relevant to society, negates freedom and the independence of the human person—and expresses and continues a state of alienation. A man cannot be a person if he is merely a cog in the mechanism of history—even if he is a conscious cog, aware of necessity and finding his freedom in acquiescing in it. Sartre felt, however, that his strictures were not directed against Marx "but against the Marxist scholasticism of 1949". He was probably correct.

Such laws are supposed to be derived by logical inference from the empirical data of society. But the laws of that society today are those capitalist economics, along with other generalisations from the same data in contemporary society. Such laws could only conform to conditions as they are. We want a theory to do precisely the opposite—to take us *beyond* existing conditions and reverse the laws derived from and constituting the existing order.

If ideas, as the older materialism and some forms of Marxism (but not Marx) believe, *reflect* objective reality, they cannot possibly help us to transcend it. They can only transfer to our minds the ideology which is natural to the ruling class, along with the contradictions, the growing irrationality and the consequent despair. Ideas which lead to liberation must not reflect but be a *critique* of the existing order and its ideology; in which case they are not limited by the conditions within which they work, for it is these they have to criticise.

It must follow that a socialist ideology[2] will not consist of empirical *laws*. A moment's thought makes it clear why. Laws are concerned with conditions that recur frequently and in which we are in control of the variables, or can neglect them as irrelevant. In history, conditions are seldom if ever repeated, nor can the independent variables be neglected. Whatever theory we produce therefore cannot be a blue-print, a long distance strategy, a prediction—it never was

[1] Henri Lefebvre, *The Sociology of Marx*.
[2] We are now using this term in a different sense from that of a false consciousness; reminding ourselves that Marx did too. Here it means a system of ideas, a world view, a philosophy of socialism.

I

so for Marx. It cannot, that is to say, be the application of scientific laws. It is directed by certain *principles* however, which are not *laws*. They will be these familiar Marxist concepts:

We see man as increasing his control of nature by improving his technology and by improved economic systems.

We see him in the future replacing class society by one which will give opportunity for the rational control now lacking.

The logic of the contemporary situation is illuminated by this understanding and now requires of us an immediate programme worked out on the basis of the logic of the actual situation. Every such programme is advanced only as working hypothesis, not as the application of fixed law. As such, a hypothesis is tested and corrected in action.

Its utility can only be of short duration, because the more effective it is the more it alters the situation, which then acquires a logic of its own, requiring new plans. We thus feel our way forward, without dogmatism, without a law system, but not without a guiding theory. This is why Marx rejects the notion of a systematic theory which has to be put into practice, and substitutes for it *praxis*: the understanding of the immediate problem and active grappling with it. The whole process being an attempt to re-organise the economy rationally, which means transcending present economic law—a paradigm shift.

This is Marx's middle way, his dialectical way, between empiricism and metaphysics (or theoretical systems), always measuring social actuality against historical possibility. This is an effective world-changing *praxis*, guided by the end of collective control in the collective interest.

Sartre puts this very well, but fails to recognise that he is describing Marx's Marxism.

"What is needed, in a word, is a philosophical theory which shows that human reality in action, and that action upon the universe, is identical with the understanding of that universe as it is, or in other words, that action is the unmasking of reality, and, at the same time, a modification of that reality. . . . The possibility of *rising above* a situation in order to get a perspective on it—a perspective which is not pure knowledge but an indissoluble linking of understanding and action—is precisely that which we call freedom."[1]

This is the kind of venture that demands not blind obedience and the faithful application of doctrinaire schemes, but the conception of an open society the course of whose development can only be decided as we venture forward, learning how to proceed by the success and failure of our provisional working hypothesis. There is nothing we can predict here except in the most general terms, which, as a guide to immediate action, would necessarily be inadequate. Even our stated aims and values are constantly being changed and developed by experience, giving rise to new demands and creating new possibilities. Man is creating both his world and himself as he goes forward. He is not imitating a plan laid up in the heavens. His goal is whatever increasingly satisfies more people, more completely and more permanently.

"What he is doing is, in effect, so to arrange the empirical world that in it man experiences and gets used to what is really human and that he becomes aware of himself as man."[2]

What kind of a world that will be, we can envisage in no greater detail than what is indicated in the basic principles of a Marxist theory of man, society and their history. We, ourselves, are the creators, the valuators, and the final judges of what is good.

In the whole body of his work Marx never lays down either a theory of historical development

"It is never possible to arrive at this understanding by using the passe-partout of some historical-philosophical theory whose great virtue is to stand above history",[3]

or a programme for the revolution. Marx could be dogmatic in the sense that he had strong convictions based on critical understanding, but he presented no dogmas, no doctrines presented as absolute and final, to be transmitted to his disciples and accepted as true for all time and all occasions. Nor did Marx present in the forty years of his

---

[1] Sartre, *Materialism and Revolution*.
[2] Marx, *The Holy Family* (Quelch translation), p. 176.
[3] Marx, letter to the Editor of *Notes on the Fatherland*, end of 1877.

I*

writing one organised theoretical position, consistent and systematised, which could be relied upon to provide solutions for all problems. That he provided "the key to all historical locks" was a claim which, as Lenin said, "was refuted by Marx instantly". On the contrary, his thought developed and changed and his formulations were directed to the successive historical situations in which he found himself, which differed drastically.

All complete explanatory systems of philosophy depend upon unquestionable assumptions as the source and guarantee of such doctrines, and there is no known system of metaphysics or logic which has ever been able to justify such claims, which are certainly not made for nor could they be justified, by science. All scientific theories are provisional, fall short of finality and absolute truth, and are verified only up to the point of giving us a working and partial truth—true as far as it goes.

This is all that we can know of the regular processes of nature, which can be repeated and are therefore capable of being verified or refuted by experiment. But social theories concern the complex reality of concrete life which involves events that are never repeated, a stream of independent variables and, above all, the infinite undependability of individual motives and judgment. Since history never repeats itself, a "theory" of history can never be tested experimentally as scientific "theories" can.

Nevertheless, in our everyday life we live by what light we have and that increases. We can feel our way forward, and we can gather wisdom from experience. The degree of our insight and the quality of our judgment must always fall short of anything like certainty, but we can be wiser after the event, when we examine the causes and effects as they have occurred, than we were before it happened.

Marx made no prediction like those we make in physics or astronomy, and left us no blue prints, no programmes, but only his method of approaching things and capacity to evaluate the logic of the situation.

Truth is to be sought *in the situation* itself, not in an abstract theory standing over against the facts. This is what Marx called *praxis*. Lenin did not find the strategy and tactics he adopted in 1917 anywhere in Marx, for Marx had never examined or anticipated such a situation. But he found enough guidance in Marx's methods to enable him to make his own judgments and stake his very existence on them. How far he was successful history has shown.

What we learn from Marx can only be whatever clarifies the situation in which we find ourselves, its value is shown even in how far subsequent experience shows that we did recognise what the situation demanded. The truth is in the facts, not in the book It is in the estimation of the balance of forces, and success depends not only on the circumstances but on the intelligence, will and courage of the men who take advantage of them. It depends on our own intervention and that of those we persuade to join us; but also on the success or failure of those who disagree with us and act against us. The factors in a physical experiment do not act in novel and unpredictable ways because they are unconscious of what is happening. The men on whose behaviour historical events depend do, and everything depends on their understanding and their responsibility. That is why you can predict with considerable accuracy the results of physical forces but historical events are not as predictable as eclipses! Even there we are lucky to reach a degree of probability.

That is also why we must continuously check and revise our political hypotheses by a self-correcting process of trial and error. When we do so, we shall find, as Lenin did, that after working for a few months on one plan, we are changing our directives and operating with new theories derived from the situation already changed by the actions based upon our original estimation. This is why 90 per cent of Lenin's writing consists of *ad hoc* estimations, analyses, interpretations and directives concerning an ever-changing situation—the situation that *he* was changing.

Marxism is frequently combed for texts to support policies bearing little relation to any situation anticipated by Marx or towards which his hopes were directed. The implied suggestion is that Marx's writings constitute a sort of Revolutionists' Handbook, with strategic plans, tactical instructions and ready-made blue prints for a great variety of "revolutions" in all sorts of conditions, none of which, as a matter of fact, were in his mind at all. He foresaw a Russian Revolution and the possibility of a transition to socialism which avoided the worst horrors of the industrial revolution, and he thought that it might be the spark to ignite the Western revolution. But his theories and his concrete studies were not concerned, as he himself said, with any overall plan for all countries and cultures, but with the development of capitalism up to the point when "*all the productive forces, for which there is room in it, have been developed*", *and the material conditions for the higher relation of production have matured.* He never says that this is just round the corner, he never suggests a sudden catastrophe and the rise of the New Jerusalem from the flames of capitalism.

The transition he suggests, may be long and difficult.[1] He does not lay down plans or give instructions for effecting revolutionary change; he does not even predict that it will necessarily be violent. Marxism is concerned with the whole historical period in which the transition to socialism takes place—which may extend to a century or two centuries. The rise of feudalism from the ruins of the Roman civilisation or of capitalism from the economy of the renaissance and the succeeding economies, were protracted affairs, yet they were, according to Marx, not nearly such radical changes as that which we are to experience in the transition to socialism.

The transition from capitalism to socialism will be a long, intricate and confused affair involving the whole thought pattern or world view now prevailing. It involves re-thinking all our categories and assumptions, a transformation of our minds comparable to that which followed the breakup of the medieval synthesis, the Renaissance, and the new world views of Galileo and later of Darwin, and greater.

It is Marx's method to unite his theoretical thinking with the march of events. That is why it cannot be separated and built into an abstract system; and why it must be developed in a concrete fashion as the actual economic, political and social world goes through the preparatory stages of development which prepare the way for socialism.

It follows that there is no *general formula* for revolution *everywhere* in Marx, and we search his writings in vain for texts to lend authority to political moves and revolutionary projects. There is no sanction for any strategy or tactic other than that afforded by the logic of the situation in question; and this throws the whole responsibility onto the shoulders of the man on the spot. All the help he will get from Marx will have been assimulated long before he is brought to the test and will depend on his own intelligent study of the Marx of the nineteenth century.

Marxism is about the coming to consciousness of people in a highly developed economic and historical situation; the recognition of its contradictions, of the structure of society in which changes are taking place, of its paradoxes and possibilities. Above all, this is a form of change not limited by existing economic laws or the categories of the existing world order, but is "the original movement which abolishes the present state of affairs".

[1] *Critique of the Gotha Programme.*

For this reason the Marxist is no Marxist if he sees his science in a book or in his mind. He has to understand what is happening before his eyes and, by participating intelligently and with comprehension, play his indispensable part in social change.

Never does Marx guarantee the success of the revolution in advance or take it for granted; because revolution does not happen automatically, or as the result of laws operating independently of the intelligence and will of man. Revolutionary consciousness is the *sine qua non* of social development. The economic forces "moving with the precision of a mechanism" only create *the situation* in which we find the possibility of supplanting them. Only in *that* sense do they work with "iron necessity towards inevitable results". But Marx never says that this necessity applies to the transformation of capitalist society.

Marx offers no guarantees, and when he lays down his pen he cannot count on us to continue his work, he can only look to the future with mingled hope and fear. When he had completed his work as theorist and revolutionary he had said what he had to say, and done what he could. The last words of his last work are these:

> *Dixi et salvari animum meam!*
> (I have spoken and saved my soul.)

INDEX